LADY QUEEN ANNE

LADY QUEEN ANNE

A biography of Queen Anne of England

MARGARET HODGES

Farrar, Straus & Giroux
New York
An Ariel Book

TO THE BRITISH MUSEUM, the National Portrait Gallery, and the New York Public Library for courteous help in making available many prints and portraits.

To Niels H. Sonne of the General Theological Seminary, New York City, for the text of the service "At the Healing."

To N. H. MacMichael, Keeper of the Muniments, Westminster Abbey, for information about the burial places of the Stuarts and the wax effigies of. Queen Elizabeth I and Queen Anne.

To Herbert Ganter and Henry Hoar of the Earl Gregg Swen Library, Rare Book section, College of William and Mary, for information about Colonel Daniel Parke.

To Daphne Carter, Fletcher Hodges, Jr., and John Hodges, for editing, research and advice.

To Canon Hugh S. Clark, Church of the Redeemer, Pittsburgh; John Clement Harrison, Graduate School of Library and Information Sciences, University of Pittsburgh; William Mc-Shea, History Department, Mount Mercy College, Pittsburgh; and Robert Paul, Pittsburgh Theological Seminary, for reading the manuscript.

To Samuel Hartwell for calling my attention to the poem, "Queen Anne's Lace," by Margaret Widdemer. To John Upson for the great line from "The Complaint of Deor." And to Peter Gray; Dr. Walter Jacob, Rabbi of Rodef Shalom Temple, Pittsburgh; Elizabeth Macfarlane; and Charles H. Moore for lending me special books which I might otherwise have missed.

To Nigel Nicolson, literary executor of Victoria Sackville-West, for permission to include the recipe for Lady Betty Germain's potpourri; and to the executors of the late Lady Waller for permission to print the recipe for "A Most Excellent Cake."

To Margaret Widdemer and to Harcourt, Brace and World

for permission to include her poem, "Queen Anne's Lace"; to George G. Harrap & Company Ltd. and to Charles Scribner's Sons for permission to quote from *Marlborough, His Life and Times* by Sir Winston Churchill; to Methuen & Company, Ltd., for permission to quote from *England under the Stuarts* by G. M. Trevelyan; and to The Viking Press, Inc., for permission to quote from *The Portable Swift,* edited by Carl Van Doren.

This book is dedicated to
Carnegie Library of Pittsburgh
with gratitude for its resources
and to its librarians,
"cheerful and discreet, obliging and very instructive,"
like Dr. Richard Bentley,
librarian to the Court of St. James's
in the time of Queen Anne

Contents

LADY QUEEN ANNE

THE STUARTS

A genealogical chart showing the family connections mentioned in this book

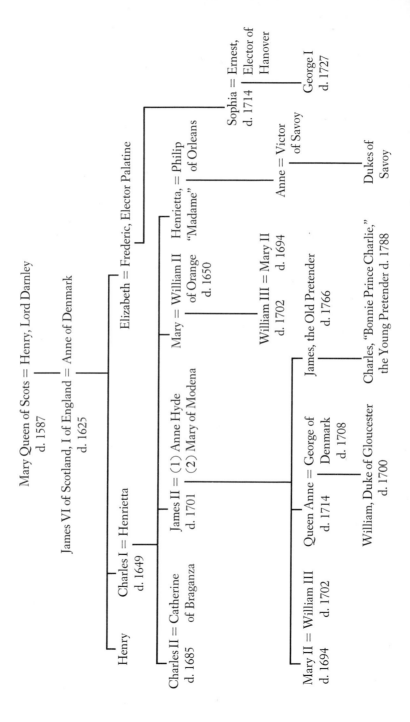

Foreword

QUEEN ANNE OF ENGLAND, the last of the Stuart monarchs, was born in 1665, more than three hundred years ago, but the issues and conflicts of her day seem strangely and excitingly contemporary to modern readers. Then, as now, there were agonies over a long, puzzling, and costly war. As in our day, honest men and solid citizens were dismayed by the flouting of moral standards and by political factions tearing at each other's throats in time of national crisis. Even the Augustans—Dryden, Pope, Addison, Steele, Defoe, and Swift—who gave Anne's reign much of its luster, were as controversial as modern authors. Some intellectual circles were pleased and stimulated by their keen judgment and polished style. Other critics, like Bishop Berkeley the philosopher, were

> . . . disgusted at an age and clime
> Barren of every glorious theme.

In the midst of it all stands the figure of Anne, who consciously or unconsciously influenced so much of the action and thought and passion of her time, because from the moment of her birth she was a possible claimant to the throne. Kingdoms might rise or fall according to her state of health, and when she died in 1714 the bells tolled for the end of the Stuart era.

After three hundred years it is not easy to see Anne as she

really was. It is as if she were hidden in the enclosure at the center of a maze, that fanciful contrivance so dear to the heart of the eighteenth-century gardener. There are dozens of tortuous and alluring paths along which the writer might wander endlessly and never find her. Documents, manuscripts, diaries, letters, histories of the period exist in great plenty, but we must follow only the paths that seem most likely to lead us to her.

For the most part, fact will be the guide rather than fancy, and the facts are voluminous enough. If followed with caution, Samuel Pepys, Daniel Defoe, and Sir John Evelyn will help us—though Pepys, even with his sharp eye for detail, could err; Defoe sometimes got information from dubious sources; the meticulous Evelyn wrote parts of his diary long after the event and so made mistakes. Abel Boyer's *Annals of the Reign of Queen Anne* are dependable, but Boyer confined his record to official and public events. Sarah Churchill, Duchess of Marlborough, sitting up in bed to dictate her memoirs at the age of eighty, pointed out many paths leading to the Queen, or so she said, but we had better not take them. Trust Sarah, trust a witch.

We can look for the Queen in some of the scenes that she knew, in palaces like Whitehall, St. James's, Windsor, Hampton Court, Kensington, reconstructing through paintings, etchings, records, and conjecture what was said and done in the great rooms, courts, gates, and gardens along the river. Some conjecture can hardly be avoided, since even the best of our sources are themselves subject to it. We must bear in mind also that London today is not the London of Queen Anne's day. Time, floods, and fires bring even palaces to ruin and decay, and what did not fall down, like London Bridge, has been torn down and built up again, over and over. We long in vain to know exactly how the room looked where, in view of the whole Court, Anne first received a kiss from that faint-hearted suitor, George of Hanover.

(Was he really "Georgie Porgie, pudding and pie" who "kissed the girls and made them cry"?) Dozens of our nursery rhymes began as clandestine political gibes during the lifetime of Queen Anne.

Certain phrases in Anne's own letters seem to reveal her feelings to the small group who knew her well, and we can use such letters as the basis for some imagined conversations. The Queen, in the seclusion of her Court, kept in touch with the colorful, noisy world through a few friends like Sarah Churchill, "meaching" Mrs. Masham, the red-haired Duchess of Somerset (whom Dean Swift called "Carrots"), eloquent Henry St. John, clever Robert Harley, and Dr. Arbuthnot, man of many talents. Through them the Queen knew something more than the palaces by the sweetly flowing Thames, the world of racing at Newmarket and of gambling at Bath. She had glimpses of the coffeehouses, the theaters, even of the prisons that she could not see for herself. She wished also to know the England that lay quiet and far-removed from "the tide of pomp," the England of country squire and yeoman, for she had a concern to serve all of her people, and the people knew it. She was often to hear them shout, "Long live Queen Anne!" They were thankful for the new hospitals and charity schools, practical results of her commitment to do the Lord's work, in the words of her beloved Book of Common Prayer, "for the fatherless children, and widows, and all who are desolate and oppressed."

The search for the Queen is sure to be rewarding as we discover why Macaulay, Trevelyan, Churchill, and other historians, her contemporaries and ours, have called her "Good Queen Anne," and have judged her reign to be a glorious one. Perhaps she will come out a little way to meet us, in spite of her shyness, though walking is painful for her.

Because she was ill for so long, "Queen Anne's dead" became

a stock phrase meaning, "Stale news. I've heard that a thousand times." But her name deserves to be something more than part of a phrase, as in Queen Anne's Lace, Queen Anne furniture, Queen Anne's Bounty, Queen Anne's War, and "Queen Anne's dead!"

Let us follow some of the most promising paths in our maze and try to find her as a living person—Lady Queen Anne, the last of the Stuarts, who had "no interest, no end, no thought" but for the good of her country, a great Queen of England, whose reign ushered in our modern world.

> Lady Queen Anne she sits in the sun,
> As fair as a lily, as brown as a bun;
> Come taste my lily, come smell my rose,
> Which of my maidens do you choose?
> The ball is ours and none of yours,
> Go to the wood and gather flowers.
> Cats and kittens now stay within,
> While we young maidens walk out and in.
>
> Old English nursery rhyme

Chapter I

Whitehall

Gay go up, and gay go down,
To ring the bells of London town.

ALL OVER LONDON the church bells were ringing. The young man heard them above the cries of gulls and the creaking of ropes as he stepped cautiously into the waiting barge, on a December evening in 1680. He was a German prince, George of Hanover, and the bells were being rung in his honor by order of Charles II, who was the titular head of the Church of England, as well as King of England, Scotland, and Ireland. Somewhere up the river a cannon boomed a welcome. Being of a cool and calculating disposition, the Prince considered the possibility that if his mission in England turned out favorably, he himself might one day be King of England, Scotland, and Ireland and in a position to order the ringing of bells and the booming of cannon.

The barge sent to convey the Prince from ship to shore was very fine. Rowed smartly by eight oarsmen wearing the livery of King Charles's household, it moved swiftly over the water. Prince George noted the forest of masts above him as the boatswain maneuvered through the shipping that lay at anchor in the Pool, the lower part of the Thames which was used as a harbor. His questions to his attendants were in French, for he spoke no English. There were sometimes as many as two thousand sails in the harbor, counting only sea-going vessels, not barges, yachts, and pleasure boats. The Pool ended at a bridge, where the water swirled under a series of pointed arches. In the fading light of the winter evening, the roofs of houses cut a row of sharp peaks against the sky above the bridge.

"It is called London Bridge," he was told. "Those are residences and shops, as on the bridges at Avignon and Florence. The Palace of Whitehall lies beyond the bridge at some distance, and we cannot safely pass under the arches because of the great rush of water. We will be met by a coach and will proceed by road along the river to Whitehall. The fortress which we are now approaching is known as the Tower of London, although your Highness will see that there are truly many towers within the walls. . . . Your Highness is correct, it has the appearance of a prison and has always been so used. It was formerly the residence of the English kings, but your Highness will find the Palace of Whitehall less formidable. And now, if your Highness pleases to disembark, taking care for the steps, which the boatswain warns are very wet, we shall find the coach waiting for us on the roadway above."

Another gentleman of the King's household joined the Prince's party at the top of the stairs and bowed him into the expected coach, which was drawn up with a line of others to receive the royal guest from Hanover and his retinue. George climbed in, followed by his equerry and the English gentleman. The heavy coach proved to be a less comfortable conveyance than the royal barge. Drawn by four matched horses and attended by coachmen, footmen, and outriders, it made a brave show as it rattled along the road above the river, but it jolted abominably.

In spite of the Prince's dry, cold manner, the Englishman did the honors of the city, chattering away in excellent French.

A seventeenth-century engraving of London **Bridge**

"Your Highness may wish to look to the right as we pass St. Paul's Cathedral. It is now being rebuilt and will be the finest church in the world."

Prince George remarked that the London church bells were still ringing. The gentleman of the royal household laughed. "We English ring bells for hours together, once we have begun. This will go on into the night. If your Highness pleases, we have reached the Palace of Whitehall and will proceed across the court on foot. Your Highness's rooms are ready."

The gateway of Whitehall Palace was imposing, built of brick and stone, with rooms and turreted towers above it, but the Prince thought that what he could see of the palace was strangely lacking in magnificence for a monarch who considered himself to be the equal of the great Louis XIV. Whitehall was not another Versailles. It was a rambling collection of buildings, mostly of red brick, but some of mere plaster and wood. Accompanied by his own gentlemen and servants, he was guided across a stone courtyard and through a series of halls, chambers, and galleries to a bedroom, where at last he had a chance to rest and collect his thoughts.

With his journey behind him, the importance of his mission was again uppermost in his mind. Prince George had come to Whitehall in order to meet the Princess Anne. a niece of King Charles, and perhaps to ask for her hand in marriage. She was now fifteen years old, and he knew that, for a number of reasons, the English king considered this a suitable match. The Hanoverians and the Stuarts were already united by family ties. Besides, King Charles himself had married a Roman Catholic, Catherine of Braganza, a Portuguese lady who had brought with her a fine dowry but had so far produced no heir to the throne. The marriage had not met with popular approval, all the less so when two years before, in 1678, a certain Titus Oates had claimed to uncover a "Popish plot." According to Oates, the objective of the plot was to return England by force to the Catholic faith through a French invasion, to murder the King, set fire to London, and start insurrections in Ireland and Scotland. Queen Catherine, if Oates was to be believed, not only knew of the plot but was conspiring to poison her husband. Fortunately, the King did not believe the accusation. But London was in a panic over the supposed plot, people were going about armed with knives and pistols, and something must be done to restore public confidence. The Protestant Succession was a principle to which most Englishmen were firmly committed. Mary, Anne's older sister, was already married to William, Prince of Orange, who was a Protestant. Another Protestant connection in the royal family would smooth troubled waters.

This much was well known to Prince George of Hanover. He may have been less aware of other rumors which were afloat at the court of Charles II—that both of the royal brothers, Charles and James, were strongly attracted to the Catholic faith. Since the death of the Princess Anne's own mother, her father, James, Duke of York, had remarried. It was being said that he was under the influence of his beautiful young wife, Mary of Modena, who like Queen Catherine was a Roman Catholic. Two Papist wives in the royal family gave rise to much nervous speculation. The specter of a French invasion by His Most Catholic Majesty Louis XIV was never far from men's minds, and a stream of Protestant refugees from France kept English feelings at fever pitch with terrible tales of persecution, even of massacre. South of the Pyrenees lay Spain, another Catholic country, which might easily be persuaded to join with France and turn England into a mere province in an empire united under Louis, the "Sun King."

Prince George decided to wait and see the English King, his

Court, and especially the Princess Anne before making up his mind. He had not yet been summoned to an audience with Charles and could put the time to use by taking an inspection tour of the palace. There was a good deal to see. Whitehall Palace covered about twenty-three acres. A long garden lay beside the river and steps led down to the water's edge. He had not yet seen the Banqueting Hall when a message came that King Charles would receive him there for dinner on the afternoon following his arrival. Being a man of rather simple tastes, Prince George was unprepared for that magnificent occasion.

Chapter II

The Banqueting House

SOON AFTER HIS CORONATION, Charles had revived the custom of dining frequently "in ancient state," a habit which delighted many Londoners, since anyone who was decently dressed could come to the palace for a glimpse of the King. Pomp and circumstance were welcome after the austerities of Cromwell. It was a great thing to stand in a gallery and wait for Charles and his Court to pass by on their way to a magnificent dinner in the Banqueting House. Sir John Evelyn, a gentleman who was intimate with the King and his circle, describes in his diary just such a dinner, at which Charles entertained the Knights of the Garter.

"The King," says Evelyn, "sat on an elevated throne at the upper end at a table alone; the Knights at a table on the right hand, reaching all the length of the room; over-against them a cupboard of rich gilded plate; at the lower end, the music; on the balusters above, wind-music, trumpets, and kettle-drums. The King was served by the lords and pensioners, who brought up the dishes. About the middle of the dinner, the Knights drank the King's health, then the King theirs, when the trumpets and music played and sounded, the guns going off at the Tower. At the banquet came in the Queen, and stood by the King's left hand, but did not sit. Then was the banqueting-stuff flung

about the room profusely. In truth, the crowd was so great that
. . . I now stayed no longer . . . for fear of disorder. The cheer
was extraordinary, each Knight having forty dishes to his mess,
piled up five or six high; the room hung with the richest
tapestry."

On the present occasion, the Banqueting Hall was filled with as
gay a company as ever graced the English Court, women as well
as men, all chirping, so it seemed to German George, like birds
in a bush, fine birds in fine feathers. The high-pitched voice of
the Keeper of the Door announced Prince George's coming,
voices were subdued, and periwigged heads bowed, as the
ladies and gentlemen of the Court made way for him to cross
the room. He recognized the King at once, not only because he
had seen portraits of his cousin but because Charles was indeed
"every inch a king." He was tall, with the eyes of the Stuarts,
debonair, so Evelyn tells us, full of a restless energy, and had,
like the rest of his family, a fatal charm. He came forward now
to greet Prince George with an easy informality that made the
young man conscious of his own awkward manner.

George presented his gifts to the King, and made a mental
note that the Keeper of the Door must have a gratuity at a suitable time. The hand of every man in the palace seemed to be
stretched out in hope of receiving what was due to his station,
high or low. Fortunately, Prince George had come well supplied
with money. He knew, moreover, that he had brought a most
acceptable gift in bringing himself, and he was not surprised
when Charles bowed graciously, leading the way toward a dais at
the end of the Banqueting Hall.

A cluster of ladies who stood near the dining table curtsied as
his Majesty approached, and George bowed over the Queen's
hand. She was small and dark, her face veiled with the dignity
which habitually covered her unhappiness. After one respectful

look, the Prince turned toward a young girl who stood at the King's side.

"The Princess Anne," said his Majesty. The face into which Prince George looked with swift appraisal was round and rather pale, framed in brown hair that hung in curls to her shoulders. Her eyes were gray; and she looked as if she might have been crying. Standing very straight and still like an obedient child, she held out her hand and the Prince took it in his. He had never seen hands more beautiful, firm, supple, and warm to his touch. Diamond bracelets encircled her round white wrists, sparkling against the brocade and lace of her dress, so that every motion of her hands was enchanting. He raised his eyes again to her face and noticed a look of reserve, somewhat akin to that of the Queen. It was as if neither of these women felt at home here. Yet, who should be more so?

"We are glad to see you," she said. "Did you have a good journey?" The words were a mere formality, prepared ahead of time by a shy person who wished to do her best, but they were made extraordinary by her voice, which had a purity and range that made every word memorable.

He mumbled an answer as the King turned and led them to the dais, seating the royal guest on his right, between himself and the Princess Anne. The Queen seated herself silently on the King's left. She might as well have dined alone, for the royal back was turned to her during the entire dinner. The lords and ladies of the Court sat at long tables below the dais. To a flourish of trumpets and roll of drums the feast began.

A similar feast, held the previous year, will serve as a sample of the menu which a distinguished guest might expect at the Court of Charles II. There was beef, mutton, duck, chicken, rabbit, and neat's tongue. Also a large "turkey pye all over gilded rubby" [ruby] . . . "a Florentine, gilded" [a meat pie baked without an under-crust], a shrimp pie "with vermiliane color," a venison pasty and three gilded trotter pies. The large "salmond" pie was also fringed with gold, and "among the lighter things were oranges, almonds, raisins, sixty pounds of comfits" [sweet fruits, preserved and dried], and 567 pounds of confections! Afterward, the goblets, still rather a rarity in England, and very expensive, were thrown about and smashed, because the guests, being "members of the upper class . . . liked the sound of breaking glass."

On the day of the dinner in honor of Prince George of Hanover there was probably less breakage, because the royal ladies were present. Even so, the scene was anything but dull. Orchestras at each end of the hall played in turn. At the long tables below the dais there was much talk and laughter; graceful compliment, wit, and artificial elegance mixed with oaths and stories that would have made a plowman blush. Table manners ranged from finicky to coarse, for many of these courtiers had made money first and acquired gentility later, and many of those to the manner born were too arrogant to care what they did.

The four royal personages seated on the dais had a less enjoyable time. Eating dinner at the head table is apt to be a rather lonely business, as those who have tried it will bear witness to this very day. Lords and servitors came and went with a succession of dishes offered on bended knee, but conversation languished.

The Queen tasted her food and sent most of it away again. This cold, grimy northern land could not produce such food as she remembered in her own Portugal, the home from which she had been torn to make a useful political alliance. From time to time she darted a glance at some of the ladies whose presence she most fiercely resented. There was the Duchess of Portsmouth, whose apartments here at Whitehall were a particular affront, being "luxuriously furnished, and with ten times the richness and glory beyond the Queen's; such massy pieces of plate, whole tables, and stands of incredible value." In this country where one looking glass was a treasure, the Duchess had a room completely lined with mirrors. The Queen had avoided visiting those apartments but could not avoid the constant sight of the Duchess's "childish, simple, and baby face," since his Majesty, with singular want of feeling, had insisted that she, as his current favorite, be appointed Maid of Honor to the Queen. True, the Queen's own bed was covered with silver on crimson velvet and was said to be worth £8,000, but it was really only a political present from the states of Holland to the English King, not truly a present from the King to her.

At another table sat Barbara Villiers, Lady Castlemaine, the Duchess of Cleveland, no longer young but still very beautiful, now supplanted by the Duchess of Portsmouth in the King's favor. Bishop Burnet called her "vicious and ravenous; foolish but imperious, very uneasy to the King, and always carrying on intrigues with other men, while yet she pretended that she was jealous of him."

It was a bitter memory to the Queen that Charles had once treated her, Catherine, with the same extravagant generosity which he now showed to such women as these. In her own honor there had once been "the most magnificent triumph that ever floated on the Thames, innumerable boats and vessels, dressed and adorned with all imaginable pomp . . . thrones, arches, pageants, and other representations, stately barges of the Lord Mayor and Companies, with various inventions, music, and peals of ordnance, both from the vessels and the shore, going to meet and conduct the new Queen from Hampton Court to Whitehall, at the first time of her coming to town." So Sir John Evelyn described it.

All of that was long past. Perhaps if she had had a child . . . But at this heathen Court, one indignity had followed another, rising to a peak of frightfulness with the fabricated "Popish plot" incident of two years ago. As a result of this dreadful affair, two loyal Catholics had died on the scaffold, others had been sent to the Tower, and all lords of the Roman Catholic faith were forever excluded from Parliament by law. She, even she, had been accused of intending to poison the King, when God alone knew her constant prayers for his life and health that he might at last be converted from his wicked ways to join her in the true Faith.

The King had nothing to say to Queen Catherine, not because he had ever for a minute believed the rumors against her but because, quite simply, she bored him. Finding Prince George a hard man to talk to, he soon began to call his special friends from their dinners to come to the dais. Charles liked to tell stories and told them well. There was always much to say; the King's interests were wide. He loved to sail, to plant, to build, and he had his own laboratory in St. James's Park, where he performed experiments in physics and mechanics. He could shoot, ride, fish, and play tennis. Londoners of high and low degree swarmed into St. James's Park to see him with his courtiers practicing "pale-maile," a game like croquet. Altogether he had earned the right to be called "the Merry Monarch." The look of melancholy which sometimes shadowed his face only added to his charm. It was a reminder to loyal followers that the King had had great misfortunes, beginning with the execution of his father in front of this very Banqueting House. Then there had been the years of exile and hardship on the Continent, where he and his brother James had been mere hangers-on at foreign courts and in low taverns. If the King now lived a reprehensible life, there were many to love him and forgive him,

King Charles II, Anne's uncle. A portrait by John Michael Wright

either because he was Charles, or because he was a Stuart, or because there were others as bad or worse in that dissolute Court. Inconstancy only made a charming subject for a poem or a song, like "Love and Life," by John Wilmot, Earl of Rochester:

> . . . Then talk not of Inconstancy,
> False Hearts, and broken Vows,
> If I, by Miracle, can be
> This live-long Minute true to thee,
> 'Tis all that Heaven allows.

The King sat at table, eating heartily and talking more than he ate, sending for one after another of his courtiers, who had to leave their dinners to cool while they listened and laughed appreciatively at the King's stories. From time to time one of the gentlemen would bow and make his escape, and the King was constantly in need of fresh recruits to the group around him. John Wilmot said, as he returned to his seat, "I wonder to see a man have so good a memory as to repeat the same story without losing the least circumstance, and yet not remember that he had told it to the same persons the very day before."

The King did not much care who came or went. "He thought," says Bishop Burnet, "that no body did serve him out of love: and so he was quits with all the world." Halfway through dinner he began to brood, and ordered his spaniels brought in. They climbed into his chair and licked his face while he cuffed them, petted them, and fed them by turns. They were the only living creatures of whose affections he was sure.

If the King himself was less than content, so were his courtiers. Even for those who had struggled hardest to rise to that lofty circle, life at Whitehall seemed like a kind of slavery. The humblest of his Majesty's subjects were more free to eat and sleep at ease than were his intimates, rising in haste from bed or board at the command of royalty. One scholarly gentleman, our friend Evelyn, wrote that a day at Court made him think of Horace's Town Mouse and Country Mouse. After seeing a lady-in-waiting leave her table still hungry at eleven o'clock at night because the Queen wished to walk in the garden, Sir John blessed God that he did not have to do the same.

Prince George, at the King's right, ate stolidly through all the courses. Since Anne too was silent, he found it simpler to eat than to struggle with polite conversation. He took special note of the Life Guards, splendid with white feathers that drooped over the broad brims of their hats, and with scarlet coats richly trimmed in gold lace and ruffles. Their weapons were even more impressive: short carbines, pistols, and swords bristling on every side. It would be a bold man who would attack a king with such guards. George thought of reviewing the uniforms and weapons of his own guards on his return home.

Servants were lighting wax tapers in silver sconces, for the dinner, which had begun at three in the afternoon, was still well under way as night fell. The glow of the candles was cast upward, and George noticed the painted ceiling. In this he had no doubt that his country could hold its own with England. He had seen many similar ceilings, painted by famous artists to honor some royal figure. In the Banqueting House at Whitehall the royal figure in question was that of King James I, grandfather of the present King. He was portrayed on his way to heaven, wafted skyward by rosy cherubs who looked quite unequal to the task. The painting was a reminder that James I had held his scepter and orb by Divine Right, and that therefore the King could do no wrong. It was clear that his grandson, Charles II, claimed the same Divine Right, but Prince George himself entertained some doubts on the subject.

The Princess Anne, like her suitor, ate steadily through the long dinner. She had early discovered this easy way to avoid the effort of making conversation, the kind of conversation known as "wit" in her uncle's Court. She could talk when there was something important to say, but she could not play with words. Besides, Dr. Compton, who as Bishop of London had guided her religious life, said she must never talk scandal. Apparently the German Prince did not care to talk either. She wondered if he liked her. The King had told her that Prince George had come with marriage in mind. If the Prince wished to have her for his wife, and if the King would have it so, she knew she must agree.

The year before, Isabella Bennet, the only daughter of Lord Arlington, had been married by the King's wish to a son of Lady Castlemaine, the bride being twelve years old at the time of the wedding and the groom only sixteen. Anne knew how frightened Isabella was at the thought of marriage. But it was his Majesty's pleasure to keep the peace with Lady Castlemaine, and that was the end of it. In any event, romantic love was considered a poor reason for marriage.

As for Prince George, Anne thought him handsome enough, and she might come to like him. Perhaps he would marry her and take her away to live in Germany. Then she would be near Holland, where her sister Mary lived with a Dutch husband, their cousin William. Anne had been in Holland the year before and thought it would be pleasant to visit back and forth with Mary. Afterward, she had gone on to Brussels for a visit with her stepmother and her father, who had had to be sent away from England because people were not fond of him at home.

Anne had liked Brussels because Sarah, her dearest friend, had been there. Sarah was now married to a gallant soldier, Mr. John Churchill. They had had such a happy time together in

Brussels. Anne had written to her friend Lady Apsley, telling all about it. "All the people here are very civil, and except you be otherwise to them they will be so to you. . . . The Park here is very pretty, but not so fine as ours at St. James's. . . . I saw a ball at court which far surpassed my expectations, for it was very well. There we had lemonade, cinnamon water, and chocolate sweet-meats, all very good. . . ." No doubt there would be parties and good things to eat at the Court of Hanover, too.

It was dreadful to know that the people hated her father. For this reason, he and her stepmother were away again, in Scotland, and again they had taken Sarah with them. Anne wondered if she would some day be able to have Sarah with her forever and ever, as she so much wished to do.

The musicians were hot and thirsty. A bowl was being passed among them, after which they began with renewed vigor, playing an old carol, "The Twelve Days of Christmas," in honor of the season. Christmas Day was not far off, and with the return of the Stuarts it was no longer a fast as it had been under Cromwell. Anne's finger tapped to the merry tune, and her spirits lifted. The King smiled and, leaning across the Prince, said, "Give us a song, my child. Play 'Greensleeves.'"

Anne blushed and begged to be excused, but when he insisted, she rose from her high-backed chair and seated herself on a stool that was brought at the King's command. A guitar was borrowed from the orchestra, while virginal, viol, recorder, and flute fell silent. All turned to watch and to listen. The guitar was a favorite instrument everywhere in England, and the Princess was known for her music. As she began her song, the faces of her audience were transformed. In this one thing, a passion for music, for "harmony, heavenly harmony," all were agreed. "Greensleeves" was an old tune to which at least a dozen songs against the Roundheads had been written, but Anne sang it now as the love song it was meant to be:

> Alas! my love, you do me wrong,
> To cast me off discourteously;
> And I have loved you so long,
> Delighting in your company . . .

The white fingers of the Princess moved quickly, lightly among the silver strings. Once having begun, she seemed to forget who and where she was. She was part of the song she sang above the rippling, running cadence of the guitar.

The King listened with his dark smile, his eyes turned now on the Princess, now on the Duchess of Portsmouth, who was refusing to answer his look. The Queen sat rigidly, looking at nothing and at no one.

Prince George was carried away by the music of the Princess. He determined to become a patron of the art at the earliest opportunity. If the English Court could be so embellished with the playing and singing of these simple old tunes, how much more could his own Court profit from the presence of a master musician. When the time came, he would arrange for such a master to live at his Court and compose the finest music.

Now the Princess was ending her song to applause and murmurs of approval. She half rose, glancing at the King, but he would not allow her to stop. She must sing something new, he said. What had she learned recently? Once again her head bent over the guitar, and the voice floated and throbbed with the sorrow of Dido, an ancient queen who had "died young and fair" for love.

> When I am laid, am laid in earth, may my wrongs create
> No trouble, no trouble in thy breast;
> Remember me, remember me, but ah! forget my fate.
> Remember me, but ah! forget my fate.

In the midst of the applause, Queen Catherine rose, signaled to the ladies, and led the way out of the Banqueting Hall, her eyes bright with tears that must not fall. The Princess followed her, full of compunction. If she had only thought a moment, she would not have chosen that song. Yet it was so beautiful, and written by a young man hardly older than herself. His name was Henry Purcell. He had composed the music for "Dido and Aeneas," to be performed by the pupils at a girls' school. The passion and simplicity of the flowing melodies and the purity of the young voices had moved all hearers to ecstasy, and Purcell became famous. This very year, he had been appointed organist at Westminster Abbey.

As Anne left the room, Charles was calling for a change of mood. Both orchestras were tuning their instruments again, and Cavaliers were shouting for a song in honor of the King:

> Here's a health unto His Majesty,
> With a fal la la la la la la.

Accompanied by her aunt, Lady Clarendon, Anne stepped into a coach which was waiting in the courtyard to drive her through the park to St. James's Palace. As they set off, the wheels of the coach passed over the spot where her grandfather had been executed. Anne had heard that story many times. She never spoke of it, but whenever she thought of it late at night, she was afraid.

Chapter III

London—1665

THE BATTLEMENTS and towers of St. James's Palace rose above the treetops in a park planted with oaks which were already over a hundred years old. The newly returned King Charles was bent on making the park even more beautiful. He had laid out a mall with rows of trees and broad gravel walks half a mile long, where he and his people could walk at leisure.

Oliver Cromwell had used the old palace hard, turning it first into a prison and then into a barracks, but now it was restored to splendor, with handsome furniture in the new manner. At foreign courts, the royal family had acquired a taste for luxury during their years of exile on the Continent. Charles brightened the dark rooms at St. James's with fine tapestries and paintings, among them the portraits of the beauties who graced the royal Court.

In one of the bedrooms the Princess Anne had been born on February 6, 1665. About the time of her birth a comet had appeared in the skies of western Europe. In London it gave rise to superstitious terror among the people. Seen through city smoke, it was "of a faint, dull, languid colour and its motion very heavy, solemn and slow." Daniel Defoe, who saw it himself, looked upon it with foreboding.

Well he might do so, for during December 1664, disaster had struck. Two Frenchmen died of the plague in a house in Drury

Lane. Another case was known in February 1665, about the time when Princess Anne was born, but the death occurred in the slums near the crowded docks, two miles away from St. James's Palace. James, the Duke of York, and his Duchess remained unperturbed for the time being.

By April 30, Mr. Samuel Pepys, at his London house, was writing in his diary, "Great fears of the sickenesse here in the City, it being said that two or three houses are already shut up. God preserve us all." He remembered the plagues of other years. On May 24, England now being at war with Holland, he wrote, "All the newes is of the Dutch being gone out, and of the plague growing upon us in this towne; and of remedies against it; some one thing, some another."

Fear was everywhere. Even St. James's Palace and Whitehall felt it. Charles and James moved their families, including the new baby, to Hampton Court, farther up the river. All over town the dreaded mark of the plague appeared on doors. On June 5, Mr. Pepys wrote, "This day, much against my will, I did in Drury Lane see two or three houses marked with a red cross upon the doors, and 'Lord have mercy upon us' writ there; which was a sad sight to me, being the first of the kind that, to my remembrance, I ever saw. It put me into an ill conception of myself and my smell, so that I was forced to buy some roll-tobacco to smell and chew, which took away my apprehension." June 15: "The towne grows very sickly, and people to be afeard of it; there dying this last week of the plague 112, from 43 the week before . . ."

If one victim was struck down in a house, that house might be sealed, and all within it doomed; whole families perished in this way. People were leaving London by every road; the river was crowded with boats full of refugees and their belongings. "Bring out your dead!" was the cry at night, as carts went

Hampton Court

through the streets to gather up corpses and carry them to great pits for burial.

The royal family, including the Duke of York and his caval-cade, moved here and there for safety as the terrible summer dragged on—to Salisbury, to York, and finally to Oxford. By August a solemn fast was declared throughout all of England, and Pepys wrote desperately, ". . . a man cannot depend upon living two days to an end." Bells tolled for the dead, by day and by night. In the third week of August 5,000 died. August 31: "In the City died this week 7,496, and of them 6,102 of the plague. But it is feared that the true number of the dead this week is near 10,000; partly from the poor that cannot be taken notice of, through the greatness of the number, and partly from the Quakers and others that will not have any bell ring for them."

Early in September, the Lord Mayor ordered fumigating fires to be lit in the streets. The burning of saltpeter was thought to be a preventive, and at St. Paul's a mixture of pepper, sulphur, hops, and incense was burned. More than one doctor made a fortune with recipes for bogus "fumes." And still the plague increased.

Pepys, who had left town, returned on September 6 to pack up and carry away some of his possessions. He saw the fires burning throughout the whole city. The next day, Sir John Evelyn came home to the desolation of a city where it seemed that no one remained except the dead and the dying. He wrote, "I went all along the city and suburbs from Kent Street to St. James's, a dismal passage, and dangerous to see so many coffins exposed in the streets, now thin of people; the shops shut up, and all in mournful silence, not knowing whose turn might be next." At Whitehall, grass grew in the courtyards.

Looking back three hundred years, with our present knowledge, it seems clear that the greatest enemy of the English people was neither France nor Holland, but the rat and the louse. The plain fact was that not since the departure of the Romans had the English people, of high or low degree, been clean. Rats ran down the hawsers from ships anchored in the Pool and swarmed into the slums, bringing lice with them. The lice brought plague and typhus as well as smallpox, typhoid fever, dysentery, and a host of other seemingly uncontrollable diseases. Mr. Pepys sometimes woke up tired because, he said, "I have had a bad night's rest to-night, not sleeping well, as my wife observed, and once or twice she did wake me, and I thought myself to be mightily bit with fleas, and in the morning she chid her mayds for not looking the fleas a-days."

The high and mighty fared little better. The State bed in a palace bedroom was completely covered with rich velvet or damask which could conceal a louse as well as did the filthy pallet of the most wretched beggar. The feathers which nodded grandly at each corner of the high tester, the valance, the embroidered curtains, gold-fringed counterpanes—all were homes for lice. There was good reason to wear a periwig, which made it possible to shave the head, and so to sleep more peacefully, but the periwig itself offered a splendid haven for lice and nits. Mr. Pepys was disgusted when he found them in a new wig which he had just bought. He took it back to the barber who had made it for him and insisted on having it cleaned. One evening, after a stylish and successful dinner party at which he entertained "my Lord Sandwich" and other members of the Court, Pepys bade the gentlemen good night and went up to his wife's chamber. He got her to cut his hair and to look over his shirt, for he had been itching mightily for six or seven days. Mrs. Pepys found about twenty lice, "little and great." Her husband did not know where he had got them, but determined then and there to keep his hair cut close, "and so with much content to bed."

England was, of course, no worse than the Continent. A young French princess, about the middle of the century, was taught as a matter of etiquette not to make a habit of scratching unnecessarily and not to kill lice or fleas in company except when she was with her nearest and dearest.

By the spring of 1666, the plague had spent its strength, and the royal families of England came home. The Duke of York's procession entered the courtyard of St. James's Palace through the old gateway in the clock tower, creating a stir of excitement among Londoners who were lucky enough to see the sight. The little Duke of Cambridge was six years old, the Princess Mary was about four, and Anne was just over a year old, able to sit up in her nurse's arms and to wear a velvet cap with feathers. The fourth child, the Duke of Kendal, was a newborn baby. Any one of them might become King or Queen, if fate so decided, but in London, two of every three children died before they were a year old. Of those who survived, two of every three died before the age of five, and the royal children had never been robust. Indeed, the two little brothers riding home to St. James's Palace in the spring of 1666 were dead when spring came again. Mary and Anne were ill so often that Mr. Pepys noted the general anxiety: "Everybody mightily concerned for these children, as a matter wherein the State is much concerned."

One wonders whether a doctor was consulted about the weak eyes of the little Princesses. If not, they were probably fortunate, since a medical remedy for sore eyes was to have a powder of hen's dung blown into them. A nursemaid might have tried the time-honored rabbit's foot, hung around the baby's neck, with better results. Whatever was tried, or not tried, the

Princess Anne had trouble with her eyes all of her life. Court gossip said that it was caused by a taint in the Stuart blood. It would be more than two hundred years before anyone would think of a poor diet as a possible reason for sore eyes. If that idea had been suggested to the Duchess of York, she would have dismissed it as ridiculous. Her baby was certainly not allowed to go hungry. The Duchess herself loved to eat, and fed the baby chocolate until she was as round as a butter ball. A fat baby should be a well baby (so the Duchess might have thought), but being a Stuart, this one was born to trouble like all the rest of them.

It would take a month of gossiping to tell all the sorrows of the Stuart family. The beautiful Mary, Queen of Scots, had been executed. Her son, James I, had an unhappy reign. So had her grandson, Charles I, whose children, the present Charles and his brother James, had lived for so many years in exile. James as a boy fourteen years old, had barely escaped with his life from St. James's Palace when his father, Charles I, had been imprisoned by Cromwell. During a game of hide-and-seek, James had disguised himself as a woman and fled in a waiting coach and ship, according to a plan made by friends of the royal family who had arranged refuge for him in Holland. Conspiracies were familiar troubles to each generation of Stuarts. So were attempts to assassinate them. None of the Stuarts had ever really known peace, but worst of all their troubles was a flaw of character which seemed to run through the family.

Henry Esmond, the young Cavalier of Thackeray's great novel, described that flaw of character: " 'Tis a wonder to anyone who looks back at the history of the Stuart family to think how they kicked their crowns away from them; how they flung away chances after chances; what treasures of loyalty they dissipated, and how fatally they were bent on consummating their own ruin. If ever men had fidelity, 'twas they; if ever men squandered opportunity, 'twas they; and, of all the enemies they had, they themselves were the most fatal."

Anne's mother too had known much sorrow. Born at Cranbourne Lodge near Windsor Castle, she was a commoner. Her name was Anne Hyde, and her father, Edward Hyde, was a gentleman of good education. He had fought bravely for King Charles I at the battle of Edgehill, and later suffered exile under Cromwell for his loyalty to the Stuarts. For months the Hyde family were literally without money, adequate clothes, or food. At the age of fifteen, Anne Hyde summed up her youth: "I lived in my own country till I was twelve years old, having in that time seen the ruin both of church and state, and the murdering of my King."

But better times were coming for Anne Hyde. She attracted the attention of James, the young Duke of York, while both of them were still in exile. He was a handsome and dashing soldier, though lacking the charm of his brother Charles. She was both intelligent and virtuous, a refreshing change from the women he had known. The result was a secret marriage, which was to cause a furor in Whitehall Palace when it was finally revealed at the time of the Restoration. True, Charles II, James's brother, was a young king who might reasonably be expected to marry and have children. But if Charles should die without children, James would be the heir to the throne, and so would his children after him. That those children should have a commoner for their mother was almost unthinkable, yet the marriage was an accomplished fact. In the long run, it had to be recognized, and Anne Hyde set about establishing her place as Duchess of York.

Her household at St. James's Palace was an elaborate one, which she presided over with such wit and determination that she was soon accepted and generally admired. Only her father, now Earl of Clarendon, was dismayed at the magnificence of his daughter's Court, and told her so. She answered that he knew nothing about the expenses of a prince, and continued to do exactly as she pleased.

It was pleasant to be home again at St. James's in the spring of 1666. James played with his children in the very garden from which he had escaped in fear of his life so many years ago. It was good to see that London was reviving after the plague. And so life went merrily on at St. James's until the night of September 1.

Chapter IV

London—1666

IT WAS SATURDAY NIGHT, September 1, 1666—a warm evening in a very dry season, unusual for London. A breeze made the weather even more pleasant. At Whitehall and at St. James's, Charles II and the Duke of York were both in residence with their Courts.

Along the river's strand, between the palaces and the bridge, lay the great houses of English noble families whose names resounded with echoes of their country's history—Durham, Worcester, Somerset, Arundel, Essex, Northumberland. Stretching down to the river's edge below these great houses were the gardens that sweetened the air for the favorites of fortune who moved through the spacious rooms or slept in the monumental beds. In some of the rooms, both above and below stairs, wax tapers were burning; it was a night for music and dancing. Candlelight was reflected in the polished surfaces of dark oaken tables and of silver braziers where coals would soon burn to ward off winter chill. The tapers illuminated the classic figures of gods and goddesses on high tapestried walls, or the portraits of ancestors, framed against wood paneling in the newer style. The glow was dimmed here and there by the perfumed smoke of cassolets set about to disguise less desirable smells that might offend noble noses. The candles were brightest where the great and near-great had gathered for dancing.

Silk, satin, and damask gleamed softly as ladies and gallants kissed in the gavotte; turned, bowed, touched hands in the stately pavane and sarabande; the light flickered in the motion of lace fans as ladies cooled their hot faces after the gay, quick courante.

Through open windows the sounds of the guitar, harpsichord, and recorder floated down to the river's edge, where music echoed back from pleasure-seeking boaters. Everyone was learning to play the guitar, "and God knows the universal twanging that followed," said the witty expatriate Count de Gramont, in his memoirs of the period.

Farther down the river, in the heart of the City, St. Paul's Cathedral was quiet that Saturday night, awaiting the service of Communion to be celebrated early in the morning. The old Gothic church had been visited earlier in the week by a party of gentlemen and expert workmen who had come to survey "the general decays" and to make plans for rebuilding. Dr. Christopher Wren, a brilliant mathematician turned architect, was in the group. They plumbed the uprights, examined the steeple, and drew up a plan to present to the Bishop. Scaffolding had already been set up in anticipation of the much-needed repairs.

Around St. Paul's the streets of the City were closed to commerce at night, but the houses were not abandoned. Rich merchants as well as shopkeepers slept above their places of business, the prosperous ones in houses of timber, lath, and plaster that might sprawl over an acre of ground, room after room ranging around a series of courtyards. Servants slept in the garrets or leaned from the windows to chat with friends across the narrow streets. Porters, messengers, and others who lived as hangers-on of the complex establishments slept in cellars and warehouses, curled up in corners or under counters.

From royal palaces and great houses, from simple courtyards

and small gardens came the sound of music. Mr. Pepys, for instance, sometimes "spent the night in extasy almost" after an evening of dancing and supper and singing. He seems to have hired his servants not for the work they might do, but for their ability to join in a family concert. In spite of lice and fleas, how delightful to spend an evening at home! "There," he wrote, "my wife and Mercer [the maidservant] and Tom and I sat till eleven at night, singing and fiddling. . . . The girle plays pretty well upon the harpsicon, but only ordinary tunes, but hath a good hand; sings a little but hath a good voyce and eare. My boy, a brave boy [another servant], sings finely, and is the most pleasant boy at present, while his ignorant boy's tricks last, that ever I saw." Sometimes, for a change, Mr. Pepys made Tom play on his lute. "So to supper, and with great pleasure to bed."

Since the days of Cromwell, Sundays had been strictly kept, and tomorrow would be a very quiet day in London. But tonight was Saturday night, and there were many other sounds besides music to hear in the streets.

At the Bear Garden there was a great crowd of men and women, gathered to see the cock-fighting, dog-fighting, bear- and bull-baiting, or all four entertainments. One night "one of the bulls tossed a dog full into a lady's lap as she sate in one of the boxes at a considerable height from the arena. Two poor dogs were killed." John Evelyn saw it for himself when he went with some friends. He thought the sports were "butcherly . . . or rather barbarous cruelties." Samuel Pepys had a stronger stomach when he went to see a prize fight at the Bear Garden. "The house was so full there was no getting in there, so forced to go through an alehouse into the pit, where the bears are baited; and upon a stool did see them [the men] fight, which they did very furiously, a butcher and a waterman. The former had the better all along, till by and by the latter dropped his sword out of his hand, and the butcher . . . did give him a cut over the wrist, so as he was disabled to fight any longer. But, Lord! to see how in a minute the whole stage was full of watermen to revenge the foul play, and the butchers to defend their fellow, though most blamed him; and there they all fell to it knocking down and cutting many on each side. It was pleasant to see . . ."

At a street corner a Punch and Judy show had all but stopped traffic, while

> Punch and Judy fought for a pie;
> Punch gave Judy a knock in the eye.

A few small children riding in the arms of their parents looked on, open-mouthed. The rest of the audience were adults, but they too were in raptures over this new puppet show that had only recently come from Italy.

Guests were leaving a party at a private house to go home with linkboys, who would light the way through the streets. For entertainment after dinner there had been a fire eater, whose performance was unforgettable. "He devoured brimstone on glowing coals . . . chewing and swallowing them; he melted a beer-glass and eat it quite up; then, taking a live coal on his tongue, he put on it a raw oyster; the coal was blown on with bellows till it flamed and sparkled in his mouth, and so remain'd till the oyster gaped and was quite boiled. Then he melted pitch and wax with sulphur, which he drank down, as it flowed." Not at all a dull party, and one which created plenty of lively talk as the guests emerged into the street.

They took good care on their way home to keep close to the houses. The streets were deep in mire and every kind of dirt. Sewers were almost nonexistent, and a shout of "Garday-loo!" ("Guardez l'eau") meant "Watch out for the water!" as the contents of bucket or pot fell from an overhanging window into the street below. A lady being carried home in a sedan chair held a perfumed handkerchief or a pomander ball to her nose. Indeed everything about her was perfumed, including shoes and gloves, but milady herself had almost certainly not had a recent bath.

Gresham College, near Bishopsgate below London Bridge, was dark on the night of September 1, 1666, since there was no lecture that evening. This was the meeting place of the Royal Society for Improving Natural Knowledge, where brilliant scientists and men of letters came regularly to read learned papers and exchange ideas. But with all of this learning available to the city of London, no adequate fire-fighting system had been devised by the night of September 1, 1666. Most houses had only buckets. There were no fire engines in London.

At about three o'clock on Sunday morning, the maid Jane called Mr. Pepys to come and look at a fire. He put on his "nightgowne" [dressing gown] and went to a window that faced toward the City. The fire seemed to be somewhere near Cheapside, among the markets and warehouses. It was too far away to be a present danger. There were fires every day in London, and they were put out, sooner or later, by the householders themselves. Mr. Pepys went back to bed. When he looked out of the same window on Sunday morning at about seven o'clock, he could not see much fire, but Jane came running to say that three hundred houses had been burned during the night. Mr. Pepys dressed and hurried out to see for himself. He was told that the fire had started in the King's baker's house in Pudding Lane. When he reached the Tower, a strong east wind was blowing, and the flames were coming toward the river. He stepped into a boat, as many others were doing. From the river he saw "everybody endeavouring to remove their goods, and flinging into the river or bringing them into lighters that lay off; poor people staying in their houses as long as till the very fire touched them, and then running into boats, or clambering from one pair of stairs by the water-side to another . . . Having staid, and in an hour's time seen the fire rage every way, and nobody, to my sight, endeavouring to quench it, but to remove their goods and leave all to the fire . . . and everything, after so long a drought, proving combustible, even the very stones of churches: I to White Hall, and there up to the King's closett in the Chappell, where people come about me, and I did give them an account dismayed them all, and word was carried into the King."

Both the King and the Duke of York were much troubled. Pepys was ordered to find the Lord Mayor and to "command him to spare no houses, but to pull down before the fire every way." Back to the City he went. There he found the Lord Mayor going about the burning streets like a man demented. On hearing the King's message, the poor man, half fainting, cried, "Lord, what can I do? I am spent: people will not obey me. I have been pulling down houses; but the fire overtakes us faster than we can do it."

The timber houses, crowded together, made a roaring furnace of street after street. Once again, as in the time of the plague, the people of London fled from their city. This time they carried with them what they could, and let the city burn. Choked by the dense smoke, stung by flaming drops of fire that fell from above, the people watched the death of their city, while night came on like no night ever seen before. The fire was "only one entire arch of flame" up and down the river. The water shone red in the glare. The King himself came by barge with his brother to direct and encourage the people. He put James in charge of the City, and one building after another was blown

Samuel Pepys, a portrait by John Hayls

up with gunpowder to create gaps across which the fire could not leap. Still it raged.

On September 3, John Evelyn wrote, "God grant mine eyes may never behold the like, who now saw above 10,000 houses all in one flame! The noise and cracking and thunder of the impetuous flames, the shrieking of women and children, the hurry of people, the fall of towers, houses, and churches, was like a hideous storm; and the air all about so hot and inflamed that at the last one was not able to approach it, so that they were forced to stand still, and let the flames burn on . . . for near two miles in length and one in breadth. The clouds also of smoke were dismal, and reached, upon computation, near fifty miles in length . . . London was, but is no more!"

John Dryden was not in the city at the time of the Great Fire, but he described it in a long poem, "Annus Mirabilis," commemorating that "Year of Wonders." He recalled how the fire had started, "in mean buildings first obscurely bred," like a usurper who emerges from a humble birthplace to destroy the peace of a kingdom. The winds, which had at first seemed to hold back the fire, were "like crafty courtesans," who were coy with the flames to make them burst out "with inrag'd desire." In his mind's eye, Dryden saw the lurid outline of London Bridge, where the heads of traitors had always been mounted on pikes. He imagined the ghosts of those traitors descending to dance with the spectral fires reflected in the river.

On Tuesday night the wind dropped. John Evelyn was thankful that St. Bartholomew's Hospital had been spared. The old building and its inmates were part of his responsibility as Commissioner for the Sick and Wounded. He thought ruefully of the treatise which he had presented to the King five years earlier on the subject of smoke control in London. Now there was smoke enough! If only action had been taken in time, as he had recommended, the coal and wood wharfs, and the stores of oil and rosin would have been moved outside the City, but it was too late now. They had burned fiercely, as had other warehouses full of combustible goods like pitch and tar, wine, and brandy. Thank God, his Majesty had ordered the houses around the Tower of London to be pulled down before the great magazine of gunpowder could catch fire and explode!

But St. Paul's was gone. The scaffolding about its walls had helped to catch the racing flames so that all blazed upward. Where Sir John and Dr. Wren had consulted only a week before about the best plan for beautifying and strengthening the ancient church, there was now nothing to beautify. The great leaden roof had melted and fallen, the stones had split asunder. "The stones of Paul's flew like grenadoes, the melting lead running down the streets in a stream, and the very pavements glowing with fiery redness, so as no horse, nor man, was able to tread on them." The entire church must be rebuilt.

The gallant behavior of the royal brothers, Charles and James, inspired many citizens to follow their example during the fire, and afterward an effort was made with emergency measures to help the destitute. Outside the City wall, camps appeared, where refugees, broken by the disaster, their faces streaked with soot and sweat, their hair white with fallen ash, sat down to weep among their bundles. But inside the City, looters began to move from house to house. They came from "Alsatia," a refuge for thieves and other lawless outcasts in the Whitefriars district of London, and to "Alsatia" they returned, leaving the refugees even more destitute.

By September 6, the fire was over. It had destroyed four-fifths of the City, leaving about three hundred thousand people homeless. The London of Chaucer and Shakespeare was gone.

Amazingly, the rebuilding began almost at once. Dr. Wren,

soon to be Sir Christopher Wren, was there to guide the planning and the building. But alas, the slums, which lay on the outskirts, reappeared much as they had been before—seedbeds of trouble full of hopeless vagabonds crowded into filthy hovels. The old prayers of the Litany were still timely for the people of London: ". . . from plague, pestilence, and famine; from battle and murder, and from sudden death, Good Lord, deliver us. From all sedition, privy conspiracy, and rebellion . . . Good Lord, deliver us."

How had the fire really started? A rumor got about that the French and Dutch had landed, entered the City by stealth, and set the fire. For a long time afterward, any Frenchman or Hollander in London let his nationality be known at peril of his life. He would be attacked without sense or reason by mobs of rioters who dispersed only when troops came to drive them away.

There were other opinions, too. Sir John Evelyn thought that the plague, the fire, and the war with the Dutch, coming one after another, clearly betokened God's punishment for a people "minding nothing but luxury, ambition, and to procure money for our vices. . . . In a word, we were wanton, mad, and surfeiting with prosperity, every moment unsettling the old foundations, and never constant to anything."

A month after the fire, a general fast was declared throughout the nation "to humble us on the late conflagration, added to the plague and war, the most dismal judgments that could be inflicted, but which indeed we highly deserved for our prodigious ingratitude, burning lusts, dissolute court, profane and abominable lives."

That year was a lesson long remembered. For the next generation the English people, especially Londoners, would think of 1666, the "Annus Mirabilis," not only as a sign of God's anger, but also as the fault of the French potentate, Louis XIV. Somehow, he must be back of all this misery. Who was the passive ally of Holland in its war against England? Louis! Who were the first to die of the plague in London? Two Frenchmen! Londoners nodded sagely. And who started the fire? Probably not the King's baker in Pudding Lane. He swore that he was in bed by twelve o'clock that night, with all of his ovens stone cold. No, the fire must have been started by Papists (backed, of course, by Louis), who undoubtedly threw "fire-balls" into the houses. One of these days there would be war with France. The people feared that thought, yet somehow knew it must be so.

At St. James's Palace, two miles away, the little Princess Anne slept in her crib, quite unaware that the events of 1666 would still cast shadows thirty-six years later, when she was Queen.

Chapter V

🌿 *St. Germain*

Pat a cake, pat a cake, Bakers man, so I will master as I can, and prick it, and prick it, and prick it, and prick it, and prick it, and throw't into the Oven.
Tom Durfey (1653–1723) *from* "The Campaigners"

BABIES DO NOT CHANGE MUCH from one century to the next, nor do the games their nurses play with them. The Princess Anne played pat-a-cake, heard about Jack Sprat and his wife, and began, as soon as she was able, to guess riddles. At night, looking out over the treetops from the window of her nursery, she was asked,

Higher than a house,
Higher than a tree;
Oh, whatever can that be?

She learned to answer, "It is a starre in the skie."

There were circle games to play too, and since the great plague there was a new meaning, some said, for one of the oldest games of all. "Ring-a-ring o' roses" meant the red rash that broke out with the coming of the sickness; "a pocket full of posies" meant the bundle of herbs which people had carried as a protection; "A-tishoo! A-tishoo!" was the sneezing which came as another symptom of the disease; and then, "We all fall down."

On going to bed there was a prayer, half Christian worship,

half Celtic magic, to be said by good children like Anne for
safety at night:

> Matthew, Mark, Luke and John,
> Bless the bed that I lie on.
> Four corners to my bed,
> Four angels round my head;
> One to watch and one to pray,
> And two to bear my soul away.

The learned gentlemen of the Royal Society talked of a uni-
verse based on scientific law and order, but there were still plenty
of people who knew better and could tell the children about

> . . . ghoulies and ghoosties,
> Long leggity beasties,
> And things that go bump in the night.

The little Princesses by the nursery fire at St. James's Palace
sat close together for comfort, yet asked for one more story.

Their mother continued to worry about their health, particularly that of Anne, who more than once was so sick that she was
not expected to live. All kinds of remedies were tried without
success. At last it was decided that a change of air might help.
French doctors might know something that English doctors did
not know. In July 1668, Anne was sent to France to stay with
her grandmother, Henrietta Maria. This dictatorial and formidable old lady had made trouble on a grand scale through meddling
in the affairs of her royal sons, Charles and James; but now she
behaved as a grandmother should, sent coaches and retainers to
meet the little Princess at Dieppe, and put her under the care
of the best doctors who could be found.

The visit of the English Princess was made with the full
knowledge and approval of the hospitable French King. The
young Duke of Monmouth had already arrived from England

and had been warmly welcomed. He was a natural son of Charles II, handsome and charming like his father. All that he needed was a little French polish, which his relatives at St. Germain were only too glad to supply, along with some ideas about ways and means of putting himself on the throne of England when the proper time came.

It was typical of the Stuart period that Charles II and Louis XIV were related by marriage, so that Louis was constantly playing a double role in the lives of his royal English cousins. Officially he was the archenemy of England; unofficially he was the host to England's royal family whenever they needed a refuge. The French had a phrase—*Cousinage fait dangereux voisinage;* Cousins make dangerous neighbors. But Cousin Louis could be a very good neighbor indeed.

There was a beautiful palace at St. Germain near Paris, which was Louis's favorite residence during the first part of his reign, while Versailles was being built. Here the little Princess Anne spent almost three years of her life. The change of air and of doctors did seem to benefit her. The sunshine poured in through the long French windows of the children's wing of the palace, where Louis's many children, the "Enfants de France," played happily. The famous gardener, Le Nôtre, had planted fragrant shrubs in the courtyard below the palace windows. Seen from above, they looked like the arabesques of a great Oriental rug. Fountains were everywhere. Terraces were planted with fruit trees, and in the Great Park a newly planted forest was spreading its green.

In the rooms of the palace at St. Germain were luxuries which England was only beginning to acquire: crystal chandeliers, floors laid in intricate patterns. English furniture was heavy, dark, built to last forever; French furniture was more gracefully designed and was often painted in pale colors or decorated with floral marquetry. Royal immigrants, arriving in gloomy mood from some political catastrophe in England, were soon cheered by all this freshness and brightness. It was really a pleasure to wait in exile at St. Germain.

This was the France where the great Jean Racine was just beginning to attract attention with his classic dramas. Molière came to St. Germain to produce one of his comedies for Louis's brilliant Court. Corneille was still writing. Jean de La Fontaine was busy collecting fables from Aesop to be adapted with a droll touch.

Another gentleman at Louis's Court was a lawyer named Charles Perrault. He had a fanciful spirit and a warm heart; it was he who persuaded the King to allow the children of Paris to play in the Tuileries Gardens. He was making a collection of stories which he found among the French people themselves. Perhaps some of the stories came from old women or young girls at work in the great kitchens of St. Germain. The tales were crude, but Perrault thought he could polish them. He may sometimes have told stories in the children's wing of the palace where the Princess Anne lived. Soon children everywhere would hear Perrault's *Contes de ma Mère l'Oye, Tales of Mother Goose*. Among them were "The Sleeping Beauty," "Cinderella," "Little Red Riding Hood," "Puss in Boots," "Bluebeard," and "Hop-o'-My-Thumb."

Not long after the arrival of three-year-old Anne, the Queen Mother, Henrietta Maria, died, but Anne was in good hands. Her aunt, Henrietta Anne, took her little niece into the nursery of the palace at St. Cloud to be brought up with her own daughter, Marie Louise. Of all the ladies at Louis's Court, none was more remarkable than this aunt, Henrietta Anne, known to all as "Madame."

Madame had great beauty and vitality; she was a magnificent

horsewoman. She was one of those women who command attention, wherever they are, whatever they do. She was the favorite
sister of Charles II, and the correspondence between them was
voluminous. He wrote to her explaining his point of view about
all important matters, and valued her opinion and approval above
all others. When France halfheartedly declared war against
England in 1666, Charles wrote to her, "I cannot tell what kind
of correspondence we must keep with letters now that France de-
clares war with us. . . . But nothing can make me lessen in the
least degree of that kindness I always have had for you, which
I assure you is so rooted in my heart as it will continue to the
last moment of my life. For my dearest sister. C."

Louis himself was not enthusiastic about this declaration of
war against England. He only wanted to do enough to fulfill his
obligations to his Dutch allies. A few naval skirmishes would not,
he hoped, annoy the English too much, for it would be disagreeable to have England take revenge by forming an alliance with
Spain. The English navy was a threat which worried him at
times, but maintaining the balance of power was important too,
and Louis could not think of everything and do everything at
once. Meanwhile, it was a piece of great good luck that Charles
and Madame were so fond of each other. These family relationships might be somewhat embarrassing and hard to explain
when war was being waged between the two countries, but
they would be very convenient when the time came to declare
peace.

In 1667 Madame seemed to be in perfect health. Then in
1670, very suddenly, she died. The cause was unknown, al-
though poisoning was suspected. Her death left the French
Court deeply shocked and grieved, but to Anne and her little
French cousin, the death of Madame was only dimly understood.
Dressed in long coats of violet velvet (which some thought in

deplorable taste), they were made to receive the visitors who came with condolences. When Lady Frances Villiers arrived with her husband to take Anne home to England, Cousin Louis parted with the child affectionately and gave her, as a farewell present, a pair of diamond bracelets said to be worth 10,000 crowns. If he had known that this frail child would live to humiliate France, he might not have given the bracelets to her.

Queen Anne as a child, a portrait by Sir Peter Lely

Chapter VI

Richmond

SOON AFTER ANNE'S RETURN from France her mother died of cancer. It was only one, though perhaps the worst, of the troubles that had been crowding thick and fast about her luckless family. Anne's maternal grandfather had fallen from power under the most humiliating circumstances. He who had been born plain Edward Hyde had risen, under King Charles's favor, to be the first Earl of Clarendon. He had been made Chancellor of the Exchequer and then Lord High Chancellor of England. The Great Seal was in his keeping. The King had no higher honor to confer. But as Clarendon grew older, changes came. He had always held very conservative convictions and had been a strong supporter of the Church of England. The first Cavalier parliament of 1661 had passed measures against Dissenters and called them the Clarendon Code. He was the natural target for criticism by the liberal faction and by men of non-conforming religious persuasion. He made no bones about his disapproval of Lady Castlemaine and of the vicious Duke of Buckingham, both members of the notorious Villiers family and both favorites of Charles II.

The King was bored with the indignant accusations of his Lord High Chancellor. He was hoping for an excuse to get rid of the old man, and the excuse came. When the extravagances of the King created a need for economy, Clarendon recommended that the cuts in expense should be made by reducing the navy to a skeleton force, barely strong enough to carry out raiding attacks on the Dutch ships. Anne's father, the Duke of York, was enraged. As Lord High Admiral he had been pursuing a vigorous course of action against the Dutch, even sending two ships to Long Island, in the New World, where the Dutch had surrendered without a blow being struck. The colony of New Amsterdam had been renamed New York in honor of James. He also recognized the importance of a strong navy for the purpose of trade with both the East Indies and the West Indies. Working with Samuel Pepys, who was the deputy of Lord Sandwich, James had reconstructed and reorganized the navy. And now this foolish old man, his father-in-law, had power enough to oppose the war with Holland and to put a part of the fleet out of commission, saying that the sailors could not be paid. Clarendon argued that the city of London had been through enough, with the plague and the fire, and could not now stand a war. The Duchess of York begged her father "that he would no more oppose the Duke in the matter," but the old man told her that she did not know what she was talking about. At this critical point it would perhaps have been better for the Earl of Clarendon to resign, but he did not know how generally unpopular he had become. Parliament blamed him because he would not let them spend the money they had voted for the support of the navy. The people blamed him because it was he who had arranged the marriage of Charles with his barren queen, Catherine of Braganza. It was even said that Clarendon had known very well there would be no children born of this marriage and that he had deliberately planned it so that the throne would go to his own grandchildren, Mary and Anne, the children of the Duke and Duchess of York.

In May 1667, when negotiations for a peace were already under way, a Dutch commander decided to take revenge for the English raid that had cost Holland her colony at New Amsterdam. One night some Dutch ships sailed into the Thames and captured or burned sixteen English ships of the line as they lay unmanned and at anchor. It was the greatest disgrace ever inflicted on the English navy, and someone had to bear the blame. The Earl of Clarendon was the most convenient scapegoat, although the King himself might have been a more logical one to blame. Pepys wrote that "the night the Dutch burned our ships the King did sup with my Lady Castlemaine, at the Duchess of Monmouth's and they were all mad in hunting of a poor moth." So, while Charles was chasing butterflies, the ships had gone up in smoke on the river. Worst of all, the *Royal Charles,* the very ship which had brought the King home in triumph from the Continent in 1660, was captured by the Dutch, and sailed back to the Hague. John Evelyn called it "a dishonour never to be wiped off! Those who advised his Majesty to prepare no fleet this spring deserved—I know what—but—" Here Evelyn's anger was so great that he could not find words to continue.

So Clarendon must go. Charles took matters into his own hands. He called Clarendon to Whitehall. For two hours one morning they talked together in the garden, beneath the windows of Lady Castlemaine's rooms. About noon she got out of bed and looked down to see how the conference was progressing. Realizing that it was all over with Clarendon, she ran just as she was, in her nightgown, to laugh at the old courtier from a vantage point in her aviary. Clarendon heard her insulting remarks as he passed by on his way out of the garden, and stopped long enough to say, "Madam, if you live, *you* will grow old."

The fate of Edward Hyde, Earl of Clarendon, was no worse than that of many others who gave their lives and fortunes into the hands of the Stuarts. Charles had a short memory for the years of devotion and faithful service of his followers.

A case in point was that of Sir Richard Fanshawe, who had gone off in 1664 to represent Charles at the Court of the King of Spain. Sir Richard had paid his own expenses, in expectation of being reimbursed for them and of receiving a small salary as well. The necessary expenses were great. To go suitably dressed meant "a very rich suit of clothes of a dark fille-morte brocade laced with silver and gold laces, every one as broad as my hand," said Lady Fanshawe in her diary, "and a little silver and gold lace laid between them, both of very curious workmanship; his linen very fine, laced with very rich Flanders lace; a black beaver [hat], buttoned on the left side, with a jewel of twelve hundred pounds value. . . . On his fingers he wore two rich rings; his gloves trimmed with the same ribbon as his clothes." The whole family, if not so splendid as Sir Richard, had to dress and live in a state of magnificence proper to their position as representatives of his Majesty King Charles, yet the money to reimburse them for their expenses was not forthcoming during the entire time of their residence in Spain.

On Sir Richard's death in 1666, his pay was £2,000 in arrears, with £5,815 more due for expenses. Lady Anne Fanshawe brought her husband's body home to England for burial and spent the next years sitting in anterooms of the palace either waiting to have an audience with the King which never took place, or receiving promises that were never kept. It was common knowledge that the Stuarts were bad masters.

In the years that followed Anne's return from France, she was old enough to see and to understand something of what went on around her. It may have been at this time that she learned to value friendship and to determine that she would be a true friend to anyone who was true to her.

Plans for the upbringing of Mary and Anne were made by their uncle, King Charles. First, it must be known by all the people that their religious life was under the supervision of an undoubted Protestant. This step, the King felt, would draw attention away from the strong Catholic leanings of their father, James, Duke of York, who was heir to the throne if Charles's wife had no children. Charles knew very well that James had been meeting with Jesuit priests, and that he intended to reveal his conversion to the Church of Rome. Charles himself was considering conversion to the Catholic faith, but he had no intention of letting it be known, since he was perfectly aware that a Roman Catholic on the throne would inevitably bring on a revolution. England was fanatically opposed to "Popery," in spite of the blameless lives and patriotic devotion of many Catholic aristocrats and others too obscure to have their sufferings noticed.

When the Church of England's Henry Compton (later Bishop of London) was appointed to give religious instruction to Mary and Anne, even the most rabid Protestants were satisfied. Lady Frances Villiers became governess to the Princesses, with her own seven children as their playmates. A music master, Anthony Robart, had been with the little girls from the time Anne was two years old. Mrs. Barry, an actress, came to give elocution lessons. This was especially for the benefit of Anne, so that her sweet voice would be trained to the best advantage. Lady Villiers was to have £1,200 a year for the "robes, linen, and other apparel" of the two Princesses.

A suitable home was found for the motherless children. Not far from London, and lying close to the beautiful Thames, were two old palaces, Kew and Richmond. Queen Elizabeth had loved Richmond, but now it was dilapidated and partly demolished. The hunting lodge remained, and it was given to the Villiers family during the years when Anne and Mary lived with them. There were swans on the river at Richmond. Daisies, lilies, and primroses grew "along the shore of silver streaming Thames." The air was mild, and the hunting lodge, perhaps because it was smaller, was warmer and more comfortable than the great drafty palaces of Whitehall and St. James's. Kew and Richmond were sweet with birdsong in the cherry trees, and with the scent of lilac. To this day it is a rare treat to "go down to Kew in lilac-time."

In the gardens and the park between Kew and Richmond, Anne grew stronger than she had ever been, and happier. Years later she still thought of Richmond as a kind of Arcadia, saying that "she loved it in her infancy and the air agreed with her." There were other beautiful houses at Richmond, along the river, "the sweetest river in the world," as Evelyn called it; houses with "parterres, flower gardens, orangeries, groves, avenues, courts, statues, perspectives, fountains, aviaries." As in Andrew Marvell's wondrous "Garden," there were sunny orchards with "ripe apples . . . luscious clusters of the vine . . . the nectarine, and curious peach . . . melons."

In this earthly paradise the children played at battledore and shuttlecock, and Blind Man's Buff. They rolled hoops along the garden paths and swung in the green and leafy shade of the old trees. The gardens and park belonged to the children unless the King came. Sometimes he arrived by barge along the river for a pleasure trip, bringing with him enough ladies and gentlemen to fill the park. Then the children were hurried off to dress in their best silks and satins, like small lords and ladies ready to bow and curtsey for his Majesty.

Anne was buttoned and tied into her finest little gown, heavy with gold embroidery and hanging in deep folds of brocade to the very floor. The peaked bodice was so stiff that she could not bend at the waist. When she was dressed, her nurses ran with her to the garden to find the King. There he was, taller than any of the rest; it was easy to find him. He had brought the little dogs. They were barking and jumping up on her dress, but never mind. They were dear little things with their shiny eyes and curly, wagging tails. They looked as if they were laughing.

Now Lady Frances was whispering to tell her that she must make her curtsey to his Majesty. But the King did not notice her curtsey. He had turned away to look at a lady who was coming across the grass. Sometimes things looked blurred to Anne. She could not quite see who the lady was until she came close. It was Lady Castlemaine, who was now the Duchess of Cleveland. Anne looked up into a beautiful, petulant face, painted very white but with red cheeks and red lips. On one cheek she wore a small black patch, shaped like a crescent moon. Her dark eyes sparkled. Lady Castlemaine touched Anne's shoulder lightly with her fan. "La!" she said, "it's the Duke's child," and walked on. The King followed her. No one was watching Anne. She went off into the park to see if she could find the little dogs. She did not like Lady Castlemaine.

Was there a man standing on the far side of the lawn? Perhaps it was her father, come to Richmond with the King. He often came to see his children and to play with them when affairs of state did not weigh too heavily on him. She was on the point of running to him when Mary came up behind her, saying, "We are to have supper now."

"But there is Father," Anne told her, pointing. "I want to see him first."

"That is not Father," Mary said, in her positive way. "It is a tree. And only yesterday you thought a tree was a man. You are stupid, Anne." Then, as they went off toward the hunting lodge together, "I learned a new verse that the ladies are saying:

Lucy Locket lost her pocket,
Kitty Fisher found it;
There was not a penny in it,
But a ribbon round it."

"It is very pretty," Anne said.

"Do you know what it means?" Mary said, in a conspiratorial tone. "Don't tell. One of the ladies said that Lucy Locket means Lady Castlemaine. Kitty Fisher means the Duchess of Portsmouth. And the pocket is the King!" She went off into gales of laughter.

"How can that be?" asked Anne.

But Mary only answered, "You are stupid, Anne."

Dr. Edward Lake was always waiting for the children when they came in to dinner. It was he who said grace, as it was he who taught them their catechism and saw that they learned the Collect for every Sunday in the year. Bishop Compton would want to know, when he came down from Oxford or London, whether Anne and Mary were well-grounded in their Bible and Prayer Book. The Bishop was "a grave and serious good man," according to John Evelyn, who was one of the same sort. But in the privacy of his own diary Evelyn confessed, with all due respect, that "this worthy person's talent is not preaching."

Compton's greatest talent, as Anne's preceptor, was in giving his young charge the strongest possible aversion to any religion but that of the Church of England. In our own time, the spirit of ecumenicism has thrown open the doors of all churches "to let in a little fresh air," in the words of Pope John XXIII. It is difficult now to imagine the atmosphere of the late seventeenth century, when political and religious persecution went hand in hand, and when hard and bitter memories were passed down from father to son, generation after generation. Catholic, Church of England, Puritan, none were guiltless. All denominations harbored their bigots and fanatics, and all nurtured many other men of tolerance and moderation.

Mr. Pepys was one of the latter. He was a good Church of England man, but he said, "The business of abusing the Puritans begins to grow stale, and of no use, they being the people that, at last, will be found the wisest." Pepys went to St. Olave's Church regularly and sat in the special gallery for naval personnel, reverently attending to the service, acknowledging and bewailing his sins and wickedness, which were indeed manifold. But one Sunday morning when he was meditating on his vows for the new year, he could not forbear to notice that "a most insipid young coxcomb preached." Pepys was only one of many who knew that there was room for improvement within his own church.

Many sermons preached from the pulpits of the established Church of England at this time fanned the flames of hatred and fear that were already centuries old. Sometimes the Puritans were reviled, but since they no longer seemed to be the chief threat to Church and State, the Papists were more often the target. As dangerous as the Papists were the Levellers. In a well-reasoned sermon against these troublemakers, Dr. John Breton preached at Cambridge, using the text of John I:27: ". . . whose shoe-latchet I am not worthy to unloose." The sermon described various fashions of shoes worn in ancient days by the Jews and other nations, a piece of research which must have kept the good doctor happily engaged in the University library for several days. He went on to develop the theme that great persons in the days of St. John had servants who took off their masters' shoes. In conclusion he approved "the lawfulness, decentness, and necessity, of subordinate degrees of men and servants, as well in the Church as State;" and he spoke strongly "against the late levellers, and others of that dangerous rabble, who would have all alike."

In another hundred years, in a colony across the sea, the spiritual descendants of "that dangerous rabble" would be writing that "all men are created equal," but even then it would be a revolutionary idea. The Princess Anne was not exposed to any such thought. She learned her religion as best she could, by the limited light of the limited minds to which her own mind was entrusted. It was a shock when Dr. Lake felt compelled to reveal to Anne that her own mother had become a convert to Catholicism shortly before her death. Anne was warned to be on guard at all times against talking to any priest whom her father might send to her. She shed many tears when Dr. Lake and Dr. Compton spoke to her about her father. Could it be true that he was a wicked man? Some even said that he was cruel. She heard people talking when they did not know that she was listening. Anne might not see very well, but she could hear, and what she heard about her father and her dead mother cast the only shadow in the bright days at Richmond. She promised Dr. Compton that she would never, never listen to a Roman Catholic priest. He questioned her about her nurses. Yes, she told him, one of them was a Catholic, but had never said a word to try to convert her. Was she sure? Quite sure. Dr. Compton appeared satisfied.

For Anne, the sun shone brightest at Richmond after the arrival of Sarah. She was Sarah Jennings, the younger sister of beautiful Frances Jennings, who had been Maid of Honor to Anne's mother. The Jennings family had fallen on hard times in the Civil War against Cromwell's Roundheads, and the appointment of Frances to a position of honor at Court was a chance to recoup some of their losses. Sarah had been left alone in the country to be cared for by servants, from whom she had learned almost, but not quite, all that she knew. Now she entered the Court circle accompanied by her mother, who chaperoned her like a dragon. Anne loved Sarah from the first moment. Sarah was four years older, but she attached herself to Anne because Mary had her own friends and paid no attention to Sarah.

Anne thought that Sarah was perfect. She was dressed simply, but her flowered silk gown fitted her slender figure admirably. She had the bloom and freshness of English country living, and she was full of ideas. She wanted to see all of Anne's dresses and asked how much they cost, not so much from envy as from an instinct for good management that ran in the Jennings family. Later, as they explored the old house together, Sarah opened a table drawer and found a pack of cards.

They sat down at the table and Sarah dealt the cards with an expert hand. "I'll teach you to play ombre," she said. "It's all the thing at Court. Frances says so. Do you have any money? It's pleasant to play for stakes." Anne had no money, but she had a lace handkerchief; Sarah had a plain one. Sarah won the lace handkerchief, and Anne agreed that playing for stakes made the game more exciting. Sarah promised that they would play again.

Chapter VII

London Again

IN THE MONTHS THAT FOLLOWED, Sarah was taken into the York household to be Anne's companion. Sarah was the leader because she was older and of an aggressive disposition; Anne was the younger, dependent, admiring. Sometimes they were at Richmond but oftener in London at Whitehall or St. James's.

Now that Anne had a friend like Sarah, it was not unpleasant to come back from the quiet of Richmond to the gaiety of London. The King could be seen almost every day, taking his little dogs for a run in the Park at St. James's, or feeding the ducks in the pond. Anne's father enjoyed the Park too, and often played with her there.

London was being rebuilt at a fast pace. Now it was harder to find fields where cows grazed within sight of the City. More than thirteen thousand houses had been burned in the Great Fire, but the astounding energy of planners and builders was more than equal to the need. Narrow streets were widened and building codes were established. Old timber, lath, and plaster houses gave way to brick houses of safer, sounder construction. Daniel Defoe thought that both servants and masters in London were still the most careless in the world about fire, but now large timber pipes brought water up from the river. When a fire occurred, a plug in the new water pipes could be turned so that water was available for the use of the new fire engines. Insurance companies employed firemen who were ready at all hours to put out fires in houses covered by insurance. Although there would still be plenty of London houses without running water or the benefit of fire insurance, standards of safety, convenience, and sanitation rose. And there was another new blessing: a source of drinking water, "very sweet and good," brought by conduits from distant springs.

But with the gains there were losses. Where one great house had stood, twenty new ones might fill the same space. The Savoy, one of the few great houses which had escaped the Fire, was "parted into innumerable tenements and apartments." Greater density of population all over the City meant more coal fires sending up smoke from a growing forest of chimneys. The streets were cleaned, but the air grew foul. Another hundred years and it would be a rare morning when a poet could look on the City and see it "all bright and glittering in the smokeless air." Still, London drew men to itself, and there would always be many to boast that "earth has not anything to show more fair" than the view of London from the river.

It was a city that seemed made for pleasure, which is "the height of what we take pains for and can hope for in this world," said Mr. Pepys, "and therefore to be enjoyed while we are young and capable of these joys." Yes, London made a joyful hubbub. More than ever, there was always some London church where bells rang gaily and incessantly. Above the rattle of wheels and hooves on cobblestones, street criers added to the din.

"Chairs to mend, old chairs to mend! Rush or cane bottom'd, old chairs to mend, old chairs to mend."

"New mackerel, new mackerel!"

"Old rags, old rags, take money for your old rags!"

"Any hare skins, or rabbit skins?"

And throughout the night sleepless citizens could be sure of hearing the watchman's call: "Past three o'clock, and a cold frosty morning. . . . All's well!"

Once again, all over London dancing and singing parties went on, far into the night. But with this gaiety went a sense of urgency, which Andrew Marvell gave voice to when he told "His Coy Mistress" that he could not wait for her forever:

> Had we but world enough, and time,
> This coyness, Lady, were no crime . . .
> But at my back I always hear
> Time's wingèd chariot hurrying near;
> And yonder all before us lie
> Deserts of vast eternity.

"We have today, enjoy it; tomorrow, who knows?" sang the Cavalier poets of the Restoration.

"Patience; God knows!" answered the Puritan. In an obscure house in a quiet London suburb, John Milton was reaching the end of his long struggle for truth and liberty against evil and tyranny, a struggle handicapped by blindness but never by despair. A slender figure in a gray cloak, he was led about the streets near his home in Artillery Walk, Bunhill, or sat in his garden, talking affably to the learned men who came to visit him. In his last dark days, waiting to enter into light eternal, his Puritan spirit of endurance under suffering was dramatically at variance with the age in which he lived:

> . . . God doth not need
> Either man's work or his own gifts. Who best
> Bear his mild yoke, they serve him best. His state
> Is kingly: thousands at his bidding speed,
> And post o'er land and ocean without rest;
> They also serve who only stand and wait.

The Princess Anne was soon to learn more about the serious-minded, God-fearing Puritans, Dissenters, and Covenanters who would one day be an important part of her kingdom. Her growing awareness of the Protestant will of England came about because of her father. He had always been kind to her, but when she was eight years old, it seemed to her that he did something most unkind. He married again.

His bride was a beautiful young Italian girl, only fifteen years old and a Roman Catholic. She was Maria d'Este, sister of the Duke of Modena, and she had never heard of England or of the forty-year-old Duke of York until his emissary arrived to arrange the marriage. She had half thought of entering a convent, but when she was persuaded that marriage with the English James would be for the good of her people and a service to God, she consented. The marriage was so unpopular with the English that when poor Maria d'Este (Mary of Modena, they called her) arrived, she found Londoners burning effigies of the Pope. Nevertheless, the wedding was solemnized. Mary and Anne were presented with a stepmother young enough to have been their sister, but the happy possibilities of the relationship were largely ruled out by the fact of her religion and that of James, who was openly confessing his own conversion to the Catholic faith.

A Declaration of Indulgence in 1672, relaxing the laws against Catholics and Non-conformists, was soon nullified; religious tension in England increased with every passing year. Behind most of the trouble was England's suspicion of Louis XIV, the Catholic King of her long-standing enemy, France. Suspicion at this time was well-founded. In 1670, Charles had made a secret Treaty of Dover, by which Louis agreed to give financial help to Charles in England's war against Holland. In exchange for this help, Charles promised to use every means in his power

The Bettmann Archive

The National Portrait Gallery

Queen Anne's father and stepmother, King James II and Mary of Modena

to bring England back to the Church of Rome. Charles was under the influence of politically minded Jesuits, and was moved also by his affection for his French Roman Catholic sister, "Madame." He misread the wishes both of the Pope and of his own English people. The English, and even their representatives in Parliament, knew little or nothing of the secret terms of the Treaty of Dover, but they did know about the conversion of the Duke of York to Catholicism. He was Lord High Admiral of the Fleet, and Parliament would not have a Catholic in a position of such power. On the Continent, every little king and princeling might admire the methods of France's Grand Monarch, Louis XIV, who ruled by the principle of absolute power for State and Church, but in England it was not so. In 1673 Parliament passed the Test Act, by which no one might hold civil or military office unless he would take Communion under the rites of the Church of England.

If Charles had had a conscience, he could not have remained King under the Test Act, for his own religious preferences were becoming more and more Catholic. Some years later James told Pepys that Charles was a Catholic but that he concealed it for political reasons. Pepys told Evelyn, and Evelyn recorded the secret in his diary. He and others like him respected James for the sincerity of his religious belief. Charles was different. The Anglican Bishop Burnet reported a private conversation with the King in these words: "He said once to my self, he was no atheist, but he could not think God would make a man miserable only for taking a little pleasure out of the way. He disguised his Popery to the last. But when he talked freely, he could not help letting himself out against the liberty that under the Reformation all men took of enquiring into matters of religion: For from their enquiring into matters of religion they carried the humour farther, to enquire into matters of state. He said often, he thought government was a much safer and easier thing where the authority was believed infallible, and the faith and submission of the people was implicit." Charles was right. It was easier for him to rule England without having Parliament probing, questioning, and interfering with his religious belief. He kept quiet, thinking privately that it must be easier to rule in France than in England.

Unlike Charles, James had a conscience. He has been called unlovable, bigoted, cruel, intolerant, slow-witted, stupid, incompetent, but these are words that routinely go with life in high places. Whatever his faults, James was open and honest in his religious convictions; he dared to confess his faith, no matter what the consequences. Parliament, whose power was growing by leaps and bounds, forced his resignation as Lord High Admiral.

No one seemed to remember the services which James had given during his years with the navy. In "Annus Mirabilis," Dryden had praised him to the skies:

> Victorious York did first, with fam'd success,
> To his known valor make the Dutch give place:
> Thus Heav'n our monarch's fortune did confess,
> Beginning conquest from his royal race.

James's "known valor" was forgotten now. So was his contribution to the victories in the New World which gave England colonies in Delaware, New Jersey, and New York. Mary and Anne could not help knowing that their father was disliked by the people he might some day rule. They could see the unfriendly looks of faces as he passed along in his carriage with his young wife by his side. Only when the two little girls were in the carriage might there be smiles from the crowds and friendly greetings for the children. The people knew that the

Duke's two daughters were being brought up as Protestants by order of the King.

Seasons came and went for Mary and Anne. There were lessons to be learned with tutors, but no school to attend. Royal children would not attend school in England until the middle of the twentieth century. Besides, few schools for girls existed. Boys might go to school, but it was considered enough for the average girl to learn to read and write, to sew and to manage a household. Some could read the Italian poets, and there were brilliant women to be met, especially at Court, but they were few.

Anne never became one of them. She did learn to read and write, to appreciate the beauty of the King James Bible and the Book of Common Prayer. She could speak French well, do embroidery, dance, play the guitar, and ride magnificently. No wonder, since the best teachers in England were only too glad to come on request and teach the young Princesses any subject or any art that was thought necessary or desirable. The King's Court itself was an education, though not always a suitable one for children. Here were gathered writers, artists, craftsmen, scientists, statesmen, all circling about the vortex of Whitehall because of the dynamic attraction of its King and Court.

It was probably the King who suggested an entertainment for the Christmas of 1675 at Whitehall. He had arranged for Mary and Anne to have some training in dramatics from Mrs. Betterton, an actress who came to the palace to help the children and their friends present a masque. Many happy hours were spent in rehearsing and trying on costumes that were being stitched up by half a dozen seamstresses. The days were full of laughter and joking as Christmas approached, and with it the night of the play.

The masque was "Calisto," written by John Crowne and

adapted by him for the use of the young performers. The scene was Arcadia; the time, "one artificial day," as the program announced. Mary played the title role, and Anne was "Nymphe, a chaste Nymph, friend to Calisto." Sarah Jennings played the part of Mercury, and young Margaret Blagge was the goddess Diana. For weeks afterward, Anne and Sarah called each other Nymphe and Mercury.

John Evelyn came to see the play. "Saw a comedy at night, at Court," he wrote, "acted by the ladies only, amongst them Lady Mary and Ann, his Royal Highness's two daughters, and my dear friend Mrs. Blagge. . . . They were all covered with jewels." They were, indeed. Margaret Blagge herself wore jewels worth £20,000, borrowed from ladies of the Court. Anne wore her diamond bracelets, no doubt, and her young stepmother had many diamonds to lend. She had never been anything but kind.

A dancing chorus caused much laughter and applause among the audience that packed the great hall to see "Calisto." The dancers were all gentlemen of the Court, among them the Duke of Monmouth, still in his twenties, handsome, and graceful. His appearance at Court always caused a flurry of speculation, since the King was known to have a special fondness for this young man, his natural son, and might yet declare him the heir to the throne. "Calisto" was such a success that the performance was repeated at Court on the twenty-second of December, as festivities reached their height.

In the safety of their own coaches, the royal family also drove out to see the Christmas merrymaking in the streets of London. The Lord of Misrule was chosen and crowned by acclaim of the crowds. His bodyguard, decked out in scarves, ribbons, and laces, pranced through the churches with rings on their fingers and bells on their toes. Costumes were a wonder to behold. The tatterdemalion procession of Christmas mummers was sure to include several small boys weaving and bobbing along the street under a dragon made of green cloth. There might be a two-legged cock horse on the way to Banbury Cross, accompanied by drummers and pipers. Booths were set up in the churchyards for a feast of bread and ale, custards, cakes, and tarts for the revelers. No one came home until morning. It was no wonder that the sober Puritans frowned on Yuletide celebration that was more like a pagan Saturnalia than a Christian holy day.

Some Puritans, of course, were more strict in their views than others. Some wanted only to purify the forms of the Church of England while remaining within the Church. Other "Puritans" were Presbyterians. Many were Free Churchmen, and these might be of various denominations, including Quakers and Baptists.

John Bunyan was a Baptist, a simple, earnest man who looked at the England of his day and called it Vanity Fair. During all the years of the Princess Anne's childhood, he and others like him had been in and out of jails, taken into custody again and again at meetings of "good people in the country" where he expected to preach. He was indicted "for an upholder and maintainer of unlawful assemblies," and for not conforming to the national worship of the Church of England. With persecution his faith only burned brighter, and in his prison cell he found new meaning in the Bible. "Those scriptures that I saw nothing in before, are made in this place and state to shine upon me," he wrote. Yet when he thought of the hardships and miseries he had brought upon his wife and children, he suffered as if the flesh were being pulled from his bones. There was a blind child who was especially dear. What hardships might she undergo while her father lay in prison? "But yet," he thought, as he considered the plight of his family, "I must venture you all with God, though it goeth to the quick to leave you. . . . I was as a man who was pulling down his house upon the head of his wife and children: yet, thought I, I must do it, I must do it."

While the London of the Stuarts was going to extremes in the search for pleasure, John Bunyan, in prison, pictured the city as a wilderness, and dreamed dreams of a man standing "with his face from his own house, a book in his hand, and a great burden upon his back." Bunyan's Pilgrim set off on a long journey, until he crossed through the deep waters of Jordan and entered a Celestial City "that shone like the sun, while all the bells of the city rang again for joy." (There was a wistful undertone in this ending of "Pilgrim's Progress," for John Bunyan had given up bell-ringing as a sin when he became converted to the religious life.) In the Celestial City the bells would ring again for those who had the patience and perseverance of a Milton or a John Bunyan. Many Puritans with less patience had already left the spiritual wilderness of England for homes in the wilderness of North America.

But even if they elected to stay in England, Non-conformists of all sects were safer than the English Roman Catholics. By 1677 the Duke of York had become an object of such general fear and distrust that King Charles arranged the marriage of James's daughter, the Princess Mary, to the Dutch Protestant Prince, William of Orange, in order to ease the tension. It seemed a reasonable move. Mary was fifteen, no younger than her stepmother had been when she came to England as a bride. William was a cousin, and Holland was not far away, but Mary wept "all that afternoon and the following day" when her uncle told her about the plans.

In due course William arrived, and Charles hurried the wedding so that William might have the pleasure of imagining himself on the throne of England. The young Duchess of York, Mary of Modena, was expecting a baby at any moment. If that baby were a boy, the Princess Mary would be one step farther away from the throne. Under those circumstances, William might change his mind about the marriage and sail home alone. However, the wedding of William and Mary was celebrated in the nick of time. The new baby, when it arrived three days later, proved to be a boy and was named Charles, after his uncle. He was not destined to live out the month. Mary remained second in line for the throne, after her father. William sailed home to Holland with his bride, well satisfied with the bargain he had made, but glad to get away. Smallpox had broken out in the palace before the wedding, and William was so nervous and sullen in consequence that the English Court privately dubbed him "Caliban" and "the Dutch monster." Perhaps they had forgotten that William's mother had died of smallpox on a visit to England, but William had not forgotten. It was not at all unusual to die of smallpox in England.

Anne was one of those who fell ill at the time of Mary's marriage to William. She was too sick to be told about the wedding and knew nothing of Mary's departure for Holland until the royal couple had left England. Dr. Edward Lake attended Anne faithfully during her illness, partly through an honest affection that is apparent in his diary, partly because one of Anne's nurses was a Catholic, who might, Dr. Lake feared, convert her to Popery on her deathbed if the disease proved to be fatal. Lady Frances Villiers, Anne's governess, died of smallpox at this time, but Anne recovered. It is not known what treatment was given, but the usual medicine for smallpox was "a black powder made from thirty or forty live toads burned to a crisp."

Chapter VIII

Newmarket

MANY A GIRL WHO ROSE from her sickbed after smallpox wore a wig for the first time, not for fashion's sake but because her own hair had fallen out. Many lost forever the fresh, delicate coloring that still makes English complexions famous. But pale cheeks could be rouged, and a beauty spot of taffeta, or even of Spanish leather, could be glued on to cover a pockmark.

Luckily, when Anne recovered from the smallpox she had not lost her looks. Besides, Sarah was her model, and Sarah needed no paint or powder. Anne followed suit and went without cosmetics, even though she lacked the high color and sparkling eyes that kept dozens of beaux dancing attendance on Sarah. As lady-in-waiting for the Duchess of York, Sarah wore her own hair simply and becomingly brushed into soft puffs above the smooth forehead behind which her busy brain was at work. At fifteen she had already met the man she wanted to marry, a young lieutenant colonel named John Churchill, eldest son of Sir Winston Churchill of Devonshire. He was ten years older than Sarah and, like her, was attached to the household of the Duke of York. He danced to perfection, and Sarah, dancing with him for the first time at a Court ball, fell dead in love with him, as had many another of his dancing partners, including Barbara Villiers.

The difference between Sarah and those others was that she

made up her mind to marry him, and when Sarah made up her mind, obstacles meant nothing. She won John's love away from Barbara Villiers, defied his family's wish that he should marry for money, and then kept him in torments of suspense. "My heart is ready to break," he wrote to her. "Since you are grown so indifferent, death is the only thing that can ease me." He need not have worried. Sarah had no intention of letting him die. When she was about seventeen, they were married. Neither had any money, but the Duchess of York, Mary of Modena, smoothed the way with a generous wedding present. Perhaps she favored the match because they were both so much in love. There was not much love in her own marriage.

Sarah's marriage was a great loss to Anne. She had enjoyed hearing whatever Sarah chose to confide about her romance, and she herself admired Colonel Churchill enormously. But after the marriage, Sarah was suddenly removed from Anne's world into the world of Court intrigue. Everything now centered around John's ambitions and her own. Anne still had a child's thoughts and feelings, still loved to take a part in plays, and called her friends by their play names long after the performances were over.

Soon came the order from Charles for Anne's father and his Court to leave England for Brussels. The Churchills went with the Duke and Duchess of York, and Anne was left at St. James's Palace, almost alone except for her own personal attendants. It was sad and rather frightening to be so much alone. Her mother was dead, her father and stepmother had been sent away. Mary and Sarah were married and gone. Everyone she loved had died or gone away.

Her visit to Brussels the following year was a help. To be with her family again made her happy. Her young stepmother was kind, as always, and Sarah looked more beautiful than ever,

The National Portrait Gallery

The National Portrait Gallery

Sarah and John Churchill, the Duke and Duchess of Marlborough

Anne thought. Sarah talked to her as if she were old enough now to understand Court secrets. She told Anne which of the Court ladies were good and which were not. She warned Anne about the Duke of Monmouth, saying that he was determined to take the throne.

"But he cannot," said Anne, in surprise. "My father is heir to the throne. It is his by Divine Right, if his Majesty the King should die."

Sarah just perceptibly shrugged. "Highness, your father is a Papist. The people will never allow him to remain King. The people will decide who shall be King."

Anne was silent. Sarah had spoken a thought too dreadful for words. It brought to Anne's mind pictures that she would rather not see, pictures which often came to her in the darkness of lonely nights in St. James's Palace. Some were from the past, of which she had been told; some from the present, which she knew from her own experience. She imagined her grandfather's head lying severed from his body under the executioner's ax; her father fleeing for his life while Cromwell's guards hunted him like a rat; the Queen's face, ageing and white with distress during the year just past, when everyone in the palace at Whitehall was afraid to eat a mouthful of food for fear it was poisoned. It should not be so. If a king ruled by Divine Right, God should keep him safe on his throne. But it appeared that God Himself could not keep a king on his throne, unless the people also willed it.

While Anne was at Brussels, word came that King Charles was desperately ill. His brother James hurried back to London, partly to express brotherly concern, partly to claim the throne in case of the King's death. Fortunately, Charles was well again, convalescing at Windsor Castle, and his old cheerful self when James arrived, full of apologies for having come without permission. Now that he was in England, he had a favor to ask of the King. Might he remove himself and his Court from Brussels to Scotland? There was always a warm welcome for Stuarts in Scotland. Charles consented. With his brother's blessing, off went James and his Duchess to Edinburgh, where Charles had spent untold amounts of money to restore and embellish the old Palace of Holyrood. The King might never be able to visit Holyrood himself; someone in the family might as well enjoy it.

Anne returned to London. So it came about that she was living alone with her attendants at St. James's Palace when Prince George of Hanover arrived at Whitehall in 1680.

On the day following the banquet where they had met, Anne went again to Whitehall at the King's request to entertain the royal visitor. She came with several of her ladies and with her aunt, Lady Clarendon, who was now her governess, since the death of Lady Villiers. Lady Clarendon wished her niece to be married, but she had no confidence in Anne's ability to attract a man. She led the way with George and his gentlemen attendants, leaving Anne to follow in her wake.

They crossed the King's private garden to examine the sundial. It was a great wonder, and gave information about geography, astrology, and astronomy, as well as telling the time. While Lady Clarendon explained all of this, George was looking about him. He saw sixteen statues, each one set in a plot of fine English grass in the formal garden, but was more interested in some white linen petticoats laid out to bleach on one of the grass plots. Anne knew that they belonged to Lady Castlemaine, whose housekeeping arrangements at Whitehall Palace were far from formal. Anne stood silent and red with embarrassment. Lady Clarendon had not failed to see the petticoats. She hurried on to the Chapel Royal, where the entire party climbed to the little gallery from which his Majesty could attend services in privacy. Mr. Purcell was seated at the organ, practicing a new anthem. Anne wished that she might have come here alone with the Prince to listen to the music, but Lady Clarendon was leading them on. Anne was thankful when it was all over and she could escape to her own rooms at St. James's.

She saw the Prince again that night at a ball, but the ball was not a great success for either of them. Anne loved to dance, and she danced well. George knew none of the dances that the English Court had imported from France. He stood beside her chair, looking and feeling like a dolt, while she, out of courtesy to him, refused other partners. George's attention wandered from one lady to another, seldom to Anne. At last, a gavotte brought him to life. It was enough like a German country dance to give him courage. He bowed, she rose, and they joined the other couples. Until he was well into it, George did not know that the gavotte was a kissing dance in England, but when he saw what was expected, he kissed her. Everyone saw it.

Then, two days later he was gone. The Court was mystified, buzzing with gossip. Someone said that George had received a letter by special messenger from Hanover. Someone else said that William of Orange had objected at the last minute to a match that would have united Hanover and England. Or perhaps George had had second thoughts about Anne's inferior background on her mother's side. Whatever the reason, the Princess Anne felt humiliated, and never forgot or quite forgave the slight. Meanwhile, Prince George returned to Hanover and shortly afterward married Princess Dorothea of Zell, whom he treated cruelly.

To be the subject of gossip at Court was not pleasant. Anne was glad when the King gave permission for her to go to Scotland the following summer. The five days' voyage was refreshing, and when she reached Edinburgh, she had a sense of home-coming. Her great-grandfather, James I, had come to England from Scotland. The gray stone towers of Holyrood Palace rose at the foot of Edinburgh's Royal Mile, backed by the King's park and the rocky outcroppings of hills higher than any she had ever seen. The old palace had been made fine with a new front. Almost every day Anne would ride out on horseback, through the great gateway and along roads where rosy-faced Scots came out of their houses to smile at the Stuart Princess. It was clear that they counted her as one of their own.

At night there were country dances or balls where she met kilted Camerons, Macintoshes, Frasers, Macleans, and Macdon-alds who swore devotion to her. Their descendants, sixty-five years later, would die at Culloden for another Stuart, Bonnie Prince Charlie.

Sometimes Irish players came to Holyrood to perform for the Duke and his Court. When winter kept the Court housebound in the cold, drafty palace, Anne and her young friends took part in a masque. She also learned to play basset, a new card game. Played for money, basset was exciting enough to warm the cold-est blood. Best of all, Sarah and John Churchill were at Holy-rood with James's Court.

The only real shadow in Anne's Scottish sojourn was her father's knack for making himself unpopular. At home in Eng-land there had recently been a Parliamentary effort to have James excluded as heir to the throne. Here in Scotland, of all places, this home of Presbyterianism, he had the Abbey Church at Holyrood made into a Roman Catholic chapel for his private use. The students of Edinburgh were so angry when they heard of it that they burned effigies of the Pope. Anne's feelings toward her father grew more and more painful. She was old enough to sense that he was leading the whole family to disaster.

Holyrood House, Edinburgh, Scotland

But the tide of public opinion could still change. James, never lacking in physical prowess, was shipwrecked on a voyage in March, 1682, and narrowly escaped death, behaving with great coolness and courage. When the family returned to London in May of that year, the people gave him a hero's welcome, and forgot, for the moment, their dislike.

London had never looked more splendid. The new streets and squares, with their fine town houses, stretched one after another for miles, it seemed. Villages, formerly in the country, were growing together. Soon, Daniel Defoe could say there was nothing like London "except old Rome in Trajan's time."

Anne was at the height of bloom and beauty, and all at once she found that she had attracted a beau. He was John Sheffield, Earl of Mulgrave. He was in his thirties, twice her age, and was known for his amorous exploits. He was full of stories about military life, having been captain of a troop of horse before he was twenty years old, but Mulgrave was not only a soldier and sailor. He wrote poetry and songs, some of them especially for her. Often he came to sit with her in her apartments at St. James's, and talked while she worked on a piece of embroidery, the bright threads following the motion of her beautiful hands. Sometimes he told her about his adventures in the navy—how he had commanded an expedition to relieve Tangiers, and how fine it was to see a dozen brave ships of the line sailing together to attack. She could imagine it very well, for she herself had often seen the great English naval vessels riding at anchor in the Medway, near the mouth of the Thames. Some had as many as thirty-six cannon on each side. The sterns were richly ornamented with carved gilt, surmounted by the royal arms.

Then he told her how he had seen a man's leg amputated. Anne would have given much not to see that picture in her mind's eye, but it stayed with her. She agreed with John

Sheffield that England should do more for the men who were wounded in their country's battles.

Mulgrave rode beside her when the Court went to New-market during the summer. One evening he was a guest at a house where Anne was spending a night on the three-day journey. He left the card table to wander about the library, and returned with a book in his hands. It was a copy of "The Compleat Angler," and seeing that she knew nothing about it, he drew her to a window and began to read aloud. "The nightingale, another of my airy creatures, breathes such sweet loud music out of her little instrumental throat, that it might make mankind to think miracles are not ceased. He that at midnight, when the very laborer sleeps securely, should hear, as I have very often, the clear airs, the sweet descants, the natural rising and falling, the doubling and redoubling of her voice, might well be lifted above earth, and say, 'Lord, what music hast thou provided for the saints in heaven, when thou affordest bad men such music on earth!' "

Then he made her listen, and presently they heard it—a nightingale singing somewhere in the darkness of the park at the end of the lawn. It was no sweeter than her own voice, he told her; and he would have led her on to the terrace if Sarah had not come to interrupt.

"Highness, my Lady Clarendon asks me to bring you to her."

Lady Clarendon's face was flushed. She looked disturbed. "Princess," she said in a low voice, "please to discourage the Earl's attentions. If you do not know his reputation, others do."

Not long afterward, Mulgrave received a new naval assignment and disappeared from Court life. Even the easy-going King was angry with him for having paid suit to a Princess who might some day be Queen of England. His niece was too desirable to remain single much longer. Awareness of life's complexities had made the expression of her face more sensitive and vulnerable, therefore more attractive. The outdoor life of Scotland had added color and sparkle.

The Court went again to Newmarket for the races in the spring of 1683. The sixty-mile journey meant three days of "dirty bad roads," where, according to an anonymous poet, one

> . . . met with rude grins,
> Bad eating, bad drinking, bad sleeping, bad inns.

But only the lesser members of the royal cavalcade would stop for the night at inns along the road, and at the right time of year the most ambitious landlords might produce roasted chickens with peas, or even lobsters and strawberries, asparagus and salmon.

Deep in the countryside the large households of the landed gentry offered beds to other members of the Duke's entourage. Neither scholars nor bumpkins, these country gentlemen spent their days in the management of their estates, made comfortable by wives with "the inward and outward vertues which ought to be in a compleat woman." These skillful ladies understood "Physick, Chirurgery, Cookery, extractions of oils, banqueting stuff, ordering of wool, hemp or flax, making of cloth and dyeing, the knowledge of dairies, the office of malting, of oats, their excellent uses in families, of brewing, baking and all other things belonging to a household."

It would be a lucky traveler who spent the night in a house where the wife was mistress of so many household arts. For added pleasure, if time allowed, the host might offer a little sport—hunting, hawking, or fishing—before giving godspeed and a stirrup cup to the departing guests.

For the royal family itself, the journey to Newmarket would be interrupted by stops at the great houses of the nobility.

Euston, the palace of Lord Arlington, was one of these. Lord Arlington could entertain at least two hundred guests, besides servants and guards who had to be accommodated while their masters hunted and hawked, returning by nightfall to play at cards and dice until the sun came up again. If the hunting party roamed too far afield to return for dinner, the landlord of the nearest inn would rejoice when he saw them coming. Bells rang from the church steeple and the poor gathered at the door of the inn with hands outstretched as the gentlemen came and went; everybody benefited.

Sometimes the King left the others to go fishing. He went, it was said, "when a dog would not be abroad," and often came back with a chill. The ladies too were avid sports enthusiasts. They spent every afternoon on horseback, but gathered with the gentlemen around the gaming tables at night. There were shuffleboard tables for those who still wanted exercise, and tables with tray tops for doing beadwork, a recent fad for the ladies. No one need be bored.

The furnishings of "the stately homes" rivaled those of a king's palace. Chairs, stools, and hangings were rich with damask and velvet, trimmed in gold and silver. Mirrors reflected the splendor and made the great rooms seem even larger. Paintings and doorways were framed in "ye finest Carv'd wood in fruitages, herbages, gumms, beasts, fowles, &c, very thinn and fine all in white wood without paint or varnish." The India and China trade was bringing in Oriental porcelains, embroideries, laquered tables, fans, and bowls of blue and white "chiney-ware." The Stuart age had given a new elegance to the life of noble households in the southern counties of England.

When at last the royal family came within sight of Newmarket, they saw the town cupped among hills, with training stables dotted around it. Newmarket had been famous for horse racing since James I had built stables there. Charles I had loved it too, and loved horses even more. He had made rules against the use of force in their training and against the use of punishing bits. Charles II inherited his father's devotion to the noble sport of horse racing. He and his brother James usually came with the Court for a few weeks every spring and autumn. Charles had bought a house for the Queen nearby in Essex, and built a house for himself in the High Street at Newmarket. Evelyn thought it "hardly fit for a hunting-house" and could not understand why the King had chosen to build "in a dirty street, without any court or avenue." But the King did not care for elegance at Newmarket. Here he "let himself down from Majesty to the very degree of a country gentleman," said Sir John Reresby, who knew him well. "He mixed himself amongst the crowd, allowed every man to speak to him that pleased; went a-hawking in the mornings, to cock-matches in the afternoons (if there were no horse races), and to plays in the evenings, acted in a barn, and by very ordinary Bartholomew fair comedians."

Some few visitors to Newmarket, like Daniel Defoe, thought it depressing to see "the nobility and gentry, as well from London as from all parts of England . . . so intent, so eager, so busy upon their wagers and bets; descending (the greatest of them) from their high dignity and quality, to picking one another's pockets . . . without respect to faith, honour, or good manners." Then as now, all sorts of people went to horse races, and for all sorts of reasons. Some went to gamble, some to see and be seen by the crowds, which included royalty as well as "legs" and crooks. Some went for the sheer beauty of the view from the race course—perfect green stretching for miles of gently rolling land, with the towers of Ely Cathedral in the distance. Some came because they loved the horses. Anne was one of these.

She had ridden from early childhood, having been put on a

pony as soon as she could hold reins. Now the chief event of every April for Anne was the journey to Newmarket for the "One Thousand Guinea" and "Two Thousand Guinea" races. October meant a return to Newmarket for the Cesarewitch and Cambridgeshire Stakes.

There were plenty of houses where she might stay, with Lady Clarendon to chaperone and with a few young lady attendants. Lord Cornwallis's house at Culford in Suffolk was convenient, but Anne liked best to stay at Little Saxham, Lord Croft's house near Bury St. Edmunds. From there she rode with Sarah into the ancient town, past the remains of the famous monastery and Abbey where Edmund, King of early Britain, had been martyred in trying to save his people from the invading Danes. It was a pleasant ride from Bury St. Edmunds to Newmarket for a tour of the King's stables.

Charles could often be found there talking to the jockeys. He raced his own horses in his own name and offered valuable new prizes, silver cups, each worth a hundred guineas, instead of the simple bells which had formerly been the prizes. Soon people would forget the very meaning of the old rhyme:

> Bell-horses, bell-horses, what time of day?
> One o'clock, two o'clock, off and away!

At one o'clock the beautiful creatures were led out of their stables—some skittish, some gentle, but all showing the effects of the great care and tenderness that were lavished on them. At Newmarket, horse racing was an art and a religion.

Leaving their own horses in the care of handlers, Sarah, Anne, and her party of attendants found places in the royal stand where they could watch the horses pass on their way to the starting line. Presently, Charles came and sat beside them. He was laughing about a conversation with a jockey in his own stables. "This is the way to win a race, the little fellow tells me. The night before, you must give your horse very little supper so that he is passing empty in the morning. Then air him for an hour or two before day, bring him in, and anoint his legs with oil. Then give him a loaf of bread cut and toasted, soaked in muskadine, laid between hot cloths and dried. You must let him rest until time for the race, says my jockey, not suffering any man to come near or disquiet your horse. When the hour has come, he says, you take your mouth full of strong vinegar and spurt it into your horse's nostrils to open his pipes . . . They're off!"

The King rose to his feet and so did Anne and her ladies. It was a fair start. The horses streaked past on the velvet turf of the Rowley Mile, named for Charles's famous horse, Old Rowley. The crowds were shouting, and on either side of the race course, gentlemen on horseback thundered by on their own mounts to see the finish. Now it was over, and Charles's horse had come in a poor fourth. "Ah, well," said the King, shrugging and smiling, "it's as my jockey says, after all you have done for the nag, you must bequeath him and yourself to God and good fortune. Today we did not have good fortune."

Mr. Sidney Godolphin came into the royal stand before the next race began, and stood talking to his Majesty. "I think, sire, that something might be done to encourage the breeding of a stout and enduring animal. My son talks of bringing in some Arabian stock to improve our own."

"Tell him to do so, by all means," Charles said pleasantly. "Now, sir, watch them! They're off!" Mr. Godolphin was a keen sportsman, but although Anne knew he shared her own love for horses and for racing, she was sorry that he had come to join them in the royal stand. He always looked stern, and he spoke with a slow and deliberate manner that was rather frightening.

He was the chief financial authority in Parliament and, as such, was a man of great importance to a king who was always short of money. Mr. Godolphin had married the beautiful Margaret Blagge, Anne's friend who had worn so many diamonds in the performance of "Calisto." Anne wondered if Margaret had been happy with a husband whose face was so dark and forbidding. She had died young. Mr. Godolphin bowed gravely to Anne and turned immediately to Sarah. Anne knew that Sarah and John counted him among their special friends and considered him a genius. Perhaps she too would learn to like and admire him. She must try, because Sarah and John were sure to be right.

Late in the afternoon she rode back to Little Saxham. There would be cards tonight and a cockfight tomorrow at Newmarket. Truly there seemed to be no end to the pleasure of Newmarket.

But the next day there was very nearly an end to Newmarket itself. A fire broke out and destroyed half the town. The King and the Duke of York decided to return to London at once, earlier than had been planned. The horses and carriages came to a narrow place in the road where a bridge crossed the river. They made the crossing safely, not knowing that if they had reached this spot at the time originally planned, they would have been met by forty armed men, some of whom were disappointed would-be courtiers, and some fanatical Protestants. These men had planned to shoot the King and the Duke, then ride to London and report that Papists had assassinated the royal brothers. In London a body of men would seize the City and the Tower, and invite William, Prince of Orange, to take the throne. It was said that the Duke of Monmouth was ready to head the rebels.

The plot was made public in June, and some of the conspirators were committed to the Tower. Anne watched the King and the Duke moving about as calmly as if nothing had happened. Dr. Compton counseled her to trust in God, but it seemed to her that her old nightmare fancies had become all too real. She could only pray that her own face would show nothing of the terror she felt.

Chapter IX

Windsor

CHARLES LOST NO TIME in finding a husband for his niece. Letters came and went from one royal court to another, and in May 1683 an envoy arrived from Denmark with a proposal of marriage between Anne and Prince George, a brother of Denmark's King Christian V. There was a slight flurry of debate as to whether or not Denmark was too much under the influence of France, but this was soon happily settled in favor of the marriage.

Two months later the Prince set off from Denmark for a seven-day sail over the stormy North Sea, arriving at Greenwich on July 19. The royal barge met him, as it had met that other Prince George three years before. Once again there were formal introductions at Whitehall. But George of Denmark was very different from George of Hanover. Tall, blond, warm-hearted, and simple-minded, he came to the court of Charles II with a naïve expectation of finding love and happiness in the match that had been arranged for him.

Charles was not impressed with the prospective bridegroom. He said he had tried George drunk and tried him sober and there was nothing in him either way. There might be nothing in George of the qualities commonly expected at Charles's court—neither wit and intellect nor malice and vice, unless one counted it as a vice that it was rather easy to "try him drunk." But George of Denmark had other qualities.

He was a gallant soldier. When the Danes had been badly outnumbered by the Swedish army at the battle of Lunden, he had cut his way through the enemy to rescue his brother, King Christian V. With his courage went kindness and a gentle, amiable disposition. Perhaps most important of all was his assumption that fidelity was a natural part of marriage.

All around Anne were flagrant examples of infidelity, but happy marriages were far more common than we, with our twentieth-century distaste for arranged matches, might guess. Love could come after a wedding, if not before. Love letters were the same then as now, and to open seventeenth-century letters is like opening a jar of potpourri from an old garden; the fragrance is still there. Here is one, written by a young wife of Anne's time, and saved by a fond husband: " 'Tis now a fortnight since my dear went, and I flatter myself that, in one month more, perhaps my happiness may appear here in you . . . Adieu, my dear, make me happy as soon as you can, for with you I can have no doubts or fears; and without you there never was, nor never can be, any real satisfaction to her who is most faithfully, my dearest, ever yours."

Another wife, Lady Anne Fanshawe, looking back on a long and happy marriage, wrote: "Glory be to God, we never had but one mind throughout our lives. Our souls were wrapped up in each other's; our aims and designs one, our loves one, and our resentments one. We so studied one the other, that we knew each other's mind by our looks."

Anne ardently hoped for such a marriage. She needed one person to whom she could be devoted, on whom her thoughts could center with affection and even worship. Until now this person had been Sarah Churchill, but as her wedding day approached she turned with a whole heart to the man she was destined to marry.

July 28 was chosen for the wedding. In the meantime, St. James's Palace was in a whirl of preparation; only Anne's own apartments remained the quiet retreat that she needed and wanted, to collect her thoughts and feelings. Never before so happy and busy, she found time to write to her friend, Lady Bathurst, "The Prince stays with me every day from dinner to prayers . . . That hour and a half which I have from prayers till I go to the Duchess [of York] I am glad sometimes to get a little of it alone, it being the only time I have to myself, and for the other part of it the Prince either comes to me or I go to him, and we stay with one another till I go out."

They did not talk much. English did not come easily to George, who was, in any case, a man of few words, but with Anne many words were not needed. The two were simply pleased to "stay with one another," walking in the gardens, playing cards or visiting the exotic animals and birds in the zoo at the Tower of London.

Every day a gentleman called at the Prince's rooms to take him out for a morning's entertainment of the kind he liked best. There was a riding academy where George joined the other young gallants for exhibitions of skill in horsemanship. The exercises, according to Sir John Evelyn, were "running at the ring, flinging a javelin at a Moor's head, discharging a pistol at a mark, taking up a gauntlet with the point of a sword; all these performed at full speed."

St. James's Park was a colorful spot, which George as a fine horseman especially enjoyed. Some Turkish horses had recently been brought to England, in accordance with Godolphin's plan to improve the breed of English horses. Here at least was an interest which George could share on equal terms with the King. They stood side by side with Anne, applauding both riders and horses. At such a time and place Prince George was in his element.

There was a cockpit at Whitehall where a cockfight could be counted on for an exciting afternoon. The sport was enormously popular with everyone "from peers to pitmen" and continued to be legal for a hundred years afterward. One old black hen, the mother of many champion fighting cocks, brought her owner twenty pounds apiece for every egg she laid. She may well have been the hen of the nursery rhyme:

> Hickety pickety, my black hen,
> She lays eggs for gentlemen.
> Gentlemen come every day
> To see what my black hen doth lay.

In the evening there was the theater to attend, perhaps at the Theatre Royal in Drury Lane or at the Dorset Gardens Theatre, where the Duke of York's Company might be playing. Anne disliked the shocking plays which were being written since the Restoration. But Shakespeare was often performed, and there were many musical plays which she loved, combining two of the arts, music and acting, in which she herself was adept. She would have enjoyed "The Virgin Martyr," for instance, with its "wind-musique when the angel comes down."

Perhaps best of all, for the taste of Anne and George, was the privacy of a theatrical performance at the Cockpit, a theater which had once really been a cockpit, on the side of Whitehall nearest St. James's Park. The new cockpit had now taken its place for cockfights, but the old name remained. The theater was only part of a small building which the King was assigning to Anne and George for their own residence.

The wedding was to take place at ten o'clock in the evening at St. James's Chapel. After an early dinner the young couple attended a play with the Duchess of York. The weather was warm, the sky clear; the streets were full of cheering people lighting bonfires; bells were ringing in every steeple. This marriage had popular approval.

The Bishop of London, that same good Dr. Compton who had been Anne's spiritual adviser since the day of her birth, performed the ceremony, a ceremony which should have given the husbands and wives of Charles's court food for thought. Matrimony, said the Bishop, reading from the Book of Common Prayer (1681), is not to be "taken in hand unadvisedly, lightly, or wantonly, to satisfie mens carnal lusts and appetites, like brute beasts that have no understanding; but reverently, discreetly, advisedly, soberly, and in the fear of God . . ."

George's voice echoed that of the Bishop, repeating the ancient vows, carefully, earnestly, in good faith. Now Anne's voice in those clear tones, which all of her life were to move her hearers: "I Anne take thee George to my wedded husband, to have and to hold from this day forward, for better for worse, for richer for poorer, in sickness and in health, to love, cherish, and to obey, till death us do part, according to God's holy ordinance, and thereto I give thee my troth."

George's voice again, as he placed the ring on Anne's finger: "With this ring I thee wed, with my body I thee worship, and with all my worldly goods I thee endow."

The King, the Queen, and all their Court stood watching, aware that the girl now kneeling beside Prince George might be a queen herself one day. Many kings and queens had lived and died in this palace. Within living memory, all of them had been Stuarts. The present Stuart, Charles, had already had a serious illness. A death here, a little political upheaval there, and Anne could ascend the throne with George as her consort.

The Bishop was intoning an ancient prayer which had special meaning for Anne and George: "O merciful Lord and heavenly Father, by whose gracious gift mankind is increased; We beseech thee assist with thy blessing these two persons, that they may both be fruitful in procreation of children . . ." Any child born to them would carry on the Stuart line. If there were no children of this marriage, Anne might well be the last of the Stuarts. Charles and his unhappy Catherine had failed to produce an heir. After years of marriage, James and Mary of Modena were childless. Anne's sister Mary and her Dutch husband William had no children. Kneeling at the altar, Anne prayed fervently that she might have a child.

Now the Bishop was giving his blessing; the bride and groom were rising and turning to receive kisses and congratulations. Anne's pearl necklace must be admired; it was a present from George and said to be worth £6,000; besides that there were a diamond pin and pendant earrings that sent the Court into a buzz of speculation about their cost. Anne and George would not be poor. The King was making a grant of £10,000 a year to Anne. There was a present of another £10,000 from her father. Prince George had £15,000 a year of his own from Denmark. They had every reason to expect a life full of pleasure.

So they were wedded. The memoirs of the Verney family describe another (and similar) fashionable wedding of the time in these words: "We flung the stocking, & left them [the bride and groom] to themselves, and so in this manner was ended the celebration of this marriage a la mode; after that we [the guests] had Music, Feasting, Drinking, Revelling, Dancing & Kissing; it was Two of the Clock this morning before we got Home." No stocking was flung for Anne and George. That old custom was dying out. No longer would the entire wedding party follow the bride and groom into the bridal chamber as in the old days, sitting one by one at the foot of the bed and throwing a stocking backward to hit the bride or groom in the face, if possible. A hit meant that the one who made the lucky throw would soon be married. A new and more decorous custom would soon come into style with the throwing of the bride's bouquet.

For the rest of the summer the Court, and Anne and George with it, went to Windsor, which Daniel Defoe, like most of his contemporaries, considered to be "the most beautiful, and most pleasantly situated castle, and royal palace, in the whole isle of Britain." Windsor looked out "over part of the finest and richest vale in the world, . . . the river, with a winding and beautiful stream, gliding gently through the middle of it." Standing on a cliff above the Thames, it towered over a pleasant little village at the foot of the hill and commanded a view of the green trees, playing fields, and fine old towers of Eton College across the river.

King Charles had recently called in artists, craftsmen, builders, and gardeners to bring Windsor Castle to a peak of perfection fit for his luxurious Court. Christopher Wren was put in charge of the repairs and improvements. Under his guidance the Italian artist, Verrio, was covering ceiling after ceiling with paintings in which the Stuarts and their consorts floated among clouds in the congenial company of classic deities and Christian angels. Sir John Evelyn had discovered a genius, Grinling Gibbons, the wood carver, to surround doorways, mantels, and portraits with his extraordinary garlands of flowers and fruit trees from whose branches little birds and animals appeared. For this palace, which Pepys called "the most romantique castle that is in the world," French cabinetmakers had produced the finest examples of their art: superb canopied beds, graceful highboys, tables of silver. Most of all, George liked the Round Tower with its display of arms: pikes, muskets, pistols, bandoleers, holsters, drums, and pieces of ancient armor, well polished. One could not come to the end of all the rooms at Windsor in a day's wandering.

When they tired of the magnificence inside the palace, Anne and George strolled on the terrace facing the river. She told him how Queen Elizabeth had had the terrace built so that she could walk outdoors even in the rain. On such days a courtier had walked close behind the great Queen, holding over her head one of the first English umbrellas. The stonework of the terrace was built so high and was so solid and well drained that it was always pleasant underfoot. Together Anne and George could just squeeze into the seat which Elizabeth had put at one corner of the terrace. The seat had a high, curved back that protected their heads from the wind, and it turned on a metal base, whichever way one wished, offering a privacy very convenient for young lovers.

Anne often thought about the glorious reign of Queen Elizabeth. She was beginning to dream more and more of the future, when she herself might sit on the throne, wear a crown, and right the wrongs of her people. Then England would be great again, as in the days of "good Queen Bess." Someday they would talk of "good Queen Anne." She had asked that Sarah be appointed to her own household as a Lady of the Bedchamber. John would tell Sarah what was best to be done at all times, then Sarah would tell Anne and Anne would tell George. So Anne planned the future as she walked with George on the terrace at Windsor Castle in the late summer of 1683.

"Explain to me these Whigs and Tories of whom I hear,"

Windsor Castle

George asked her one day, as they walked down from the terrace into the park.

"Those are new names," Anne told him. "Tories are men who uphold the power of the Crown. Whigs prefer the Parliament."

"Then the Whigs are dangerous men?" he inquired.

"No, I believe not," said Anne. "My friend Lady Churchill says that the Whigs detest the Papists, and they are, of course, in the right about that."

George looked puzzled. "But if they prefer Parliament to the Crown? It is difficult to understand. I do not know what to say when I am asked about these matters."

"It is difficult for me, also," said Anne. "It is best to say as little as possible until one is quite sure that one is in the right. I depend entirely on Lady Churchill. When you are not sure, you might say, 'Really?' or '*Est-ce possible?*' and walk away."

" '*Est-ce possible?*' and walk away. Yes, I will do that," said George, well satisfied.

Windsor Little Park was delightful. Anne and George often rode together down the new avenue, three miles in length, planted with elms and limes by order of the King. Beyond lay the Great Park, almost thirteen miles around, stocked with deer and all sorts of game for the pleasure of his Majesty and the Court. A touch of the heel would start their horses into a canter or a gallop under the great oaks for a closer glimpse of a deer's antlers, half hidden in distant foliage. George was blooded for the first time in England when he joined the hunt one day with a party of the King's friends.

They thought him a good fellow, and he enjoyed their company for sports, or gambling, or drinking. He was not so much at ease with English jokes, and never understood the point when someone recited John Wilmot's quip in his poem "Upon Nothing":

French Truth, Dutch Prowess, British Policy,
Hibernian [Irish] Learning, Scotch Civility,
Spaniard's Dispatch, Dane's Wit, are mainly seen in thee.

As he sat at the table drinking with these English gentlemen, there might be winks or grins among them about "Dane's Wit," but George never noticed it.

Chapter X

The Cockpit

Here lies our sovereign Lord the King,
Whose word no man relies on,
Who never said a foolish thing
Nor ever did a wise one.
                    Earl of Rochester, "On Charles II"

LATE IN AUGUST, Charles made a royal progress to Winchester, where English kings had held court from time immemorial. Since the fire at Newmarket, Charles had been considering a new palace at Winchester, where he might enjoy racing, hunting, and beagling every autumn. The indispensable Christopher Wren had orders to plan a palace that would rival Versailles. The extravagance of the plan deterred Charles not a whit, especially since an ambulant Court was the best way to let the people see their king in various parts of his realm. King Henry VIII had spent half of his time in the saddle for this reason, and owed part of his popularity and power to the custom. A sovereign who kept himself mewed up in one palace in London not only suffered from boredom but risked weakening the bonds between himself and his people.

An important event of the visit to Winchester was the celebration of Divine Service at the ancient cathedral, where the Bishop bestowed a special blessing on "the Prince and Princess

of Denmark," as Anne and George were now titled. The beautiful old windows of the cathedral had been broken to bits by Cromwell's Puritan vandals before Anne was born; it made her angry even to think of it.

Most interesting to the Prince of Denmark was the grave of King Alfred near the Abbey. Although Alfred had beaten the Danish invaders in ancient days, George had learned as a boy that his own ancestors had given the English king a good run for it. Now with George's marriage to Anne, the Danes would have a new and glorious part in English history!

They visited the Hospital of St. Cross, where thirteen aged inmates were cared for in decent comfort. The Hospital provided dinner every day for as many as a hundred of the needy. There should be more hospitals like this one, thought Anne. No one in England should go cold or hungry.

More than any day at Winchester, George enjoyed an excursion to the nearby ports of Southampton and Portsmouth, with a sail along the south coast in the royal yachts. The Danes had always been great sailors, and he had been brought up to know and love the sea. There was time at Southampton to wander along the wharves, where ships from all over the world were riding at anchor. The King expressed an interest in a merchantman from India, and some of the gentlemen, including George, were made welcome on board. They went down into the hold and observed, as Samuel Pepys had done on another occasion, ". . . the greatest wealth lie in confusion that a man can see in the world. Pepper scattered through every chink, you trod upon it; and in cloves and nutmegs above the knees; whole rooms full. And silk in bales, and boxes of copper-plate . . ."

Anne waited on the wharf with some of her ladies until the King's party returned. Half-grown boys, ragged and barefoot, gathered around, smiling and staring at the royal visitors. There were always boys on the wharves, especially when an East India ship came in. They hung about, waiting to talk to the sailors and to hear stories of flying fish, of kings who rode on elephants, of snake charmers, and of a temple with a golden roof and walls set with precious stones. English boys who heard such stories would be longing to set sail one fine day to see for themselves if the stories were true. Anne listened and watched, thinking to herself that as long as English ships were filled with English boys, eager for adventure, England would prosper.

The Prince and Princess of Denmark found their new home in the Cockpit at Whitehall beautifully fitted up and ready to receive them on their return to London. The winter was severe, the coldest that Anne could remember. Fires were kept burning in every room of the royal residence, but the cost of fuel was so high that charitable contributions were taken up again and again to keep the poor from freezing to death. The unusual number of fires created a dense smog that settled over the city, week in, week out, bringing much sickness along with the misery of the cold.

The Thames, which normally felt the ebb and flow of the sea for sixty miles inland, was frozen solid and was the scene of much novelty and pleasure. The cold was forgotten by anyone well enough to enjoy being on the ice. The frozen river made a smooth new road for coaches, the horses picking their way among sleds and skating children. There were even coach races, which drew a great crowd. Some enterprising showmen set up a ring for bull-baiting on the ice. Puppet shows appeared and every sort of food was for sale, so that all up and down the Thames "it seemed to be a bacchanalian triumph, or carnival on the water," as Sir John Evelyn saw it.

In February the royal family came to visit the booths and shops erected on the ice. A crowd gathered wherever the King's tall, slender figure could be seen. He stopped to watch a whole ox being roasted at a turnspit; he ate roasted chestnuts. From the afternoon on the river, Anne brought back a memento presented to each of the King's party at a printer's booth. It was a sheet of paper inscribed with the names of the royal visitors. Among the names were those of Anne and George.

"And print 'Hans in Kelder,'" said George, his face beaming with good humor and red with cold. "Hans is here, too." It was George's joke, meaning that Anne was expecting a baby. So the words were printed with the other names, "Hans in Kelder."

It had been a happy day. But no one could forget for long the suffering of all England that winter. At many isolated farms, both men and cattle perished from the cold. Trees were split with the weight of ice. In all the great houses and parks, exotic plants and birds died. Anne thought often of the poor who huddled in the suburbs of London, many of them without so much as a roof over their heads.

At the end of March the weather was once more bearable, but there was still no sign of spring. Charles announced that he would "touch for the evil" in the Banqueting Hall on the 28th of March. Prince George had never seen this ceremony, and Anne asked him to attend it with her in the balcony of the hall, where they could sit for a while and then leave when the air grew too foul and stifling. "There will be a great crush of sick persons below," she told him.

She was right. The Royal Touch always brought a throng of ailing people to the palace to be healed of the "King's Evil," or scrofula. During his reign, Charles had touched almost a hundred thousand people in this healing service. The sufferers were led up, one by one, to a throne at the end of the Banqueting Hall. The King touched the face of each one with both of his hands, while a chaplain, standing at the King's side, repeated over and over again, "He put his hands upon them and he healed them." When all had been touched, they returned to the throne and received an "angel," a piece of money strung on a white ribbon and empressed with the figure of an angel. A church service followed, with special prayers for the sick. On this occasion in March 1684, perhaps because of the long hard winter just past, there was such a great crowd of people asking for the free tickets at the door of the King's doctor that six or seven people were crushed to death.

This tragedy grieved the King and others of his Court who believed in the efficacy of the Royal Touch. As for Whigs, who denied the Divine Right of Kings, as did Non-conformists of every stripe, they were more than ever convinced that the service of "touching for the Evil" should be omitted from the Book of Common Prayer and from Whitehall.

On the twelfth of May, Anne's first child, a daughter, was born dead. It was a sorrow and disappointment to George as well as to herself, but infant mortality was such a common experience that it could only be accepted as a cross which every parent should expect to bear. A child might die, but there would be other children; in many families, one almost every year. Anne wondered if she had done anything to injure this baby and thought of the riding and hunting at Windsor, the beagling at Winchester. She would give up sports, she decided, and live very quietly, so that the next child would have a better chance to survive.

Now more than ever, George was kind and gentle to her, but she felt, too, the need of a woman to whom she could talk during the hours when she lay convalescing in her bedchamber at the Cockpit, or began to walk about the gardens and the park again. There was no one like Sarah, no one so cheerful and entertaining.

"Stay with me always," Anne begged. "And do not call me Highness at every word. Be as free with me as if I had no title." A sudden fancy struck her. "Do you remember how we used to call each other 'Calisto' and 'Nymphe' when we were in the play? Let's choose some such names now. I shall be plain Mrs.— Mrs. Morley. There's a good sensible name. And you will be—"

"Mrs. Freeman?" suggested Sarah, with a tilt of her head.

"Good," said Anne. "It's a name that goes well with your free, open nature. And it will remind you to be free with me."

So Mrs. Morley and Mrs. Freeman it was, from that time on. In accordance with her new name, Sarah took Anne at her word, saying what she thought without restraint. Anne felt herself to be the most fortunate woman in the world with such a friend and adviser. Sarah received £200 a year as a Lady of the Bedchamber. Anne planned to give her more, as soon as possible. But the Cockpit, with all its comforts and luxuries, was expensive to maintain. New clothes seemed to cost a great deal, and an evening at cards could make her heart sink the next morning when she looked at the debts she had jotted down. Then there was nothing to do but ask her father for help, which he always supplied very generously and with an affectionate smile. It was painful to accept the help and not be able to return the look and the smile, yet the old secret distaste for her father and all that he stood for was still there, the old fear and distrust. Silently, she would determine to play cards no more, but it was of no use. The tables were always set, the ladies and gentlemen ready to play; it was the accepted, almost the *only* way to pass the time indoors.

"If my eyes were stronger, I might read more," said Anne to Sarah, as she paid what Sarah had won from her the night before. "There are many good books."

"Books!" said Sarah. "Don't talk to me of books. I know only cards . . . and men."

During the autumn the King looked ill. All the Court noticed it, but no one dared mention it to him. As for Charles himself, he continued to live exactly as he always had, indulging every whim and behaving in general like a gay blade, twenty years younger. He played tennis regularly and always stepped on the weighing machine at the edge of the court before and after a game, expressing great satisfaction if he had lost a pound or two. George cared nothing about his own weight and left tennis to others. During a fast game he would shake his head, watching the King's usually pale face turn as red as a turkeycock.

George was not surprised when, a few months later, a page-boy came breathlessly to the royal apartments at the Cockpit with dreadful news. The King, while being shaved, had had an apoplectic fit. Luckily, his doctor happened to be in the room, and he immediately bled his Majesty. James came to his brother's bedchamber with such dispatch that he arrived wearing one shoe and one slipper.

The entire palace was in a ferment of anxiety as the apoplectic symptoms returned and further treatments were tried. The attack had occurred on Monday, February 2. On Wednesday, Charles was cupped and was bled again from both jugular veins. He was also purged and made to vomit. On Thursday he seemed better until about noon, when he felt feverish and was given a powder, which made him worse. That night he complained of a pain in his side and was bled again. The pain continued. The following morning, Anne's twentieth birthday, word flew through the palace that the King was struggling for breath. The Queen was with him. He had asked her pardon for all his offenses toward her, and then offended her once more by speaking with his last breath of his current favorite, Nell Gwynne.

"Let not poor Nelly starve," he said, and gave up the ghost.

The shock of the King's death was immediately followed by a rumor that Charles had been received into the Catholic faith on his deathbed. Astute politician that he was, he had once said lightly to Bishop Burnet that he was no atheist, but he could not think God would make a man miserable for taking a little pleasure out of the way. This gave the impression, as perhaps it was meant to do, that Charles had no serious religious feeling. He did not intend to be a factor in religious controversy. But now at the last moment, when it could no longer have political significance, the truth came out. England had had a king who was Catholic at heart. It would now have one who was Catholic in fact.

Preparations for the coronation of James and Mary of Modena went on through the spring; they were crowned King and Queen on April 23, 1685. Mary's crown, together with her jewels and pearls, cost well over £100,000. The crown was of gold, encrusted with jewels and encircled with large pearls. Four gold bands covered with diamonds and pearls enclosed the red velvet cap. At the peak was an orb, covered with diamonds and topped with a diamond cross. Today it lies with the other crown jewels in the Tower of London.

Anne, as the King's daughter, was part of every ceremony, although she was expecting a child very soon. Her robes were heavy, standing tired her, and her heart was full of doubts and fears. A month after the coronation she went with the new Queen to the House of Lords at Westminster and stood by the throne which had been set for the King. Her father entered, wearing his crown, and was acknowledged with ceremony. He made a speech, promising to support the Church of England and the property of the people. He asked the Lords to settle his revenue for life. His brother had had to ask for money constantly, and James did not propose to do the same if he could help it. The speech was received with loud huzzas and a general shout of "Vive le Roi!" at the end. The popularity of his dead brother was standing James in good stead.

But Anne was not deceived. She knew that her father had already had Mass celebrated in the chapel at Whitehall. Everyone in the palace knew it, and soon the word would fly over the city and then over the kingdom. There would be a price to pay in terror and bloodshed.

Now, after years of delay, Titus Oates, whose dastardly plot had caused the death of Catholics, received his punishment. He was whipped at a cart's tail from Newgate to Aldgate, and two days later was whipped again as he was dragged on a sledge to Tyburn. Somehow he survived, and even lived to enjoy a pension from the Whigs who had aided and abetted his plot in 1678.

On June 1, Anne's second child, another girl, was born and was christened Mary. The baby was small and weak, but Anne and George might have rejoiced in her if other events of June had not burst on England like a clap of thunder.

At Lyme Regis, on the southwest coast, the Duke of Monmouth, natural son of the late king, landed from the Continent with a fighting force of a hundred and fifty men and proclaimed himself king. With consummate arrogance he offered a reward for James and accused him of having caused the Great Fire of London and of poisoning his brother Charles. Monmouth's idea was to use the strongly Protestant feelings of the simple country people for his own purposes. He hoped to raise a great army of malcontents with which to march on the capital and seize the throne.

When the news of Monmouth's landing reached London, James took immediate action. He offered £5,000 to anyone who would kill Monmouth, and he sent an army, headed by John Churchill, to meet the invading pretender. During the days that followed, Anne lived in painful suspense. She remembered Monmouth well from the days when he had been a part of her uncle's gay Court. As handsome as a young god, he had danced with other gentlemen in the performance of "Calisto." He was an undoubted Protestant. All of this prejudiced her in his favor and against her own father. Yet to invade the realm and rouse the peasant farmers to sedition was an act of treason which could not be condoned. John Churchill was now marching to meet him with an army of about twenty-seven hundred. Monmouth had raised eight thousand men in his march through the southwest counties. Anne must simply await the outcome with prayer.

On July 6 the two armies met at Sedgemoor, and two thousand men died in bloody battle. Monmouth was defeated and fled, disguised in a poor man's coat. His luck had run out, and with it, his manhood. He threw away the George, the medal which identified him as a Knight of the Garter, and hid in a ditch. They found him and took him to London, where he fell on his knees before the King, weeping and begging for his life. Only at the end, on Tower Hill, his courage returned. He gave a piece of gold to Jack Ketch, the executioner, telling him to do his work quickly. But Ketch was not at his best that day. He made five chops before the beautiful head fell to the ground.

Monmouth had been "the darling of his father and the ladies," said Evelyn, "being extremely handsome and adroit; an excellent soldier and dancer, a favourite of the people; of an easy nature, . . . seduced by crafty knaves. . . . See what ambition and want of principles brought him to!"

His followers, who were neither ambitious nor wanting in

principles, suffered an even worse fate. They were earnest Puritans, liberty-loving and brave, who had risked their lives for a leader not worthy of their idealism. James ordered the monstrous Judge Jeffreys to punish them. More than eight hundred were shipped off to slavery in the Barbadoes. Three hundred were hanged and cut up in pieces to be displayed at all the crossroads and market squares of southwest England. Flogging and imprisonment were meted out to many more. When John Churchill heard of it, he struck the mantelpiece with his fist and said, "This marble is not harder than the King's heart."

Many had hated the Puritans, remembering the grim days of Cromwell and the desecration of churches and abbeys all over England. Many had laughed at strange Puritan customs and eccentric names; like Praise God Barebones and his brother, If-Christ-hadst-not-died-thou-hadst-been-damned. Some good men, Catholic and Church of England alike, said privately that it was a wonder no Puritan had yet called himself Holier-than-thou. But Puritans proved themselves heroes as they went to their death, praising God, in Judge Jeffreys' Bloody Assize. Most of the men involved in Monmouth's Rebellion were unlearned; but they knew one book, the King James Bible, which had been in every cottage since their grandfathers' days. The beauties of that Bible opened simple English hearts to another book. The second part of "Pilgrim's Progress" had been published by the Dissenter, John Bunyan, only the year before, in 1684. Bunyan too had been in prison for his faith, and the new martyrs treasured his testimony:

> He who would valiant be
> 'Gainst all disaster,
> Let him in constancy
> Follow the Master.

> There's no discouragement
> Shall make him once relent
> His first avowed intent
> To be a pilgrim.

The Protestant followers of Monmouth had been a relatively small group, but their fate united Protestants all over England as nothing else might have done.

James II seemed bent on alienating the affections of all his subjects. He now demanded the repeal of the Test Act, which required that holders of government office, either military or civil, must be Church of England men. Instead of pleasing his people with this apparent show of leniency and tolerance, he only succeeded in angering men of all faiths. The Established Church was affronted because its position was weakened. Dissenters were displeased because they felt they were being used as a cover for the King's real intention of strengthening the Church of Rome. Catholics disliked being associated with a king who had shown himself to be cruel in the very first days of his reign. Nevertheless, with the repeal of the Test Act, James set about finding Catholics for high position both at Court and in the army.

The effect was not long in making itself felt. During the next two years the rebels grew in strength and number. They looked for a leader strong enough to drive James from his throne, and responsible enough to rule wisely himself. The man they favored was Anne's brother-in-law, William of Orange.

James began not only to promote Catholic interests, but to take more oppressive measures against Protestants. Adding insult to injury, he brought in boatloads of the "wild Irish," used them to help build up his own army, and had about thirteen thousand men camped just outside London, to keep order. At the same time the persecution of Protestants in France became so severe that forty thousand went to Switzerland and more than a hundred thousand to Holland, Denmark, and Germany. Some fugitives trying to escape to England were taken from British ships by the French. There were even stories of French Protestants who tried to escape by being shipped out in crates and barrels.

James seemed unaware of or unresponsive to the mounting tension. He even made the mistake of trying to convert his two staunch Protestant daughters. Anne's chaplains had neither the wit nor the learning to defend Protestant theology effectively, but this was not necessary. She had made up her mind about her faith years before, and now wrote to Mary, "I am resolved to undergo anything rather than change my religion. Nay, if it should come to such extremities, I will choose to live on alms rather than change."

Of course it did not "come to such extremities." James was much too indulgent a father to force her obedience to his wishes. Outwardly, life went on as usual. Another child was born to Anne and George, a healthy little girl, named Anne Sophia. The older child, Mary, was still weak and constantly ailing, but perhaps with time and good care she would be well.

Early in 1687, Prince George became so ill that he was hardly expected to live. Anne nursed him herself, sitting beside him day after day in the darkened room. Purges were tried, leeches were applied, plasters were laid on his chest to blister it. He was also given "quinaquina," a new medicine which an apothecary had used with success when called on to cure Charles II of malaria. (It would later be called "Queen Anne's Mixture," and still later, quinine.) Somehow, in spite of the doctors, George lived through his illness and began to improve.

Then on February 6, Anne's twenty-second birthday, the baby Anne died. Her little sister Mary outlived her by only a few hours. The strain of nursing her husband, the sleepless nights, the death of her two children, one after the other, was too much for Anne. Another child had been expected, but it too was lost without living to be born at its full term. From this time on, Anne's face had a different look—quiet, impassive, and rather remote. She did not cry outwardly or demand sympathy at the expense of those around her. Her tears were silent and inward.

"It is very strange," Sarah wrote to John Churchill, "the Princess does not weep. She seems quite indifferent about the death of her children. I believe she has no deep maternal feelings." Anne had already promoted Sarah to be First Lady of the Bedchamber and was constantly planning new ways to help dear Mrs. Freeman. She would have been stunned if she had read Sarah's letter.

As spring came on, Anne and George were well enough to drive out one day with Sarah through the streets of London. The handsome modern townhouses with their gray stone or red brick fronts, their high casement windows and classic doorways, lined the new streets and squares. Now the carriage was rattling along past St. Martin's-in-the-Fields. Anne looked out of her window to see where Dr. Tenison, the rector, might possibly put the public library for which he had asked. Sir John Evelyn and Sir Christopher Wren were helping with the plans. Dr. Tenison had thirty or forty young men studying for the ministry in his parish, and was distressed by their habit of gathering in taverns and coffeehouses. A public library might solve the problem. Anne thought it an excellent idea. She was saddened by the knowledge that some young men in orders were not as dedicated to their high calling as they might be. Someday, she thought, she would like to strengthen the Church by helping to strengthen the clergy.

At St. James's Church, Piccadilly, they stopped the carriage and went in to say a prayer and to see the altar. Sarah begged

Queen Anne and Prince George of Denmark

leave to wait in the carriage. Sir Christopher Wren had built the church, which was still quite new and much admired. The altar was of white marble, richly carved with Mr. Grinling Gibbons' garlands of fruit and flowers. With his quaint fancy, he had carved a pelican, her young at her breast, just over the altar. It was a symbol of charity, as the rector reminded Anne.

"Would not Lady Churchill like to see the church?" he asked her.

"She prefers to remain in the carriage," Anne told him.

She could have told him more, for she knew that Sarah was indifferent to religion in any form. Sometimes Anne's ladies-in-waiting gossiped about it, calling Sarah a free thinker, or even an atheist, but Anne always defended Sarah, saying, "The less show one makes, the better, in my opinion. As for moral principles, it is impossible to have better ones than she does. And without that, all the lifting up of hands and eyes, and going off into church, is nothing." Her ladies would smile knowingly behind her back, as soon as it was turned. The devout Princess and her agnostic lady-in-waiting differed in their religious views, but in "Mrs. Morley's" eyes, "Mrs. Freeman" could still do no wrong.

Even in that day of violent religious factions, there were many instances of friends who remained devoted although their faiths were poles apart. A curious case was that of the Catholic James II and the Quaker William Penn, who was perhaps the King's closest friend. Penn's father, Sir William Penn, had served as an admiral when James had been the Duke of York. His son William had been given a sound Anglican background at Chigwell Grammar School in Essex, and later at Christ Church, Oxford, a stronghold of Anglican faith, suitable for the training of scholars and gentlemen. But at Oxford, the handsome and brilliant young Penn had come under the influence of a Puritan divine, had developed a taste for radical religious notions, kicked over the traces, and been expelled. That this ardent young reformer should then turn up at Court and become the trusted friend of the much reviled James, remains a mystery to this day. Penn rejected all the popular arguments against having a Catholic in power.

"The King will put his crown in the Pope's pocket!" his Protestant friends would argue. "And if the King believes the Pope to be infallible, what becomes of our religious liberty?"

"Ah," Penn would say, "but see how it works out in fact. Dost thou know that the people of Coventry have sent an address to his Majesty, thanking him for their liberty of conscience? Is the King to have no credit for his Declaration of Indulgence? A thousand men signed the Address from Coventry, Church of England men, Presbyterians, Independents and Anabaptists alike." But few at Court, or elsewhere, would listen to the young Quaker.

At about this time Anne began to notice a certain tune whistled and hummed in the streets of London. She seemed to hear it everywhere.

"The tune is called 'Lillibullero,'" Sarah told her. "Henry Purcell wrote the music and Lord Wharton has made some words for it, satirizing his Majesty and the Catholics. Yes, you will hear it everywhere these days. When the people don't dare to sing the words, they whistle the tune."

"And what are the words?" asked Anne.

"Oh, there are all sorts of words," Sarah told her cautiously. Then, unable to contain herself, she burst out, "'There was an old woman tossed up in a basket, Seventeen times as high as the moon.' They sing those words to 'Lillibullero.' It means that they want to send his Majesty, your father, away."

Anne turned pale. "What else do they sing?"

"There are many verses," said Sarah. "Some of Lord Wharton's verses concern my brother-in-law, Dick Talbot. He is gathering an army for his Majesty in Ireland. I have no use for Dick, you know. He is a Papist, so I don't mind what anyone says about him." She began to sing, rather tunelessly, but with spirit,

> There was an old prophecy found in a bog,
> Lillibullero, bullenala,
> "Ireland shall be ruled by an ass and a dog,"
> Lillibullero, bullenala. . . .
> And now this prophecy's come to pass,
> Lillibullero, bullenala,
> For Talbot's the dog and James is the ass,
> Lillibullero, bullenala.

"There is another verse of 'Lillibullero' that says,

> O, but why does he stay behind?
> Ho! by my soul, 'tis a Protestant wind.

Can you guess what they mean by that?" Anne shook her head, returning Sarah's confident look with one of fear.

Sarah lowered her voice. "They mean your brother-in-law, the Prince of Orange, and the Protestant wind is one that would blow him to England to take the throne with your sister, the Princess Mary."

Faint with the shock of Sarah's revelation, Anne seized her friend's hands for comfort. "Mrs. Freeman, this means—a revolution!"

Sarah was undaunted. "A glorious one, if it succeeds, my dear Mrs. Morley. And you, with your devotion to your Church, will want to help, will you not? My husband has thought for weeks that you should know and be prepared."

"You are asking me to betray my father," Anne said miserably.

"You are only asked not to give aid and comfort to one who is destroying his country," Sarah returned. Then she continued, taking Anne's hands more firmly in her own, "Mrs. Morley, the time will soon come when you must be able to leave this place quickly and in secret. Allow me to have a little staircase built from your apartments to mine on the side nearest the park. No one need know why it is done. We can say that it is for convenience, and that will be true."

Silently, Anne nodded. There could be no harm in building a staircase. Sarah went away, leaving the Princess to absorb the meaning of all that had been said. Anne was in an agony of indecision. She owed her loyalty to the man who was both her father and her king. The Stuarts had always been loyal to one another. And besides, did not the King rule by Divine Right?

Anne knew that her sister Mary was passionately attached to her grumpy little husband, William of Orange. It was said that he did not return that feeling, and Anne owed nothing to him. He simply represented a principle in which she earnestly believed—the Protestant succession of the throne of England. She remembered too how only recently at Whitehall the Bishop of Bath and Wells had dared to preach a sermon exhorting a congregation of the greatest nobility to cling to the Protestant faith as taught by the Church of England, "concluding with a kind of prophecy, that whatever it suffered, it should after a short trial emerge to the confusion of her adversaries and the glory of God." Surely, if all the Protestant faithful were true to their belief, the present turmoil would pass!

But it did not pass. Everyone, everywhere now seemed to be singing "Lillibullero." Bishop Burnet said that "perhaps never had so slight a thing so great an effect."

During the winter a new rumor flew through Whitehall, making the situation far more serious. From all appearances, Mary of Modena, James's queen, was expecting a child. It was not the first time that this had happened, but in fifteen years of marriage none of her children had lived. If she should now produce an heir to the throne—a Catholic heir, at that!—the evils of the present time would continue indefinitely. All doubts as to the course of the rebels were swept away by this impending birth. James must go! But was not the timing of this birth almost beyond belief?

Anne in fact found it very hard to believe. The Queen seemed as kind as ever to her, but Anne began to doubt the sincerity of that kindness. In her own mind a peculiar set of suspicions began to form, fed by the usual palace tittle-tattle. The Queen, it was said, was not really pregnant, but only gave the appearance of pregnancy so that when the proper time came, a child (someone else's child), could be presented to the people as the true and lawful heir, establishing an English Catholic succession. Anne watched her stepmother at every opportunity.

"I will do all I can to find it out," she wrote to her sister, "and if I should make any discovery, you shall be sure to have an account of it."

 *Bath*

Hush-a-bye, Baby, on the tree-top,
When the wind blows, the cradle will rock;
When the bough breaks, the cradle will fall,
Down will come Baby, cradle, and all.
                    Old English Nursery Rhyme

IN APRIL 1688, Anne was hoping for another baby. In spite of
the anxiety and excitement at Whitehall surrounding the expected birth of a possible heir to the throne soon to be born to
the King and Queen, it was decided that Anne and George
should go to Bath to improve their health and spirits. Her stepmother's child would be born in July. There was always a room-
ful of official witnesses on such occasions, and Anne was determined to witness the birth herself. But there was plenty of time
for a visit to the famous spa where, it was said, almost any
disease could be cured.

In Anne's day the springs drew hopeful sufferers from all
over England. Drinking the water and bathing in the springs
was recommended for "obstructions of the viscera, the palsy,
gout and rheumatism, the colic and jaundice, white swellings,
the leprosy, hysteric and hypocondriac complaints, spasmodic
diseases, affections of the head and nerves, and almost all cases
where a powerful stimulus is wanting." Surely somewhere on

this list might be found the reason for the ill health that plagued the Prince and Princess of Denmark.

Ordinary travelers went to Bath by stagecoach. Anne and George were not ordinary travelers, but even in their own private coach, the trip was strenuous. They jolted and lurched along the toll road which one critic called "the worst public road in Europe, considering what vast sums have been collected from it."

The view of the English countryside through the coach windows made up for these discomforts, for the road to Bath rolled through a landscape of unparalleled beauty. Anne and George, followed by their retinue, left the Cockpit at an early hour, passing Westminster Abbey as the sun rose. Soon the city was behind them. When Kensington appeared they were already in open country. George remarked that the air at Kensington always seemed drier and healthier than town air. He had been suffering from asthma. Anne looked thoughtfully at the chimneys of Nottingham House, a fine old manor, rising above green lawns, great trees, and spring gardens in full bloom. Was it too much to hope that they might some day leave the Cockpit forever, and find a home that was spacious, beautiful, and comfortable; a home with privacy, where the air was good, where children could grow and play and thrive?

She looked fondly at her husband. The Court had a poor opinion of George; she knew it, and it did not matter. The gentlemen at Whitehall constantly used their sharp wits to cut reputations to bits. George was not spared. He was the butt of many sarcastic comments; it only made her love him more. Sitting beside her, solid, strong, good-humored, affectionate, he seemed to her infinitely superior to all the rest.

They spent the first night at Windsor in a mood of contentment and hope. Anne found her old guitar and sat down with it after dinner in a window that looked out on the river. Behind her, stars appeared in the evening sky, the Thames darkened, lights began to shine from villages across the river. She tried one or two of her old songs, but she had not sung for a long time. The words escaped her. Presently she called a curly-haired page boy to her.

"Will you sing us a song?"

"Yes, madam, if you please."

"What will you sing?"

"I'll sing you twelve O," he answered with a joyful smile.

"Ah!" she said, with pleasure. "We must all sing with you."

He began at once, to the rippling accompaniment of the guitar, and one by one the others joined their voices in the simple tune. Each verse repeated what had gone before, so that at the end, all knew the words.

> I'll sing you twelve O
> Green grow the rushes O
> What are your twelve O?
> Twelve for the twelve apostles
> Eleven for the eleven that went up to heaven
> Ten for the ten commandments
> Nine for the nine bright shiners
> Eight for the eight bold rainers
> Seven for the seven stars in the sky
> Six for the six proud walkers
> Five for the symbol at your door
> Four for the Gospel makers
> Three, three for the rivals
> Two, two for the lily-white boys
> Clothed all in green O
> One is one and all alone
> And evermore shall be so.

When the voices were silent again, they all sat for a while, talking quietly. Someone murmured, "Sweet Thames, run softly till I end my song." Anne kissed the page boy and thanked him. She was no longer the girl she had been, but tonight she looked as if she were the same.

The next day the cavalcade moved on through Berkshire, where Lord and Lady Clarendon had a beautiful house called Swallowfield. The gardens with their aromatic plants delighted Anne, and the well-stocked fish ponds pleased Prince George. But even more, they were moved by glimpses of the people in villages nearby.

A girl came to the great house in the morning, just as the royal party was preparing to leave. She carried a basket of wool, spun at home and dyed the color of English violets. She stood in the spacious hall where a servant had told her to wait for Lady Clarendon. The ladies and gentlemen from London were standing there while the coaches were brought to the door. Anne came down the broad stairway and heard Sarah Churchill talking to the girl.

"Is this how you earn a living, my child?"

"Yes, madam, by spinning wool from my father's sheep."

"You spin a very fine, smooth thread," said Sarah, fingering the wool. "Who taught you?"

"My mother taught me."

"And how much do you earn in this way?"

"Four pence a day, madam."

"That is not much. How do you manage?" Anne's party were gathering around to listen.

"I manage very well, madam. I live at home with my father and mother. I have enough to give alms to the poor." Her eyes, serene and beautiful, looked into those of the great lady before her.

"And how do you spend your days?"

"I work, I pray, I read."

"Do you expect to marry?" Sarah asked, taking in the grace of the girl's figure and the freshness of the flower-like face.

"Perhaps, madam. I don't know." Seeing Lady Clarendon on the stairs, the girl curtsied and turned away to wait until the mistress of the house had time for her.

Farewells were said, and the coaches moved off, given godspeed with harp, trumpets, and bells played by servants at the door. Anne never forgot the girl she had seen that morning at Swallowfield. The memory stayed with her like a talisman. Like that girl, she herself was English, entirely English in her heart, and this was England, the real England; not Whitehall and the sophistication of the Court, but the English counties, transformed by the work of English people into the rich and genial countryside through which they were passing. The English family, that greatest of all institutions in the land, was more important than the King; the working day of the ordinary English family suddenly appeared to Anne as enviable compared to the idleness of the Court where her own life was spent.

"I work, I pray, I read." What did that girl read? Not much except the Bible, perhaps, but that was an education in itself. And there was education in being taught by a loving mother to do something well and to take joy in it.

A great flock of pigeons flew with a rush of wings from a woods near the road. For a moment the sky was dark with them. This land was rich with crops and flocks and herds and wild life! George pointed out two farmers with guns over their shoulders, each carrying a brace of birds for the turnspit and the pot on the hearth at home. As evening came on, they saw milkmaids, homeward bound with their foaming pails. Little boys skipped and whistled and piped before them on the path. Anne knew the tune. She had often heard the dairymaids at Richmond sing the song when she was a child:

Come, butter, come;
Peter stands at the gate
Waiting for a butter cake;
Come, butter, come.

Then from the top of a hill they saw the walls of Bath in the distance, glowing with a pale gleam of gold as the sun set. The river Avon shone like a thread of gold below the stone walls. Periwigged heads leaned out of carriage windows to give the coachmen cries of encouragement. The journey was almost over. The last hill was so steep that everyone had to get out of the coaches while the exhausted horses stood shivering in the traces and the servants put their shoulders to the wheels.

When at last the royal coaches rumbled through one of the city gates and clattered over the paving stones of city streets, the travelers were aching in every bone. A long soak in the hot waters of Bath would be the greatest luxury of the following morning.

By invitation of Thomas Ken, Bishop of Bath and Wells, Anne and George stayed at the Abbey House, close under the walls of the ancient Abbey, with a few friends especially chosen for the honor of attending the Prince and Princess. Anne had asked no questions about arrangements for the rest of her household until she called Sarah to join her by the fire for a bowl of hot caudle, prepared by the good brothers for the royal guests.

"I like something sweet," said Anne. "I hope that rooms in the town were found for all to be as comfortable as we are."

"No one thought of it in time to write ahead," Sarah answered, "but some lodgers can be moved to make room, if need be."

Anne looked distressed. "Mrs. Freeman, do you mean that others may be turned out of their rooms on account of our attendants?"

"Of course," said Sarah. "Why not? No one of importance need be moved."

"I should not like anyone to be disturbed," Anne said. She seldom disagreed with dear Mrs. Freeman, but on this occasion she must differ with her friend. "Please bring me a pen and paper so that I can write a note about it."

Sarah thought that it was perfect nonsense. She stood tapping her foot while Anne wrote that "the Place was a Rendezvous for People indisposed; that She and the Prince came there only to enjoy the common Benefit of the Waters, and not to hinder any Body from the same Privilege; and that she understood her Attendants should make shift for Lodgings, as well as herself, without turning others out of theirs." The note was sent off to an equerry at once. As a result, the Prince and Princess of Denmark became enormously popular at Bath.

The first business of the next day was to drink the waters. Most of the travelers sallied forth before breakfast by sedan chair to the Pump-Room, where they stood about, sipping, and exchanging "How d'ye do's" with the company.

In the warm bright light of early spring, nothing could be more charming than the view of Bath, pearly gold in the morning sunshine. The city was small; there were no more than fifteen streets, as many lanes, a few open spaces, terrace walks and private courts, but Bath was far more elegant than London. Already its simple rural pleasures were giving way to fashionable ones. Besides the people who drank the waters or bathed in them for health, London society now came for other reasons too. Charles II had visited Bath with Catherine of Braganza, on the advice of her physician; James II had come with Mary of

Modena. They brought with them the craze for gambling. It was "How d'ye do?" all morning and "What's trumps?" all afternoon. The idle and indolent of London had found a place where, as Oliver Goldsmith put it, "they could have each other's company and win each other's money, as they had done during the winter in town." The price of lodgings had risen to a guinea a night, but with a little luck and a pair of loaded dice the expense of the trip might easily be defrayed.

At noon every day the fashionable world appeared in full dress with elaborate wigs, face patches, and paint, to meet friends and enjoy a Bath bun or a buttered roll with chocolate, tea, or coffee at one of the eating houses.

There was music in the Pump-Room all day long, and bells rang in the streets at the least excuse. A young visitor wrote home to Mother:

> No city, dear Mother, this city excels
> In charming sweet sounds both of fiddles and bells;
> I thought, like a fool, that they only would ring
> For a wedding, or judge, or the birth of a King;
> But I found 'twas for me that the good-natured people
> Rang so hard that I thought they would pull down the
>   steeple, . . .
> Yet some think it strange they should make such a riot
> In a place where sick folk would be glad to be quiet.

"Sick folk" went religiously to the baths every day, and others went merely for the novelty and pleasure of it. The King's Bath, the Queen's Bath, and the smaller Cross Bath—all must be seen. Anne on her first visit to the Cross Bath felt an inward pang at the sight of a new stone cross recently erected in the middle of the pool by order of her father. The cross commemorated the benefits received by Mary of Modena after bathing there, benefits resulting in the expected birth of a child and heir to the throne. Anne too wished to bathe in the Cross Bath. For this occasion the bath may have been temporarily closed to the public. Even Samuel Pepys, who was not squeamish, took one look during his visit to Bath ten years earlier and wrote that "it cannot be clean to go so many bodies together in the same water." There was a rule that no person should "thrust, cast, or throw another into any of the said Baths, with his or her clothes on." Another rule forbade anyone to "cast or throw any dog, bitch, or other live beast into any of the said baths." Such high jinx were known to have happened.

The Cross Bath was recommended to Anne and George as more moderate in temperature than the others, but even so, said Pepys, "the springs so hot as the feet not able to endure." He was very nearly parboiled. The Prince and Princess of Denmark and their party dressed for the bath in special canvas garments that filled with water "so that its borne off that your shape is not seen. The gentlemen had drawers and waistcoats of the same material." Celia Fiennes, a spirited young lady who traveled all over England on horseback, noted exactly how one took the baths.

"There was a cross in the middle of one bath with seats round it for gentlemen, and round the wall were arches with seats for the ladies, with curtains in front. They all sat up to their necks in the water." There was a gallery around the top for the company to come and view the proceedings. In the King's Bath the water was hotter and you could have it pumped on you. If you did, you wore a broad-brimmed hat. "To go out of the baths," said Miss Celia, "the ladies passed within a door and went up steps and let their canvas bathing clothes slip off." Meanwhile your maid put "a garment of flanell made like a Nightgown with great sleeves over your head, and ye guides take ye taile and so pulls it on you. Just as you rise ye steps, and yr other garment drops off so you are wrapped up in ye flannel and your night-gown on ye top, and your slippers, and so you are set in chaire which is brought into ye roome. Ye chaires you go in are a low seate. And with frames round and over ye head and all covered inside and out with red bays [baize]." So to the lodging "where you go to bed and lye and sweate. . . ." Celia Fiennes was not strong on syntax or spelling, but she had sharp bright eyes that missed no detail.

Dinner was served about four o'clock in the afternoon, followed by evening prayers and then a round of visits to the Pump-Room, tea, dancing, perhaps a theatrical performance, or a game of cards. "From the Court to the scullery everyone gambled," said one observer, "and scarcely any two persons could meet without one or the other suggesting cards or dice." But sceptics wondered why physicians sent their patients to Bath to sweeten their blood by drinking the waters if they also allowed them to sour it by upsetting their nerves with gambling losses.

In May, news reached Bath that the King had ordered his Declaration of Liberty of Conscience to be read aloud in all the churches of England. The Archbishop of Canterbury and six bishops, including the Bishop of Bath and Wells, refused and were sent to the Tower. They said that they were not opposed to Dissenters but thought the King's order illegal. For the next month at Bath, the trial of the bishops was the subject of every conversation; something new to talk about was always a great blessing at Bath. There was general rejoicing when the defendants were found not guilty.

In the middle of June, John Churchill arrived. He had come on horseback at top speed with more distressing news for Anne.

"Prepare yourself, Princess," he said. "The Queen is delivered of a son."

"Mr. Freeman! Impossible! And I not there to witness it! It is a month before her time."

He looked at her with sympathy. "Dear Mrs. Morley, I am afraid it is quite true."

John then disclosed one of the strangest tales in all the annals of Stuart history. The Queen had been brought to bed suddenly on June 10. Official witnesses were called into her chamber, but among them were no Protestants, no representatives of either Anne or her sister Mary. In the midst of the proceedings a large warming pan was brought into the room and put into the Queen's bed, under the covers. A few minutes later the attending physician showed the company a live male child and announced the birth of a Prince of Wales.

"But," said John Churchill, "even Catholics consider it a miracle, and Protestants are calling it 'the warming pan baby.' They say it is not the Queen's child, but a cheat, done to set aside you and your sister and establish a Catholic succession to the throne."

Anne was much shaken. "It seems so very strange," she said. "A month before the time expected, and all as if secret, while I was out of town. I do believe that my father would resort to almost any ruse to secure a Catholic succession to the throne."

"There are many who believe that," Churchill told her. "Mrs. Morley, I must ask you to hear something further, which may be painful to you. Leaders of both Whigs and Tories have united to invite Prince William, your brother-in-law, to take the throne of England."

Anne sat looking at him. She felt cold and sick. "And my father?" she asked.

"No harm will come to his Majesty, I swear it," he told her. "Only an accident, quite unforeseen, could put him in the least physical danger. But he must, of course, leave the country."

"Dear Mrs. Morley," said Sarah, taking Anne's hand in hers, "be guided by us. Believe me, if you truly love your country, there is no other way."

"What must I do?" Anne asked in a dry, hard voice.

"Rely on me," said Sarah, confidently. "You have nothing to fear, nothing to think of. The plans have been laid. We only wait for the right moment."

Anne and George returned at once to London. All over the city there were the usual signs of rejoicing for the birth of a Prince of Wales, and bells rang from church steeples. Bonfires burned in the streets. But if one walked through those streets, one heard whispered talk about the fraud of "the warming pan baby," and "Lillibullero" was whistled and sung by day and by night. A tide of rebellion against the King was sweeping the country.

Anne wrote to her sister Mary about the peculiar circumstances surrounding the birth of the new Catholic heir to the throne: "I shall never now be satisfied, whether the child be true or false; it may be it is our brother, but God only knows. . . . After all this, 'tis possible that it may be her child; but where one believes it, a thousand do not."

Samuel Pepys was one who believed it. He interviewed Margaret Dawson, formerly a servant of Mary of Modena. She was an eyewitness to the birth, and Pepys carefully quoted her evidence: "I did alsoe see fire in that faimose warming pan, soe much talked on, and I did feele ye heate of it."

During the rest of the summer Anne tried to behave as if all were well, but she found it hard to "put on a face of joy when one's heart has more cause to ache." French refugees continued to arrive in England with tales of horror. What if a Catholic king, her own father, should spread persecution throughout England as Louis XIV had done on the other side of the Channel?

What if religious freedom should disappear from England with the establishment of a Catholic succession through the supposed fraud of "the warming pan baby"? Anne's doubts and fears multiplied daily. Sarah was always at her side, reassuring, persuading. Anne must not think that she was deserting and betraying her father. She must only think what was best for England.

In September, reports of William's imminent arrival continued. Whitehall was in a panic. It was said that William had gathered a fleet and was about to sail for England. He was only waiting for a favorable east wind. James put a large weathercock on the roof of the Banqueting House opposite his own private apartments, and watched it anxiously every day. With his genius for doing the wrong thing, he called in five thousand Irish and four thousand Scots to build up his army outside London, and continued to remove Protestants and put Papists in positions of trust. "It brought people to so desperate a pass, that they seemed passionately to long for and desire the landing of that Prince, whom they looked on to be their deliverer from Popish tyranny, praying incessantly for an east wind."

In the streets of London men took off their hats to feel which way the wind was blowing. The favorite verse of "Lillibullero" was:

> O, but why does he stay behind?
> Ho! by my soul, 'tis a Protestant wind.

And still the wind blew from the southwest, while all England waited in vain for the coming of William. At last, on October 14 Evelyn wrote in great excitement, "The King's birthday. No guns from the Tower as usual. The sun eclipsed at its rising. . . . The wind which had been hitherto west, was east all this day. Wonderful expectation of the Dutch fleet."

Deliverance from the rule of the hated James seemed at hand.

But a terrible storm wrecked William's fleet so that he had to return to Holland to repair and replace his ships. It was not until Guy Fawkes Day, November 5, 1688, that he was able to land at Torbay on the south coast of England with a fleet of nearly seven hundred sails. John Churchill immediately sent a letter to the King relinquishing command of his brigade, and rode off to join William. George was still with the King, but Anne knew that he too was planning to desert to William's forces. She lived on at the Cockpit in a state of nervous suspense mixed with feelings of guilt.

James joined his army at Salisbury to face William in battle if need be, but every day he heard of desertions from his ranks. As each name was reported, the King shared the bad news with Prince George, who only responded with a guarded, *"Est-ce possible?"* Within a few hours George himself had gone to join William. "Is *'Est-ce possible?'* gone, too?" asked the King. If even the faithful George had gone, James knew that his cause was hopeless.

In London an order arrived from the King for the arrest of Sarah, but her well-laid plans stood her in good stead. On a night of rain and fog, Anne left her bed and went quietly down the little staircase leading so conveniently to Sarah's apartments. She wore her dressing gown and slippers. Together, wrapped in dark cloaks, they left the Cockpit with two of Anne's attendants. Charles Sackville, Lord Dorset, was waiting for them at the door. They splashed through the wet. One of Anne's slippers sank into the mud, but Lord Dorset took off his white glove and put it on the foot of the Princess. In the darkness ahead was Charing Cross, where a coach waited. Lord Dorset saw them safely into the coach, off to the house of Anne's good old friend, Bishop Compton. From there they were driven to Lord Dorset's beautiful house in Epping Forest. The Bishop traveled with them, carrying a sword and pistol as in the days of his youth. Armed forces turned out to guard the Princess until she could reach Oxford and rejoin Prince George. Like other Stuarts before her, she might be in danger of her life. When thrones fell, heads were apt to fall. Face to face with real danger, she did not fear it as she had feared danger in her dreams, but her conscience was uneasy.

Unlike Anne, the Bishop enjoyed every minute of the journey, and Sarah was in her element. At a banquet given for them in Nottingham, Colley Cibber, the actor, had the honor of waiting on Sarah. "Such a commanding aspect of grace!" he sighed. "Such beauty, like the sun, must shine into equal warmth the peasant and the courtier." Her brilliance quite eclipsed the shy and silent Princess.

While Anne and her friends continued on their triumphal progress, Mary of Modena fled to Portsmouth for safety with the unlucky little Prince of Wales. She had not gone far enough to please the incensed English. Even in the streets of Portsmouth she heard a taunting rhyme:

> Lady Bird, Lady Bird, fly away home,
> Your house is on fire, and your children will burn.

Dismayed, the poor Queen set sail for France. Two days later James left Whitehall disguised as a servant. By coach and boat he escaped, throwing the Great Seal into the Thames as he went. Discovered by fishermen before his ship could reach France, he found himself once again at Whitehall, more a prisoner than a king. Official arrangements were made for his second departure, since his subjects wanted nothing better than to speed him on his way. The only one who mourned his going was his old friend, William Penn. On Christmas Day, James landed in

Brittany and was soon reunited with his family, as guests of cousin Louis, in that dependable asylum at St. Germain.

The wind had blown, the cradle had rocked. Then the bough broke, and with it the Glorious Revolution ended. Down came baby, cradle, and all. By December 18, William of Orange was at St. James's Palace, and Whitehall was filled with Dutch guards. Anne and Sarah returned to London. At Sarah's suggestion they attended the theater decked out in orange ribbons.

Anne was ashamed of wearing the orange ribbons. But perhaps the new year would bring happiness. She was already expecting another child. If the magic of Bath worked for her, this child might live.

An artist's rendering of the flight from England of Mary of Modena, wife of King James II, with her "warming pan baby"

Chapter XII

Hampton Court

Mary, Mary, quite contrary,
How does your garden grow?
With silver bells and cockle shells
And pretty maids all in a row.

IN THE GREAT KITCHEN at Hampton Court a boy stood by the fire with a warm silver dish in his hands. The cook, one of several brought from France in the days of Charles II, hovered over a saucepan in which the first peas of the season were being prepared for the royal table.

It was the spring of 1689. William was King, Mary was Queen. They had been invited, indeed almost elected, to take the throne. England had gone through great turmoil to be rid of James. With his departure the "Divine Right of Kings" had gone too; English people had a king of their own choosing. Even so, they were not enthusiastic about William. Most people adopted a wait-and-see attitude, merely noting that he was "very stately, serious and reserved." They knew that he had Stuart blood. They would soon find that he had some of the Stuart vices. But he lacked the Stuart charm for which the English had forgiven so much.

He was decidedly cool toward his adoring wife, who towered over his slight, hunchbacked figure. As for Mary, having left

England in floods of tears at the time of her wedding, she re-turned "laughing and jolly," much to the disgust of some ob-servers, including John Evelyn, who thought she should have shown "some seeming reluctance at least, of assuming her father's Crown." But not at all. "She rose early the next morning and . . . went from room to room to see the convenience of Whitehall; lay in the same bed and apartment where the late Queen lay, and within a night or two sat down to play at basset."

A month after William's arrival, a Convention Parliament had met to decide on the succession, and Anne, on the advice of the Churchills, had subordinated her rights in order to smooth the way. The throne would belong to William and Mary jointly as long as both lived. William demanded that he should rule alone as King, if Mary should die first. Not until his death would the throne go to Anne.

If Anne had insisted on her claim to the throne, in the event of Mary's death, she might have made great trouble for William. Her flight during the previous winter had proved her popularity with the people, as she moved from city to city and town to town. Because she had not made trouble but had stepped aside in Wil-liam's favor, it was particularly galling to find herself and George treated like poor relations by both William and Mary in this first year of their reign. Parliament, which was now supreme in money matters, had asked William to give Anne an allowance, but he had not yet done so. It was humiliating to live month after month at Hampton Court as guests, and not very welcome guests; it was impossible to return to the Cockpit without money to maintain it.

Money was not the only cause of ill-feeling at Hampton Court that spring. Anne had looked forward to a fond reunion with her sister. Now it appeared that there was room in Mary's affections

The crown offered to William III and Mary II by the Lords and Commons, 1689. An engraving after a fresco by E. M. Ward

only for the disagreeable William and for the crown on her head. Anne could not forget the long coronation ceremony in April. Almost overcome herself by the heat and the crowd of people, she had whispered to Mary, "I pity your fatigue, Madam." She would never forget Mary's face, flushed with heat and triumph, nor her answer, "A crown, Sister, is not so heavy as it seems to be."

Soon afterward, William and Mary came to Hampton Court. William had asthma and found Whitehall unbearable. At Hampton Court he could breathe. His courtiers grumbled about the time-consuming journey by road or river, to and from London, and Londoners missed the excitement of having a king in residence at Whitehall. But William cared nothing about English opinion. He disliked England and longed every day for Holland. He had married an English princess and ascended the English throne for one reason only—to strengthen the alliance among the enemies of France and to break the power of France forever.

William was silent and morose as he sat at table with his Queen and the Prince and Princess of Denmark. Only Mary chattered amiably with the ladies-in-waiting who stood about, ready to serve her. From the far end of the Great Hall a constant succession of attendants came with dishes. Flagons of beer and ale, William's preference, were kept filled.

In the kitchen, the French cook removed a limp lettuce leaf from the saucepan of peas and poured them into the waiting silver dish. The kitchen boy clapped a silver lid on the dish and ran up the steps, through a cloister, and up another flight of steps to a great oak screen. There a gentleman took the dish from the boy's hands and hurried with it down the length of the hall to the dais where the royal table stood under the towering stained-glass window. With a flourish, he lifted the lid and set the dish on the table between the King and the Princess of Denmark. The peas were perfectly fresh, just picked in the famous kitchen gardens of the palace. They were flawlessly cooked and looked meltingly tender; in a word, fit for a king. And the King ate them. Before the astonished eyes of his Court, he gobbled up every one of the peas. Mary thought nothing of it. In her opinion, if William wanted all the peas, he should have them. George hardly noticed the incident. He was applying himself to the ale. Only Anne was red with anger and resentment. For this boor she had given up her right to the throne! Because of him, she and George were penniless dependents. And the Dutch monster had not even the common courtesy to share those peas! It was too much to bear. She excused herself and left the table.

William finished his dinner, pushed back his chair, and looked about the Great Hall. The mellow light of early afternoon brightened the paneled walls. Above them, like a golden honeycomb, rose the Tudor arches that supported the blue ceiling. Henry VIII had built this hall and here he had dined, keeping open table for a household of five hundred lusty followers. There was room for them all at Hampton Court and for two hundred eighty strangers besides, if so many had ever arrived at one time. Every bed was covered with velvet or satin or silk, both hangings and coverlets embroidered with the finest needlework. Hampton Court had been a palace worthy of Henry's magnificence and splendor. But now, thought William, it should have a rebirth under a king as great as Henry. The best of these buildings, including the Great Hall, should stand. The rest must be torn down and replaced with new buildings of the greatest dignity. Hampton Court should rival Versailles, with gardens in the Dutch manner laid out in every courtyard and around the palace as far as the eye could reach. In this scheme Mary would be invaluable. William found her chatter tiresome, but he fully appreciated her taste in furniture, in objects of art, and above all, in gardening. The work must begin at once. He himself would be abroad much of the time, bringing about the downfall of Louis, but he would employ that architect, Wren, and Mary must keep an eye on the man.

That summer at Hampton Court, Anne used to waken in the middle of the night. She would lie staring through the dark, wondering what had wakened her. Perhaps it was the ghost of Henry VIII's Jane Seymour, who was said to wander about the galleries of the old palace. But what really haunted Anne was the thought of her own father. She knew, as everyone knew, what he had said when he heard of her escape from the Cockpit at the time of William's landing: "God help me, my own children have forsaken me." By day she could push that thought to the back of her mind, but it kept her awake at night; she was racked by guilt and shame. She must write to her father and ask his forgiveness.

He was in Ireland now. He had been there since April, gathering followers. There were many in England too who had not forgotten their oath of allegiance to James and who considered themselves still bound to him. Some were saying that James might have been a good king but for the baleful influence of Louis XIV. The followers of James called themselves Jacobites. In London they sang ranting songs. Even in the seclusion of Hampton Court, Mary and Anne heard the words, repeated by courtiers who "thought they would want to know."

> What is the rhyme for porringer?
> What is the rhyme for porringer?
> The king he had a daughter fair
> And gave the Prince of Orange her.

And, still worse,

> William and Mary, George and Anne,
> Four such children had never a man:
> They put their father to flight and shame,
> And called their brother a shocking bad name.

Was that "warming pan baby" really their brother after all? He was now a year old, and visitors to St. Germain since James's abdication reported that the little boy undoubtedly had "the Stuart look."

During July, the old Tudor gardens at Hampton Court were torn up, and new gardens appeared. Plants were set in beds of geometric design; the spaces between were filled with colored sand, with brick dust, or with crushed cockle shells. Two landscape gardeners, London and Wise, came out from town to supervise the work, while men with clippers trimmed trees and shrubbery into cubes, cones, globes, and the shapes of fantastic birds and beasts. There was talk of fountains and statuary, of a greenhouse and an orangery. Tree-lined avenues and broad terraces were laid out. William gave orders for the construction of a maze, like those in the great gardens of Holland, where one could wander and be agreeably lost among high clipped hedges of green or flowering shrubs. William liked the smell of box because it reminded him of Holland; all the garden paths at Hampton Court were to be edged with it. Of course no one consulted Anne.

Sir Christopher Wren arrived to present plans for the new buildings. Almost every day his thin little figure could be seen walking about the grounds, accompanied by the tall Queen and followed by his assistants. He looked remarkably young and cheerful for a man who carried the responsibility of rebuilding so much of London. To rebuild Hampton Court was only one

Queen Anne's bed at Hampton Court

more opportunity to create something of beauty, of seemly proportions and classic grace. In his mind's eye he saw Hampton Court as it would be when finished, the new buildings blending with the old, gardens on three sides and the Thames flowing by. William and Mary gave their enthusiastic approval.

Physical changes at Hampton Court were less disturbing than other kinds of change. William intended to let his power be seen and felt. The pious and benevolent Bishop Ken was deprived of his bishopric because he maintained that his Consecration Oath bound him to James as long as he lived. John Dryden, England's chief poet and literary critic for almost forty years, was dismissed as Poet Laureate. Dryden's recent "Song for St. Cecilia's Day" might extol harmony, "heavenly harmony," but William was deaf to the harmony of a Poet Laureate who could harmonize with every head of state from Puritan Cromwell to Catholic James. Loyalty should not be so easily swayed.

Foolish old English traditions must go too. When a crowd of "poor scrofulous wretches" came out from London to Hampton Court to be touched for "the King's evil," William said brusquely, "It is a silly superstition. Give the poor creatures some money and tell them to go away." Many people agreed with his action, but his tone gave offense. Those who did not know the Dutch custom were offended again when the King walked into the Chapel with his hat on, and kept it on.

Next, the King turned a cold appraising eye on the Churchills. He had made John Earl of Marlborough as a reward for his services, but Mary was increasingly antagonistic to Anne's friend Sarah. Perhaps Mary was right. And what of John's present activities? Was it true that he was persuading Parliament to grant Anne a yearly income, making her independent of William's grace and favor? One night in the drawing room, Mary approached Anne about the matter.

"What is the meaning of these proceedings in Parliament?" she asked, coldly.

Under the attack, Anne stifled her resentment and managed a mild answer. "I hear my friends hope to make me some settlement."

"Pray, what friends have you but the King and me?" Mary retorted, and turned away.

Both Sarah and John Churchill heard it. So did many others. All agreed that Mary's insult was prompted by jealousy of Anne's popularity. In spite of the King and Queen, Parliament voted an income of £50,000 a year to Anne. It came as a godsend, for at the end of July she gave birth to a boy, and with an assured income, she could prepare to leave Hampton Court.

Surprisingly, the King asked that the child be named for him. He stood as godfather, and immediately gave his nephew a title—Duke of Gloucester. All England rejoiced at the news that the well-loved Princess Anne had borne a son who was likely to live. It was not generally known that Anne was slow to recover from her confinement and that the little William was weak and sickly. His head was too large for his body, and his limbs were feeble. Doctors who came to examine the child commented privately on the unhappy Stuart family taint. Faithful George was not to blame, but the little Duke of Gloucester was suffering for "the sins of the fathers" on Anne's side of the family tree. Still, he was alive, and there was always hope.

Anne would have liked to live at Richmond for the health of her child and for sentimental reasons, but William had already given Richmond to one of his favorites. Anne and George moved back to the Cockpit. Their first thought was for their child. Since the Duchess of Portsmouth was long since gone from Whitehall, her grand apartments were turned into nurseries for the little Duke. Anne's next plan was to share her improved fortunes with her friends. She wrote to Sarah, "I have had something to say to you a great while, and I did not know how to go about it. I have designed, ever since my revenue was settled, to desire you would accept a thousand pounds a year. I beg you would . . . never mention anything of it to me; for I shall be ashamed to have any notice taken of such a thing from one that deserves more than I shall ever be able to return."

For the moment, Sarah declined the offer, but was soon in need of other help. Mary reached such a point of exasperation with the Churchills that she ordered Anne to dismiss her dear Mrs. Freeman. Anne refused. Mary insisted. Neither would give way.

Meanwhile, George was receiving his share of slights and insults at the hands of William. When the King sailed for Ireland to confront James with an army, George offered his services and raised an auxiliary force of seven thousand Danish soldiers. William would not allow George to command the Danes, but George swallowed his resentment and fought bravely at the Battle of the Boyne. James was defeated; he sailed back to France. After the victory, George climbed happily into William's coach, only to be told that the King did not want his company.

The following year, William prepared to attack Louis and the French allies on the Continent. Deciding to forgive and forget William's contempt, George once more offered help. He would go as a volunteer, not asking for any command, and would provide his own arms and supplies. William accepted his help, but when George's gear was put on board the King's flagship, he was told to remove it.

Seen in perspective, the motive for William's strange and harsh behavior is clear. Born and bred in the atmosphere of Continental intrigue, suspicion, and jealousy, it was almost impossible for him to trust anyone. He had not forgotten an unprovoked attack on the Dutch republic made by France and England at the time of the secret treaty of Dover. William thought "perfidious England" well named. Besides, George of Denmark had deserted James in favor of William. In William's view, a man who would desert once would do it again.

William was more and more disliked in England, and knew it. The English hated paying taxes for "King William's War." They hated having their army commanded by Dutch officers. Anne, the heir presumptive, was loved. George was her husband, John Churchill her friend. What more likely than a plot hatched among them to overthrow William and put Anne on the throne, with help from James? William knew that Anne was once more writing to her father. The danger seemed acute. He dismissed Churchill from all his appointments.

Anne refused to desert her friends. She wrote to Sarah in a passion of loyalty and devotion, "No, my dear Mrs. Freeman, never believe your faithful Mrs. Morley will ever submit. She can wait with patience for a sunshine day, and if she does not live to see it, yet she hopes England will flourish again."

In a final clash of wills between the two sisters, Anne and George left the Cockpit, taking the Churchills with them, and borrowed or rented houses near London for themselves, their attendants, and their son. Not long afterward, a fire broke out at Whitehall in the deserted nurseries of the little Duke, who might have died in the flames but for the quarrel between Anne and Mary. The Queen had to escape in her night clothes.

The quarrel continued. Mary, fearful of Anne's power to rock the throne, withdrew the royal guards who had always been assigned to the household of George and Anne. The Princess went about town with no more protection than any private person. Pickpockets and highwaymen were a constant threat. One night on a dark road Anne's carriage was attacked and she was robbed.

She had few visitors from Court but there were always some loyal friends, and her devotion to the Churchills was boundless. "Dear Mrs. Freeman," she said, "be assured your faithful Mrs. Morley can never change."

With Sarah and John as constant companions, Anne was happy in her quiet life. It was enough for her to watch over her husband and child, to go shopping, to attend a play, to make a little trip to Bath or Wells. Handling the reins herself, she often drove out in a light chaise. Along the roads there were friendly smiles and bows from strangers, ordinary English people who took comfort in a glimpse of their own English Princess during this reign of the unwelcome "Dutch monster." Anne found she could get along very well without Court ceremony.

But Sarah and John were restless in retirement. They longed to be in control of important events. Instead, there came a frustrating period in which the career of John Churchill appeared in a murky, uncertain, and puzzling light. Now he worked with the Tories, now with the Whigs. By turns, he was in power and out of it. He held civic and military honors, then lost all of them and for more than a month was even imprisoned by William in the Tower. He returned to favor and once more assumed his duties. Some called him a traitor, others a great patriot.

William's motives and actions were equally complex. To reach his goal he would form any alliance, accept or reject any friendship. His goal was the same as Churchill's. Both wanted to destroy the power of France. But William dared not trust Churchill in a major military or political role. He was sure that Churchill, like Anne, was corresponding with James in his exile at St. Germain. William was quite right; Churchill was at the center of a plot to restore James to the throne, for he now thought the old King more likely to give him authority than the new one. His own brilliance and utter self-confidence demanded nothing less than supreme command of England's military affairs and a guiding hand in her diplomatic relations as well. This, William would not give. Year after year, he waged his war against France without the services of his ablest soldier.

One of the houses rented by Anne was Camden House, a delightful old place near Kensington, where the little Duke of Gloucester could have his own establishment. Here everything centered around his health and well-being. He could drive through the park in a little coach drawn by two tiny horses. On cold or wet days, he could sit on the floor by an open fire, playing with his toy soldiers.

Anne often stayed at Camden House for weeks at a time. "How is my boy?" was her first question, on entering the house. She would lie on a couch, watching him at play. Like most small children, he learned to make animals of clay, to cut out colored paper mats, and to weave strips of bright paper into baskets to be given to his mother. His frail body carried a bright, eager spirit, quick to learn. A horn book hung by a ribbon around his neck with printed alphabet verses to read in any idle moment. Sometimes "A was an Archer who shot at a frog"; sometimes "A was an Apple-pie."

Young Peter Bathurst often came to play. It was hard for William to play ball games, or Blind Man's Buff, or leapfrog like other boys. But he and Peter could blow soap bubbles or play marbles and jackstones, sitting on the floor. The toy soldiers were the best game of all.

The soldiers were beautiful, all carved of wood, each one different, with painted uniforms and shiny swords. There were foot soldiers, grenadiers, and men on horseback. There were mortar pieces too, that shot out toy bombs, and there were bridges to cross and forts to take. Sometimes the Earl of Marlborough hung his wig over the back of a chair and crawled about on his hands and knees to show the boys why King William had lost the latest battle on the Continent and how he could have won it. They soon learned to tell a scarp from a counterscarp and knew all about a glacis and a covered-way.

The Queen would come to see little William, driving the short distance to Camden House from Kensington, where she and the King had bought Nottingham House. They were adding new wings to the old building and turning it into a palace. King William had a nagging cough, and the fine dry air at Kensington was good for his asthma—more helpful, he thought, than the doctor's prescription of a glass of wine with woodlice steeped in it.

Followed by her attendants and guards, Mary would sweep into the room at Camden House where the little Duke was playing. If Anne was present, the Queen might pass her without a glance, but she was always kind to William. He stood and made his bow, as he had been taught.

"And what have you learned, child, since my last visit?"

"I have learned a new alphabet, madam."

"Then let me hear it, by all means."

"In Adam's fall, We sinned all . . ." With his hands clasped behind him, he went on without a mistake, to the very end. "Zaccheus he Did climb a tree, Our Lord to see." But William's eyes were busy with every detail of the uniforms worn by the Queen's guards.

Mary praised him, gave him a gold piece, and patted his thin little shoulder. As she turned to go, he said, "Your Majesty's guards are very fine. My mama once had guards, too. Why doesn't she have them now?"

During long months when they did not meet, Anne wrote to Mary again and again. Sarah "thought the Princess did a great deal too much," hoping to heal the breach with her sister. Mary answered coldly, or not at all. She was busy with affairs of state, for she was Regent when William was away from England, conducting the war on the Continent. The palace and gardens at Kensington were to be finished before his return, and the Queen supervised the work. Besides, she was often at Hampton Court, inspecting her model dairy or the rare plants in her hothouses, or arranging for her pretty ladies-in-waiting to have their portraits painted. The portraits decorated the Water Gallery, her own charming retreat, separate from the rest of the palace. It was already filled with her embroidery, and a choice collection of Delft ware and China ware was on display. With all her activities, Mary had no time for Anne, who was always ailing these days, and was dull company at any time. If Anne wished to live with her stupid husband and those treacherous Churchills, let her do so, but she need not expect a visit from Mary.

In the winter of 1694 there was a severe epidemic of smallpox. Mary had never had smallpox; she fell desperately ill. Anne wrote, offering, even begging to come to Kensington, but the doctors advised against the visit. William, home from the wars, knew too late that Mary had been a good wife. He moved a camp bed into her room and sat beside her, stifling his cough so that she might sleep. His own mother had died of smallpox in England. He felt sure that he would lose his wife in the same way. With disgust and despair he watched the doctor measuring out a black powder to be mixed with wine. Toads had been burned alive to make that powder. These English!

A few days after Christmas, Mary died. She was only thirty-two. Anne was too ill to attend the funeral, but she came afterward to see William at Kensington. She was carried upstairs in a sedan chair. William, broken with grief, took her hands in his and they wept together, he for the wife he had not loved enough; she for the sister she had perhaps loved too well.

With Mary's death, family relationships improved. William gave Anne some of her sister's jewels and invited her to live again at St. James's. His change of heart may have been prompted by a sense of justice or by sheer loneliness. Besides, William was a diplomat. He knew that James was preparing for another attempt to invade England. Anne's friendship could bolster William's position on the throne. She had better be given every inducement to do so. But William continued to treat George with cold contempt.

Many courtiers who had deserted Anne came scurrying back. Others who had remained faithful asked her to remember their services. Everyone was aware that she was now one step nearer to the throne. In spite of gout and dropsy, which made walking painful, Anne's spirits improved. The little Duke was growing up, a mischievous, lovable child who showed great promise. A young Huguenot refugee, Abel Boyer, was appointed as his French teacher and began to work on a French-English dictionary for his small pupil, who must be as fluent and widely read in French as in English. Boyer also prepared a special lesson book, *The Complete French Master,* for the five-year-old child. Latin was taught with the help of another grammar, *A Delicious Syrup newly Clarified for Young Scholars that thirst for the Sweet Liquor of Latin Speech.*

The toy soldiers were as well-loved as ever, and little William also had a whole regiment of friends who drilled in the gardens at Camden House, trampling down flower beds and making a general nuisance of themselves. With the help of John Churchill, Earl of Marlborough, soldier without a command, courtier out of a job, they fought mock battles and followed all the misfortunes of King William.

When the King was not campaigning in Ireland or in Flanders, he often came to see his young nephew, whose discreet and forbearing mother had kept the family quarrel from the child.

One day in 1697 the King came riding through the gates of Camden House on his favorite horse, Sorrel. He looked tired and ill, but he smiled and drew rein to watch the boys drilling under the eyes of the little Duke and the Earl of Marlborough. When Churchill saw the King, he bowed stiffly and bit his lip, while the boys tossed their feathered hats into the air and cheered the King. Young William called his troops to a halt and came running to greet his Majesty.

"I am glad to see you, sir. Is the war ended?"

The King leaned down from his saddle and patted the child's head.

"The war is not ended, but there has been a treaty," he said.

"And you have won?"

"I have neither won nor lost, but I cannot find anyone with the will to fight on."

"Someday my regiment and I will serve you in Flanders, sir."

"Thank you," the King said gravely. "I will need your help." Then, speaking above the child's head, he called to John Churchill, "My lord, I appoint you governor of this child. Teach him your own accomplishments, and he will do very well."

He gave his namesake a gold piece and touched Sorrel with his spur.

"Thank you, my dear King," cried little William. "Now I can pay my troops." He ran back to his regiment, shouting, "Play 'Lillibullero'!" Wooden whistles and toy drums struck up the famous air. Some of the boys who played "Lillibullero" that day would live to have grandsons in the American colonies across the sea. Those grandsons would march to another jaunty tune,

Michael Dahl's portrait of Queen Anne with her son, the Duke of
Gloucester

"Yankee Doodle." As "Lillibullero" had "played King James out of three kingdoms," so "Yankee Doodle" would spark another revolution in the same independent spirit.

That day at Camden House marked the beginning of Churchill's return to favor at Court. William soon recalled him to high military command as well. Besides Churchill, the King also appointed other teachers and mentors to train the little Duke of Gloucester. One of these was Bishop Burnet, who read and explained the Scriptures to him, instructed him in ethics, in history, geography, politics, and government.

William was only nine years old when his serious studies began. Bishop Burnet told him what it meant to be a Knight of the Garter and someday perhaps Prince of Wales and heir to the throne. The boy tried very hard to live up to all that was expected of him. His mother thought he worked too hard, but everyone was pleased with his progress. The Bishop reported that his pupil had mastered all of Plutarch's *Lives*, Greek history, and Roman history. The Princess Anne was told that her boy found his studies easy.

The events of the last few years had been too turbulent to give her much time or taste for reading. Now, as the little Duke came to her with questions for which she had no answers, Anne began to feel her own ignorance as never before. In the apartments next to hers at St. James's Palace lived Dr. Richard Bentley, who had been appointed by William as Keeper of the Royal Library, housed in one wing of the palace. Dr. Bentley was a happy man, rearranging, cataloguing, and only emerging from the library twice a week to spend an afternoon over a pot of tea in his own rooms with a few special friends. The Princess Anne and Prince George soon became a welcome part of the little gatherings. They were both good listeners. Among the ones who talked were Sir John Evelyn, Sir Christopher Wren,

John Locke, and Sir Isaac Newton, all members of the Royal Society, all scholars and gentlemen. So great was the zest of the Society's members that they had undertaken to study the whole field of knowledge; nothing should escape them. Evelyn told about their latest discussions and experiments, such as methods of making smokeless coal; perpetual motion machines; the mechanics of a new, easily carried *camera obscura* for observing what went on in the streets, and a new improved telescope for observing what went on in the skies.

John Locke talked about his "Essay Concerning Human Understanding," and advised the Princess to read history. Newton, absent-minded, mild, and pleasant, nodded and smiled, only half listening while he contemplated the infinite variety of discoveries yet to be made. "I do not know what I may appear to the world," he once said, "but to myself I seem to have been only like a boy playing on the seashore, and diverting myself in now and then finding a smooth pebble or a prettier shell than ordinary, while the great ocean of truth lay all undiscovered before me." Newton became a devoted friend of Prince George, who was far from stupid when he felt at ease. Anne decided that if her eyes were strong enough to do embroidery, they were strong enough for reading, and with Dr. Bentley's help she began. The books and the quiet afternoons with the cheerful, learned gentlemen opened new worlds in which Sarah did not care to join her.

In 1698 most of the palace at Whitehall burned to the ground. This time nothing much remained but the Banqueting House and the Cockpit. The fire started when a Dutch servant was drying clothes too close to an open fire. Without a tear, William began to hold Court at St. James's Palace, but Londoners were not pleased. They said that if they had had a proper English king, with proper English servants, the fire would never have happened. The "Dutch monster" and his Dutch servant had swept away another cherished tradition.

The century ended in gloom. "King William's War" had broken out again on the Continent. The mood of England was one of bitterness and disillusionment. John Dryden summed it all up with his "Secular Masque":

> 'Tis well an Old Age is out,
> And time to begin a New.

But 1700, the first year of the new century, brought only a new grief to the nation. On July 24 the young Duke of Gloucester was at Windsor for his eleventh birthday. In the evening he stood with his friend Peter Bathurst on the terrace beside his father and mother. Across the Thames at Eton, bonfires burned in honor of his birthday. Fireworks rose from barges on the river and burst into flowers and fountains in the darkening sky.

"Ah! See that one, Peter! Ah! There's another!" The eyes of the little Duke were glittering, his face pale with excitement. They could not get him to sleep that night. The next day he had a sore throat and a high fever. His mother nursed him, without sleep herself, watching in anguish the treatments prescribed by the doctors. Within a week he was dead.

The small leaden coffin was brought from Windsor to London by barge. A torch-lit procession bore it on by night to Westminster. There for two days the people of London filed past to see him, "the Most Illustrious Prince, William Duke of Gloucester, Knight of the Most Noble Order of the Garter, only Son of the High and Mighty Princess Anne, by His Royal Highness Prince George of Denmark."

The following winter Anne's father, James, died at St. Germain. Mary of Modena continued to live there with "the warming-pan baby," as the skeptical English still called him. Louis had visited James on his deathbed, and announced that he would uphold James's son as King of England. He was calling the child "James III." This enraged the English, since Louis was bound by treaty not to interfere in English affairs. As a further offense, he put his grandson Philip on the throne of Spain. All England was stunned at the threat of an empire headed by the French tyrant and stretching from Dunkirk to Gibraltar.

With this turn of events, William at last found himself king of a nation resolute for full-scale war against France. Forgetting their former differences, he recalled Marlborough to full power; when fighting men were needed, nobody could surpass Marlborough. William made him Commander-in-Chief of the English forces in Holland. Now things would be better.

Late in February, 1702, a small accident changed English history. William was riding his favorite horse, Sorrel, in a stag hunt at Hampton Court. It was a rare moment of relaxation for this hard-working sovereign. The horse stumbled in a mole hole, throwing the King, whose collarbone was broken in the fall. It would not have been a serious injury for a well man. For William it was fatal.

Chapter XIII

Westminster

Boys and girls come out to play,
The moon doth shine as bright as day.
Leave your supper and leave your sleep,
And join your playfellows in the street.
                    Old English Nursery Rhyme

THE ROOM WAS CHILLY. Heavy curtains were drawn against the night air, but at St. James's Palace the candles always guttered in the draft. The Princess Anne saw that the fire on the hearth had dwindled to embers. She spoke softly to a waiting-woman who dozed on a stool at her side. "Hill, make up the fire and bring me a little chocolate. I am cold." All night long, messages had been arriving from Kensington Palace. The King was not expected to live until daybreak. She pulled her black cloak closer about her shoulders. She was in mourning for her son and for her father.

Sarah slept soundly in a high-backed chair on the other side of the hearth. Sarah could sleep anywhere, Anne thought, with a fond look. She had nerves of steel. Not a curl was out of place, but she must be worn out with this long night watch. Fortunately, Abigail Hill moved quietly and was not likely to waken dear Mrs. Freeman. Deftly she made the fire blaze up and brought the silver pot with its satisfying and comforting hot drink. Anne asked, "What time is it, Hill?"

"Three o'clock, Highness."

The Princess dismissed the serving woman and returned to her thoughts. On this day, Sunday, the eighth of March, 1702, unless the will of God intervened, Anne would become Queen. The Protestant succession would be secure as long as she lived. But there was no child to follow her to the throne. Little Gloucester was dead, and she began to think she never would have another living child. So many of her children had been born dead or had lived only a few hours, and her own health had been damaged by bearing them. She was the last of the Stuarts, except for that child, the Pretender, in France. Would he perhaps take the throne when she died? But this was not the time to think of her own death. It was the time to plan the first official acts of her new life as Queen of England.

She would find ways to honor dear Mr. and Mrs. Freeman as they deserved. There had been so little that she could do—dowries for their daughters, a few gifts for themselves through all the hard years when they had been loyal to her, sharing in her disgrace. Now they must come into their own.

And at long last, George must be recognized. She would put all military affairs on land and sea under his care. What indignities he had suffered! William's treatment of him had been both spiteful and petty, but George had borne it all with such good nature that her own long years of neglect and deliberate insult from William and Mary had been bearable. All of that was over. Never again would the little King walk through the halls and gardens at Hampton Court, leaning on the arm of his tall, stout Queen. Mary was dead, William was dying, and Court gossip said that all England was toasting the mole, "the little gentleman in black velvet" into whose hole Sorrel had stumbled. Anne did not find that amusing. This was a time to forgive and forget past grievances, to remember the undoubted accomplishments of the reign that was ending.

It was also a time to remember other friends besides the Churchills who had helped her. Mr. Godolphin, in spite of his forbidding look and unprepossessing manner, had never wavered in his loyalty. He must have a new title and other more substantial honors as well. He would make a splendid Lord Treasurer.

Then there was John Sheffield. His youthful indiscretions were ancient history now. As Earl of Mulgrave he had served his country during the reign of her father and of William too. She had not seen him often during the past years, but whenever she thought of him a warm and pleasant feeling crept up around her heart. She would never forget that he was the first man who had loved her. Not long ago a singer had entertained the Court with a simple little Scottish air, written by a rejected suitor in honor of the daughter of Sir Robert Laurie of Maxwellton in Dumfriesshire. John Sheffield had looked across the room at Anne with smiling eyes as they listened to the song:

> Maxwellton braes are bonnie
> When airly fa's the dew,
> And 'twas there that Annie Laurie
> Gave me her promise true.

John Sheffield had married twice, but he had not forgotten Anne Stuart, and to him her face was still "the fairest that e'er the sun shone on." He would find that she remembered him too. He had ability, and from early experience he knew the navy well. England needed such men now. There was a war to fight.

In inheriting the throne, she was inheriting the war, but it was no longer "King William's War." Now that Louis XIV had dared to recognize the Pretender as King, the will of all England was behind the war. Anne had only to approve it as "just and necessary" and to keep Marlborough in full command of her forces abroad. He would bring the war to a speedy end so that years of peace and plenty could mark the reign of "good Queen Anne."

With full daylight came the expected message from Kensington Palace. It was Bishop Burnet who came hurrying in to kneel at Anne's feet with the news that William was dead. Anne could hardly bear to let him kiss her hand. In her eyes, he would always be connected in some way with her son's death. He was the taskmaster whose long hard lessons had pushed the child beyond his strength. It was too ironic to hear him say, "Long live the Queen!" But the steady stream of courtiers who followed the Bishop found Anne able to smile and return a gracious speech, as one after another of the great English lords knelt to profess their fealty and acknowledge her sovereignty. It was a long and tiring day, but George came to stand at her side, and John Sheffield was a welcome visitor early in the morning. The Churchills were in their glory. There was much to do and to decide.

The Lords met Commons in joint session and announced, "That whereas it had pleas'd Almighty God to take to himself the late King William, of glorious memory, the Princess Anne being the only Rightful and Lawful Queen of the Realm, the Lords had thought it fit to acquaint the Commons, that Orders were given in the usual form, for Proclaiming her Majesty at Three of the Clock that afternoon."

At the outer gate of St. James's Palace, trumpets sounded, a troop of palace officials issued forth, and a crowd of the nobility gathered round to hear Anne's sovereignty proclaimed in a loud voice. For this great occasion gentlemen dressed in their finest —silk coat, embroidered satin waistcoat with gold and jeweled snuffbox in the pocket, feathered hat, and perhaps an amber-headed cane to raise as they shouted with the crowd, "Long live Queen Anne!"

A great lady came hurrying across St. James's Park, "full Sail, with her Fan spread and Streamers out, and a Shoal of Fools for Tenders," as William Congreve, the dramatist, described his "Mrs. Millamant." She had spared no pains to make herself grand for this momentous day. Her face was bleached with a wash, then whitened yet again with paint before the finishing touch of red dye was applied to add a becoming blush. There were no "cracks discernible in the White Varnish," said Congreve, though she "lays it on with a Trowel." On the left cheek, to show that she was a Tory, she always wore a tiny black patch, perhaps a crescent moon, a star, or a diamond. Ladies with Whiggish sympathies wore theirs on the right. Lace handkerchiefs waved in hands that had been whitened with "a paste of almonds, oxgall, egg yolks mixed with oil of Tartar, and raisins."

Ladies' hair was done up so high that it took a wire frame to support it. Congreve's lady, Mrs. Millamant, who came sailing through the park, curled her hair around love letters that she had received, and thought the ones containing poetry gave the best curl.

At Charing Cross the Queen's sovereignty was proclaimed again. There Abel Boyer was on hand to note down the events and copy the official documents of that day and of all the important days that followed. He was the same French tutor who had been hired to teach the little Duke of Gloucester. Daniel Defoe was another reporter who made notes on the spot, wrote his articles at top speed, and had them fresh off the press, ready for coffeehouse tables within the week so that London could "read all about it."

On such a bright day as this, with the sun shining and a

benevolent new Queen on the throne, Londoners thought themselves the luckiest people on earth. They felt rich and happy. "This whole kingdom," wrote Defoe, "as well the people, as the land, and even the sea, in every part of it, are employ'd to furnish . . . the best of every thing, to supply the city of London." William's reign had seemed like a long hard winter. Today, spring flowers filled the open windows as the cavalcade from the palace marched along the streets to Temple Bar, followed by wave after wave of cheering people. At Shire Lane near Temple Bar, the members of the Kit-cat Club joined the crowds in the streets. Christopher Catt, pastry cook and patron saint of the club, had made a monstrous mutton pie to celebrate the day, and the members of the club would retire to his house to eat it as soon as the procession went by. Among them were the essayists Richard Steele and Joseph Addison, the playwright William Congreve, the eminent architect John Vanbrugh, and the Whig statesman Sir Robert Walpole—intellectuals all, but not too world-weary to crane their necks and cheer like every other Londoner.

Bright young blades down from Oxford or Cambridge climbed lamp posts and balconies to catch a glimpse of the Sergeants at Arms and the grenadiers marching past. Later the students would go to coffeehouses to argue far into the night, debating the state of the nation, for politics ran high at the universities. On this day of the Queen's accession, it was startling to hear a few young extremists of Jacobite persuasion making speeches in favor of the Pretender at St. Germain. Before the night was out, some heads might be broken. The older, more sober-minded patrons would be glad when the hot-blooded students returned to college, to cool down with a game of cricket or football, leaving the coffeehouses for those who liked to sit by the fire, read the papers, and have a quiet dish of coffee for a penny.

The parade moved on. At the sound of the trumpets, humble people poured from narrow side streets and alleys into the main thoroughfares. Among them were many a "bulk and file" (a pickpocket and his mate), who had their own way of life and their own language. They would take this excellent opportunity to "heave a book" (rob a house) while all the citizens were in the streets. Or perhaps, in honor of the day, a "maunder" might take a vacation from thievery and simply burst into verse in praise of his "strawling Mort," finding her prettier than any fine lady in the crowd:

> Doxy, oh! thy glaziers shine
> As glimmar; by the Salomon!
> No gentry mort hath prats like thine;
> No cove e'er wap'd with such a one.

In the sludge at the very bottom of the social whirlpool lived the "Mohocks," who took their name from terrifying stories about the North American Indians. The "Mohocks" too were ready to play their part in the festivities, to rob, to loot, overturn carriages and sedan chairs, slashing with razors, breaking noses, or chasing a victim into a dark alley where he could be forced to do a sword dance for the brutal amusement of his tormentors.

Even the patients in the madhouse at Bedlam heard the clamor of the cheering crowds, the roll of drums, and the sound of silver trumpets. So did prisoners at Newgate. As Princess, Anne had given money to the poor and had arranged for the release of many a poor culprit. Now convicts, wretched debtors, gentlemen thrown into the old jail for dueling, all raised a shout of "God save Queen Anne!" and hoped for pardon.

Crowds came into London from the country for the great day. They stayed on, filling the inns to overflowing, until they had seen all the sights of London, visited Bedlam to laugh at the lunatics, watched a fire eater at the bear garden, or a rope dancer precariously balancing high above the street. Everyone who could afford it planned to stay in town through the coronation.

The pages of the *Post Boy* expressed conventional regrets for the death of King William, whose burial took place with minimal fanfare, but attention was naturally focused for the most part on the new Queen, who would soon be crowned in the greatest splendor. "If any thing can make us amends for so considerable a Loss," said the *Post Boy*, "it must be the Lawful, Wise and gentle Government, of our Gracious Lady Queen ANNE, whose Reign, all true English Men, ought to wish may be as Long and Prosperous, as that of the famous Queen Elizabeth."

Through the eyes and ears of Abel Boyer, we seem to be present in the Painted Chamber at Westminster Palace when Anne drove there to speak to Parliament on the Wednesday following William's death. Prince George and Sarah Churchill walked at her side as she entered the House of Lords. John Churchill walked before her, carrying high in both hands the Great Sword of State. Sarah, newly named as Groom of the Stole, Mistress of the Robes, and Comptroller of the Privy Purse, had chosen Anne's robes of purple velvet, ermine, and gold. Queen Elizabeth herself had once worn similar robes, and Sarah knew that Parliament would be pleased with this subtle suggestion that Anne wished to be another Elizabeth, to serve her people in the same way, so that England might be great, as it had been in the glorious days of "good Queen Bess." The Mistress of the Robes spared no pains to make the new Queen look the part she wished to play.

Already a new and glorious day seemed to have dawned. Bright sunshine streamed down from the high windows as the

Queen walked the length of the great chamber and took her seat on the throne. For many in Parliament that day, it was the first time they had heard her voice. Over the past thirteen years, William's cold, dry tones had become more and more distasteful, symbolic of the relations between him and his subjects. As Anne began to speak, a new feeling spread through the hall. This was the official speech prepared for her by the proper authorities, but she read it in the voice that had moved so many listeners. Remembering the day long afterward, the Speaker of the House of Commons wrote, "I never saw an audience more affected: it was a sort of charm." And when the official speech had ended, Anne added a few words of her own: "As I know my heart to be entirely English, I can very sincerely assure you that there is not one thing you can expect or desire of me which I shall not be ready to do for the happiness and prosperity of England." Even the substance of the official speech was satisfactory. It stressed the importance of preparations for opposing the power of France. It took note of the Queen's hope for "Attaining an Union between England and Scotland." It promised that the Queen would take no action without asking the advice of her Council and both Houses of Parliament. It assured the country that their established religion and their laws and liberties would be preserved.

For those in the know, the whole month was filled with excitement. John Churchill was elected at last into the Most Noble Order of the Garter, an honor which William had refused to give him. The following day he was appointed "Captain General of all her Majesties Forces in England, or which were to be employ'd abroad in Conjunction with the Troops of her Allies." This reassured Holland, which had feared that the new Queen might not honor William's commitments. Churchill was dispatched to Holland to plan war tactics, while in England the

Secretary of the French Embassy branded England and Holland aggressors. England's response was an indignant denial in Parliament. It was clear that both sides intended to fight.

With preparations for war in the able hands of Marlborough, Anne turned her own attention to religious matters. Before the end of March she made proclamations giving her strong approval of the recently founded Society for the Propagation of the Gospel in Foreign Parts. She was thinking particularly of the American colonies. There were other proclamations "for the Incouragement of Piety and Virtue, and for the Preventing and Punishing of Vice, Prophaneness, and Immorality" as well as "for Restraining the spreading of false News, and Printing and Publishing of Irreligious and Seditious Papers and Libels." This last was prompted by vicious stories that sprang up concerning the Queen herself. According to one report, papers had been found in King William's strongbox "whereby it appeared that he had form'd the Design of Advancing The Elector of Hanover to the Crown, to the Exclusion of Queen Anne." The Elector of Hanover was none other than that George who had come to England twenty-one years before to seek the hand of the Princess Anne in marriage and returned to Germany without asking for it. The rumor about the papers in the strongbox proved to be false, but Anne was angry.

It was unpleasant enough to know that the House of Commons had passed an Act of Settlement the year before, naming the Dowager Electress Sophia of Hanover as Anne's successor. By the same Act, the powers of the Crown were to be limited. How greatly the power of Commons had grown in a few short years! Where other Stuarts had ruled much as they wished, and by Divine Right, the last of the Stuarts found her rights spelled out by her own subjects, who even presumed to anticipate her death and arrange for her successor. All of this was unpalatable enough without George, Elector of Hanover, being discussed in the streets as a possible sovereign in place of herself. She wished never to hear of him again.

The spring days grew longer and the weather warmer. At night, children danced and sang in the streets, too excited to sleep, as April 23 drew near—St. George's Day, the day Anne had chosen for her coronation. In choosing this day she did honor to the patron saint of England and also to her own dear George.

Preparations for the coronation filled every moment at St. James's Palace. A dozen seamstresses under Sarah's direction were finishing a gown of brocaded cloth of gold, to be topped with robes of crimson velvet.

"I hope that it will make the people think of the psalm," said Anne. " 'The king's daughter is all glorious within: her clothing is of wrought gold.' " Suddenly, tears filled her eyes as she remembered another verse of that psalm—"Instead of thy fathers shall be thy children, whom thou mayest make princes in all the earth." She did not speak this thought, but continued aloud with the last verse: " 'I will make thy name to be remembered in all generations: therefore shall the people praise thee for ever and ever.' "

Sarah stood waiting with tilted head until the Queen had finished speaking. Then she said, "Your Majesty must wear all of your jewels, as well as the Collar of the Order of the Garter. Tomorrow we must arrange your hair as it will be on the day. They will bring the circlet in the morning and we should try the effect." At the high point of the coronation ceremony, the crown would be set upon the circlet of gold and diamonds.

In the Tower, jewelers were polishing the regalia. In great houses all over the land, peers and peeresses were examining their coronets for loose diamonds and their velvet and ermine robes for moth holes. The choir of Westminster School was practicing a coronation hymn. The Archbishop of Canterbury reviewed every detail of the coronation service with the Dean of Westminster Abbey and lesser clergy. All England rejoiced. Political factions relaxed, at least for the moment. Here was a Queen under whom the Tories could serve, since her loyalty, like theirs, was to Crown and Church. The Whigs too were pleased. The Queen's dearest friend, Sarah Churchill, was a Whig who respected the power of Parliament and believed in prosecuting the war against France. Above all, Anne was faithful to her family, and would not tolerate a profligate Court. This pleased Englishmen of both parties and of every faith.

The great day dawned, bright and clear. The whole world seemed bent on reaching Westminster to see "good Queen Anne go to her crowning." Only the great would be inside the Abbey to witness the coronation and follow her to Westminster Hall afterward for the coronation banquet, but all could try to squeeze close to the roadway or even find a front place near the path of the Queen as she walked in procession from Westminster Palace to the Abbey.

People in the streets had no knowledge of the consternation in the Queen's chamber on the morning of April 23. The Queen had awakened with an agonizing attack of gout. When she got out of bed, she could not bear to stand. Her feet were frightfully swollen. One by one, her clothes were handed to her by sympathetic ladies-in-waiting, but the shoes seemed impossible.

"What shall I do?" she cried. "I cannot walk in the procession."

"You must do it," said Sarah. "You know that you must do it."

"I cannot."

"Then you must have a chair," Sarah decided; and she ordered one, her annoyance barely concealed. She was never ill herself and had no patience with people who were. The chair was brought, balanced on two poles. Anne seated herself in the chair with her crimson robe flowing behind. At the last moment, Abigail Hill knelt before the Queen; gently prodding and pushing, she managed to get the swollen feet into the shoes. The Queen was carried to her coach, moved painfully into it, and rode to Westminster Palace through cheering crowds who had been waiting since dawn to see the royal procession. They had no notion that the Queen was in torment as she smiled and waved from her coach. It was a lesson she had learned well, from early youth, to cover pain with a smile.

In the ancient palace were gathered a throng of England's high and mighty lords and their ladies, already being put in proper order by the heralds when the Queen arrived. There was some dismay at the news that the Queen could not walk and must be carried to the Abbey, but even the greatest lords were more concerned with their own appearance and responsibilities than with those of the Queen. Each article of the Regalia must be presented to her, then delivered to the lords who would carry them to the Abbey. Heralds ran to and fro, wild-eyed, consulting long lists of names. Barons, viscounts, earls, countesses, dukes, and duchesses milled about anxiously. It seemed a miracle when at last the procession emerged from the dusk of the hall into the sunshine outside. At first sight of the drums and trumpets, a shout went up from the crowds in the streets as the long line of dignitaries, with looks both solemn and joyful, began to move along the great blue carpet that stretched from Westminster Palace to the Abbey.

Here came the choir boys, Children of Westminster School and of the Queen's Chapel, who would sing their hymn prepared for the occasion. They were half-sick with the long wait and with fright. Proud parents waved and smiled, but no boy turned his head; it would be a misdemeanor to do so. Now the peers swept past, two abreast, bareheaded, with their coronets in their hands. Now the Archbishop of Canterbury, followed by Prince George, his train borne up by gentlemen of his suite.

A long moment of anticipation—the lords who bore the Regalia were coming: the Earl of Dorset with St. Edward's Staff; the Lord Viscount Longueville with the Spurs; the Earl of Huntington carrying the Scepter with the Cross; and now three earls carrying three swords—the jeweled Sword of State, the Sword of Spiritual Justice, and the Sword of Temporal Justice. Ah! A great shout went up for the Lord Mayor of London. Now the Great Sword of State, most significant of all the swords, borne by the Earl of Oxford, whose hands must not tremble and whose arms must not fail under its great weight. Another shout. Three dukes had stepped into view, bearing the Scepter with the Dove, the Orb, and between them, on a cushion of gold cloth, the Crown itself, its jewels flashing. Now the people were bowing as three bishops came from the palace with the Bible, the Paten, and the Chalice for the service of Holy Communion, which would end the coronation ceremony.

A pause, while hearts beat high. "There she is!" It was she at last. "Long live Queen Anne! Long live the Queen! . . . But they are carrying her. Can she not walk? Is she ill? No, she is smiling. See, there is the Queen! Can you see her now, my child? Come, I'll lift you up so that you can see her. You will never forget this day. Long live the Queen!"

Those who did not see her might read about the entire ceremony in the *London Gazette* which carried the news of April 23–27. The great Queen Elizabeth had not looked more splendid than did Queen Anne, under a canopy carried by twelve lords, "in her Royal Robes of Crimson Velvet, wearing the Collar of the Order of the Garter . . . and on Her Head a rich Circlet of Gold and Diamonds . . . Thus the whole Proceeding marched on foot upon Blue Cloth to Westminster Abbey (only the Queen had the Conveniency to be carried in a low open Chair all the way) and the Houses on each side being crowded with vast numbers of Spectators, expressing their great Joy and Satisfaction by loud and repeated Acclamation."

So it was that Queen Anne came to the Abbey for her crowning. The great doors were opened to receive her, and she heard the boy choirs singing like angels, "I was glad when they said unto me, let us go into the house of the Lord." She knew now that she could finish the day and do all that she must do—kneel in prayer, stand, even walk. Dazed with emotion, she no longer felt any pain.

When the lords had taken their places, the Archbishop of Canterbury turned to the north, then south, east, and west to call in a loud voice, "Sirs, I here present unto you, Anne, your undoubted sovereign: Wherefore all you who are come this day to do your homage and service, are you willing to do the same?" Four times the walls echoed with the answering shout, "God save the Queen!"

She took the oath, promising, with her hand on the open Bible, to cause law and justice in mercy to be executed in all her judgments and to protect the Church and its clergy.

Now came the anointing. This was the most sacred moment of the coronation ceremony. Of all the objects used in the crowning of the sovereign, only the Ampulla, the vessel used to hold the oil, remained from ancient days. The rest had been melted down and sold by Cromwell, who somehow neglected to destroy the Ampulla when he vowed to destroy every vestige of monarchy in England. With the Restoration, new Regalia had been made and purchased at a great price, but none of these could compare with the Ampulla and its holy oil. Some said that

Thomas à Becket had received the vessel and the oil from the Virgin Mary herself, who came to him in a vision. All agreed that the anointing of the sovereign was the source of the long-held faith in "touching for the King's evil." In the old days, newly crowned kings had found crowds of the sick waiting for them at the doors of the Abbey to be touched before the holy oil was dry.

Kneeling at the altar, feeling the sweet drops of oil upon her head and hands, Anne knew herself to be a consecrated person. She felt sure of what she must do. She would "touch for the evil." As long as she lived, no sick person should be turned away from her door with only a piece of money. Each one should have the ancient blessing too, as it had been given by other Stuarts before her.

The long ceremony went on. For Anne it was a kaleidoscope of colors and shapes, flashing, moving, often only dimly seen, except when, one by one, the revered objects of the Regalia were placed in her hands. And at last she was seated in the Coronation Chair with the Stone of Scone beneath it. Edward I had brought the stone from Scotland four hundred years before, and English kings had been crowned on it ever since to show that they were kings of Scotland as well. Still there was no real union with Scotland. As the Archbishop raised the crown above her head, it came to Anne, like a revelation, that the Scottish people were truly her people. If union with Scotland could come in her reign, she would wear her crown with joy. She felt its weight upon her head. The cry of "God save the Queen!" surged in a great wave of sound from every side and echoed from the rafters high above. The silver notes of trumpets pierced the din, and gold glinted above crimson as the nobles placed their coronets on their own heads. Outside, a signal was given, and guns thundered from the Tower of London.

It was four o'clock, and still the ceremony went on. Prince George, the archbishops, the bishops, and all of the temporal lords must come to kneel before the Queen, place their hands between hers, kiss her cheek, and touch the Crown. Finally, Anne received Holy Communion and was vested in robes of purple velvet for the return to the Hall of Westminster Palace and the coronation banquet.

The old palace had been the scene of six hundred years of English history. Kings and queens no longer lived here, but they returned to feast in the great hall after being crowned. On each side, for two hundred feet of its length, tables were spread with a banquet for the noblest of the realm. At the far end of the hall under a canopy sat the Queen with His Royal Highness Prince George at her left. Galleries on both sides were packed with minor nobility. The sunlight still shone through the high windows, and over all, from the beams beneath the roof, carved golden angels spread their wings and gazed down in wonder.

All, perhaps even the angels, were waiting for the most dramatic moment of the traditional feast. This was the entrance of the Queen's Champion. The first such Champion had appeared on Christmas night, 1066, after the crowning of William the Conqueror. The festivities of his coronation feast had not disguised the fact that the mutinous Saxons hated their new Norman king. All at once, above the sound of the music, they had heard a pounding at the great door. In charged a knight on horseback, clad in full armor. He threw his gauntlet to the stone floor and cried, "Oyez! Oyez! If there be any person, of whatever estate or degree he be, that will say or prove that William, Duke of Normandy, is not the rightful King of England, then here am I to say that he lies and to challenge him to combat on behalf of my Lord and Sovereign!" It was Robert de Marmion, whose descendants still held the lands with which the grateful William had rewarded him. After the crowning of a sovereign, one of those descendants (now with the name of Dymoke) still knocked at the door of the banqueting hall to throw down the gauntlet and issue the traditional challenge.

Said the *London Gazette*, "Just before the Second Course, Charles Dymoke Esq; Her Majesties Champion, in Compleat Armour, between the Lord High Constable and Earl Marshal, performed the Challenge." The guests at Queen Anne's coronation banquet were almost the last to hear the thrilling knock at the door and to witness the entrance of a Champion with shining armor and white horse. The time came when the nation looked at the bill for the coronation banquet of George IV and thought it too high. By the twentieth century there would still be a Dymoke as Queen's Champion, but he would merely carry a banner in the coronation procession. English hearts would not thrill as they once had at the clatter of a steel gauntlet flung on a stone floor to the sound of deafening cheers, the drinking of toasts, and much breakage of glass.*

It was after eight o'clock when the Queen returned to St. James's Palace with Prince George. She could hardly believe that the day begun in agony had ended in such a blaze of glory. Still, she was exhausted, aching for rest. George was beaming, ready, so it seemed, to go on forever. She asked him to come to bed.

"I will only come if the Queen commands me," he said with his broad smile.

"George, I command you to come to bed," said Anne, and once more gave herself up thankfully to the kind ministrations of Abigail Hill, who knelt to remove the Queen's tight shoes.

---

* See page 265 for an eighteenth-century English menu.

Chapter XIV

Blenheim

"Great praise the Duke of Marlborough won,
And our good Prince Eugene."
"Why, 'twas a very wicked thing!"
Said little Wilhelmine.
"Nay, nay, my little girl," quoth he,
"It was a famous victory!"
Robert Southey *from* "After Blenheim"

WITHIN A FORTNIGHT after the coronation, war was declared on France. There was some debate, says Boyer, on how deeply England should commit herself, but Marlborough carried the day, contending that "France could never be reduc'd within due Bounds, unless the English enter'd as Principals in this quarrel. . . . Her Majesty gave Directions for drawing up a Declaration of War against France and Spain."

The motion for war was carried. The charges formally brought against Louis XIV were: that he had exercised "an Absolute Authority over the Spanish monarchy; that he had seized Spanish dominions, Milan and the Spanish Low Countries [Belgium], Cadiz, entrance to the Mediterranean, ports in the Spanish West Indies; and had recognized the Pretender as King of England." The conflict is known in history as the War of the Spanish Succession.

On the heels of this Declaration of War, Anne proposed the

Union of Scotland and England "for the Security and Happiness of both." Many Scots had fond memories of her visits to Holyrood in her youth. When the document with the Queen's letter was read in the Scottish Parliament, they responded well to a heart-warming phrase in favor of "a Princess who has been amongst us, and has a particular regard for us." There were repeated assurances in the proposal that the Presbyterian government of the Church would be maintained in Scotland when the Union became effective. A gracious reply was returned from the Scottish Parliament. Thus events were set in motion for one of the most important achievements of Anne's reign.

Some Scots from the Lowlands predicted that under "one Queen, one Parliament, one Flag," Scotland would enjoy improved roads and favorable trade agreements, without which she could never escape from grinding poverty. Others could see only the objections and none of the advantages of union. They would rather be dead than live under the Union. What of Wallace and Bruce? Would their glorious memory grow dim in a new day of commerce and industry? Was the ancient feud with England about to end, now and forever? Those debating the Act of Union could not know that there would be one more bloody fight with "the damn'd English." Another Charles Stuart was to come a generation later and ask the help of the clans in upholding the claim of his father, the Old Pretender, to the throne and crown of England. For almost a year, in 1745, "Bonnie Prince Charlie," the Young Pretender, would be able to revive the clan spirit. Fiery crosses would burn on the hills, and Wallace and Bruce would seem to live again.

Meanwhile, in 1702 the Scottish and English Parliaments began to build the instrument, the Act of Union, that would make the two countries one in fact as well as in form. An event of such magnitude could not take place at once, but as debate went on and on, the wheels began to turn in that direction.

It was at this stressful time that the past returned to help the Queen. Her grandfather Edward Hyde, the Duke of Clarendon, had died in exile when Anne was still a girl. His last years had been devoted to the writing of a book which he called "The History of the Rebellion and Civil Wars in England." In this first year of Anne's reign a volume of Clarendon's great work had been published at Oxford. From the librarian at St. James's Palace came a note inquiring whether her Majesty would care to see a copy. Anne's answer was prompt, and her grandfather's book was soon in her hands. He had thought of history as the result of a struggle between individuals for power or for principles, as well he might—this poor old gentleman who had walked out of the King's garden with the laughter of Barbara Villiers in his ears. The "History" was a Stuart portrait gallery, extraordinarily vivid. Looking eagerly through its pages, Anne remembered face after face from her young days, and she determined to right the wrongs of those bad old times. Once again she resolved that there should be no more corruption, no more peddling of influence. She would not surround herself with vicious and profligate courtiers. She would not be found with a butterfly net in her hand while her navy went up in flames.

Pressing forward to set the affairs of the kingdom in order, Anne began to think of financial burdens which the war was sure to bring. Parliament had voted her the same income as that granted to the late King William. She could now play at basset as much as she liked and pay for her losses without a care. But how could she ask her people to pay taxes if she too did not sacrifice for England? She thanked the House of Commons for their generosity and then astounded Parliament by adding, "I will take great care it shall be managed to the best advantage; and, while my subjects remain under the burden of such great taxes, I will straiten myself in my own expenses. . . . I will give directions that £100,000 be applied to the public service, in this year, out of the revenue you have so unanimously given me."

Sarah promised to manage the robes with utmost care. And she said that much more could be saved by putting an end to bribes that were offered to palace officials by tradesmen who came to sell goods of every sort. Anne agreed and added that she wished advancement at her Court to be through merit and not through the peddling of influence.

At the end of June, George and Anne were not at all well. The Prince's asthma had become chronic, and Anne herself was exhausted by the heavy responsibilities of the first months of her reign. Summer at Windsor brought no improvement for George, and for Anne it meant daily trips to Hampton Court, where the Privy Council was meeting. One hot day, after a long and tiring Council meeting, the smell of box in the gardens seemed overpowering. Soon afterward, Henry Wise, the landscape gardener, received an order from the Queen to dig up all of the box hedges at Hampton Court and replace them with some other plant. Box reminded her too much of the unhappy summer at Hampton Court during the first year of the reign of William and Mary. Her sister had said, "A crown is not so heavy as it seems to be," but Anne was finding it very heavy at times. She was wounded too by vicious rumors that floated about and came to her ears.

"Every coffeehouse and drawingroom is full of tittle-tattle," Sarah told her. "And a scandalous book about me is the talk of the town."

Anne's face flushed indignantly. "In that case, dear Mrs. Freeman, I shall take action. I will not allow you to suffer again for my sake. That book must be burned by the common hangman."

At the end of August she decided to get away for a little rest.

Ten years before, Bath had been delightful. They would try it again. But this year's visit was very different from the one Anne remembered so pleasantly. On that earlier visit, the Mayor of Bath had been forbidden by Queen Mary to attend Anne and George with any respect or ceremony. As a result, they had had a perfect rest. Now, on every mile of the journey they were attended with respect and ceremony, and there was no rest. Even before they reached Oxford, University officials in academic robes came on horseback to meet them. There were speeches in English and speeches in Latin; degrees were conferred; poems were recited. It was the same all along the way. At Bath the welcome was overwhelming in order to make amends for the neglect of 1692. A contemporary reporter wrote, "One hundred young men of the city, uniformly clad and armed [like Grenadier Guards], and two hundred young virgins dressed as Amazons and equipped with bows and arrows" met the royal coach and marched with it through the city gates, followed by pipers, dancing nymphs, satyrs, shepherds, and other classic figures that were sure to appear in any fashionable parade or pageant.

Anne looked from the window of her coach, smiling and waving, but said to Sarah, "Do they imagine that I was vexed when we came here before? If so, they are much mistaken. There was a privacy then that is missing now. I suppose I shall never again have privacy. I must learn to do without it."

The house of a prosperous doctor had been fitted out for Anne and George, and with their arrival, the reputation of Bath was made. They put the stamp of royal approval on a town already famous for its doctors.

There were glowing reports of the benefits which Prince George was receiving from daily bathing in the King's Bath, and from treatments by "dry pump." Visitors would have paid a high price to see the Prince emerge from his dressing room, clad in a canvas bathing robe, and descend majestically into the water. Afterward, sitting beneath the pump in a private room, he exposed his fat chest to the comforting jets of steaming hot water under the ministrations of a solicitous attendant. From fifty to two hundred strokes of the pump were prescribed. The Prince always seemed to breathe more easily after the treatments. It was felt that Bath needed only a little social polish to make it quite perfect. Beau Nash, the dandy, would soon see the opportunity and supply the polish.

Anne's visit made Bath fashionable, but gave her little relaxation. Ministers came with important papers to be signed. Messengers arrived with news of army engagements in Flanders and the naval campaign off the coast of Spain, where a fleet of Spanish treasure ships had been burned to the water's edge. There were reports of successful engagements by the English navy against the French all up and down the American coast from Newfoundland to the West Indies. The East India fleet had reached English shores with nine ships, "richly laden." The Virginia fleet of more than a hundred vessels had come into port loaded with cotton, indigo, and tobacco from the Southern colonies. Thirty vessels of the Russian fleet brought important naval stores. At home, the best harvest of many years was being gathered. All of this was good news indeed. On the Continent, Marlborough had captured several fortresses and relieved Dutch fears of being invaded by the French armies. But in Spain, the allied troops of English and Dutch soldiers had conducted themselves disgracefully, looting and plundering two towns, where they desecrated churches and attacked helpless nuns in their convents. If there had been any chance that Spain might desert Louis and join England in her war against France, that hope was now destroyed. Still, much had been gained during the summer. Wherever they drove through the countryside, cheering crowds greeted the Queen and the Prince.

"They say it is a pleasant drive to Lyncombe," Sarah suggested one day. "There is a kind of inn, I believe, most attractive. They call it 'King James's Palace.' His late Majesty, your father, took refuge there after his abdication, or so the story goes. Would you care to see it?"

"Thank you, no," said Anne. "Please tell the coachman to turn back to Bath. I have had enough for today." Sometimes dear Mrs. Freeman seemed almost lacking in tact, if such a thing were possible. But of course she could not know the painful train of thought that was always set up by any mention of Anne's father. It was but one step from James to the old sad recognition that she had not loved him as he had loved her. One more step and she was deep in shame for having deserted him and his cause. The last step, and the worst, deluged her with the overwhelming problem of what she should think and feel and do with regard to James's son, the Pretender at St. Germain. With every year that passed, she became more and more sure that he was indeed her half-brother, and a Stuart. What if he could be persuaded to renounce his Catholic faith? Would he not then be a far more acceptable king than George of Hanover? This thought brought her up hard against the contemplation of her own death.

"When we reach Bath I think I should like a bowl of posset," she told Sarah, "and perhaps a slice of cake."*

"It is fattening," Sarah answered. "All that sugar."

"I want something sweet," said the Queen.

"You will be having some fittings when we return to London," Sarah reminded her. There would be a public day of solemn thanksgiving for the military successes and other blessings, and

* See page 266.

the Queen's robes were Sarah's responsibility. "If the waist must be let out again, the lines of the robe are spoiled," she said.

"I have ordered three bolts of lace," said Anne. "I have forgotten to tell you until now. I thought that I should like to have a headdress like the ones my sister used to wear. She was very fond of lace, you know. She was large too, and the lace was . . . helpful. I might have a scarf about my shoulders, and perhaps a ruche, tucked in at the neck and sleeves. I like to help our lace-makers."

Sarah made a face. "Please do not order things. Let me do it. Unless you inquire most carefully, you may not be buying English lace at all, but something smuggled in. How much did you pay for it?"

"Almost £250, I believe," said Anne, feeling guilty.

"Smuggled," Sarah told her in a positive tone. "Besides, lace only ends by looking dowdy, and concealing nothing. I want your robes to be very simple." Then she added, "I cannot imagine your wanting to wear anything like your sister's robes. Have you quite forgotten her treatment of you? Pretending to be devout, yet behaving as if you were her slave? I could not forgive it."

"She has been dead for a long time now, dear Mrs. Freeman," Anne said gently, "and I am Queen. I can forgive her. She was always fond of my boy, you know."

Sarah only answered, "Instead of lace, you should have diamonds. They are not even an expense. They are an investment."

"I am not fond of jewels," Anne said doubtfully, but Mrs. Freeman was so often right that she let herself be persuaded. Besides, Anne wanted more than ever to be on terms of perfect harmony with her closest friend. Sarah must not know how much Anne minded the appointment of John Churchill to the position of commander-in-chief for the allied forces of England and Holland. It was the position that Anne had wanted for George. True, he was nominally the head of the English forces and was Lord High Admiral as well. But Churchill had been appointed supreme commander. In the eyes of most authorities at home and abroad, he was the man best fitted to meet the demands of diplomacy, organization, and military acumen. The slight to George rankled in Anne's mind, and for that very reason she determined to move ahead quickly with the long-planned gifts and honors for John and Sarah. They would find her unchanging in her friendship. She was considering a motto, *Semper eadem*—"Always the same." It had been Elizabeth's motto, and it might suggest to Parliament and the people the position she wished to take, standing firm in the midst of political intrigue, "always the same" in good fortune or bad.

On their return to Windsor in October, Sarah moved into the Royal Lodge in the Great Park, a gift from Anne to "dear Mrs. Freeman for all her days." With the palatial house went a yearly income for the Rangership of Windsor Park, bringing Sarah's total income from her various Court duties to about £7,500 a year. John's income was enormous. Besides his military and Court appointments in England, there were other sources too numerous and too devious to be told. One source which traditionally went to the commander-in-chief was a commission on all bread bought for the army. He had an arrangement with a Jewish army contractor, Solomon de Medina, whereby the commission received by Marlborough was used for intelligence service. Solomon de Medina was reliable, diligent, patriotic, and in possession of capital. He accompanied Marlborough on his campaigns, advanced him funds from time to time, and supplied provisions for the troops. He was an invaluable aide to a commander like Marlborough, who took endless pains over every detail of his men's care and equipment. The government intelligence system was slow and bungling compared with that set up by Solomon de Medina, whose services were soon rewarded by a knighthood, the first ever conferred on a practicing Jew in England. In the course of these vast operations, a good deal of money was changing hands, and some of it seemed to stick to Marlborough's fingers. At the moment, there was no open objection. He was the necessary man, the man of the hour.

Criticism buzzes around success as flies buzz around honey. So it would happen for Churchill. He was no plaster saint. Even in his youthful poverty he had known how to turn the weaknesses of royalty to his own advantage. He saw rich men get ahead, and determined to get ahead by becoming rich himself. He would work with anyone, or against anyone, if it suited his purposes. In this policy he had plenty of company. "Caress the favorites, avoid the unfortunate, and trust nobody," was a saying at Court. Yet John did not always avoid the unfortunate. He had been faithful to Anne in her misfortunes, and he was compassionate toward his fellow man when he met him face to face. The plight of old soldiers and old servants moved him; he helped them when he could. Unlike the practical Sarah, he did not investigate hard luck tales or take time to expose a beggar as a "sturdy rogue."

His most distinguished descendant, Sir Winston Churchill, quotes from the *Memoires* of Sicco van Goslinga for the personal impression which John Churchill made on his contemporaries: "He is about the middle height, and the best figure in the world, his features without fault, fine sparkling eyes, good teeth, and his complexion such a mixture of white and red that the fairer sex might envy. . . . He expresses himself well, even his very bad French is agreeable. As a speaker in his own language he is reckoned among the best. His address is most courteous, his perfect manners and his gentleness win over even those who start with a prejudice or grudge against him."

On this man the Queen now proposed to confer a dukedom. Sarah was at Windsor, where she had been spending more and more time of late. On October 22, Anne wrote to her from St. James's Palace, making the offer in terms dictated by her own perfect manners and gentleness: "Though I think it a long time since I saw you, I do not desire you to come one minute sooner to town than it is easy to you, but will wait with patience for the happy hour. . . . It is very uneasy to your poor unfortunate faithful Morley [so she had called herself since the death of her son] to think she has so very little in her power to show how truly sensible I am of all my Lord Marlborough's kindness, especially at a time when he deserves all that a rich Crown could give. But since there is nothing else at this time, I hope you will give me leave, as soon as he comes, to make him a Duke."

John would soon be home from the Continent. Winter was the time for planning campaigns, not for fighting them. Even a hundred years later, Napoleon still found General Mud and General Winter his bitterest enemies. Bad roads and poor forage were insuperable difficulties. Leaving his troops to live off the land in winter quarters, Churchill returned to England at the end of November, well pleased with the honor that the Queen had prepared for him. It was Sarah who foresaw that there would be increased expense in maintaining themselves as Duke and Duchess of Marlborough. It was she who stated the problem to the Queen. Anne responded by giving John another £5,000 a year for life, and would have settled the amount on his heirs forever if Parliament had not objected. There was a general feeling, as Tobias Smollett tells us, that Churchill had already been well paid "by the profitable employments which he and his duchess enjoyed."

With Parliament in a mood for economy in order to finance the war, Sidney Godolphin, as Lord Treasurer, advised the Queen to be content with the lifetime grant for the new Duke of Marlborough. Reluctantly, she agreed, but asked Godolphin to help with another project dear to her heart: "to find out means for Lowering the Price of Coals . . . for the Relief of the Poor." When she drove through the City on the Lord Mayor's Day at the end of October, groups of children from the work houses were given the great treat of seeing the Queen from the vantage point of wooden platforms raised above the level of the street, "from whence one of 'em made a Speech to her Majesty," says Boyer. When he had finished his speech, the child made a low bow and handed to the Queen the paper on which it was written. He had nothing else to give. His voice, clear, sweet, and sad, touched the Queen as no other honors of that day had done. She told Godolphin that he must find money for more free schools. She would contribute to the cause from her own purse.

Over the years, Godolphin, in spite of his severe expression and "quick, piercing eye," had become Anne's close friend. He was often one of the Queen's party when she went to Newmarket for the races. Before each of her visits to the House of Lords, he explained in detail the important issues which would be discussed. In token of their intimate and fond relations she called him "Mr. Montgomery," making him part of the inmost circle that included "Mr. and Mrs. Freeman, Mr. Morley" and "poor unfortunate faithful Mrs. Morley." Sarah had already negotiated a marriage between young Francis Godolphin and the Churchills' eldest daughter, Henrietta. Sarah was never happier than when she was matchmaking, and this particular marriage, uniting the Churchills with another powerful family, gave her great satisfaction.

"Unfortunately," she confided to John soon after his return,

"Mrs. Morley does not always take my advice, and I cannot endure to have her do anything that I would not do in her place. She is unreasonably opposed to the Whigs, and nothing that I say seems to make the slightest impression. I never thought that she could be so stubborn. Since you have been gone, the whole complexion of Parliament has changed from Whig to Tory under her influence."

John understood Sarah's impulse to direct and rule everyone around her; he had the same impulse. Coupled with it was the conviction, common in men of genius, that what he wanted was bound to succeed and that what benefited him would inevitably benefit everyone who favored his interests. In his own eyes, what he did he did for England.

His politics were moderate, so he was able to answer his wife in a reasonable tone. "The Queen thinks of the Tories as the Church Party, and devotion to the Church goes very deep with her, as you know. In her mind, the Whigs give encouragement to atheists and Dissenters and Non-conformists of all sorts. Bishop Compton fixed her views from early childhood. And you must remember that Whigs were in power during all the ill-usage that she and the Prince suffered under her sister and King William."

When she would have answered, he stopped her, first with a hand on her lips, then with a kiss. He had had enough of politics for the moment.

"Your hair is so bright," he said, touching her curls. "When I am away, I wonder if you are growing old, and when I come back, I find you are as young as ever."

She laughed. "I lead an easy life. Only it is very hard to get away from the Queen, even for a day. She depends on me so." The next day, they escaped together to Holywell House,

Sarah's old home in the country near St. Albans. It was their last happy visit there.

Early in November the Queen proclaimed the promised day of thanksgiving for the successful progress of the war. St. Paul's Cathedral was still unfinished, but it was the scene of a magnificent assemblage: the House of Commons, the House of Peers in their robes, the Knights of the Garter with their Collars of the Order. The Duke of Ormond received special honors for his naval triumphs. Anne, "habited in Purple," as Boyer described her, came "in her Body Coach, drawn by eight Horses," with the Countesses of Marlborough and Sunderland.

Riding by the side of the Queen in the coach to St. Paul's, Sarah was triumphant but not entirely at ease. There was an epidemic of smallpox at Cambridge, where the Churchills' only son, John, was a student. He was seventeen, amiable, bright, high-spirited, and popular. He was now Marquis of Blandford, the darling of his father and mother, whose hopes and plans centered on his inheriting the Marlborough lands and titles. Young John had talked of following his father in the campaigns, but Sarah would not have it. John must go to college. In the autumn of 1702, when smallpox broke out, Sidney Godolphin invited the boy to visit him at Newmarket until the epidemic was over, as a measure of protection. The invitation was accepted, but after Christmas, John returned to Cambridge. In January, his mother and father had word that he was sick. Sarah went at once to nurse her son. Anne sent her own physicians by royal coach. Everything was done that could be done. The Duke was urgently needed abroad to take command in the field, but he delayed his departure as the tone of the news from his son's bedside became more and more anxious, then despairing. Late in February young Blandford died. It was a heavy blow to his father, but the responsibilities for conduct of the war had to be shouldered in spite of personal grief. In March the Duke sailed for Holland, leaving Sarah at St. Albans.

Anne wanted to come to her friend. She had lost her own son and never felt closer to Sarah than now, but Sarah refused to see anyone, least of all, the Queen. "It would have been a great satisfaction to your poor unfortunate faithful Morley if you would have given me leave to come to St. Albans," wrote Anne, "for the unfortunate ought to come to the unfortunate. But since you will not have me . . . God Almighty bless and comfort my dear Mrs. Freeman." The last thing in the world that Sarah wanted was to have Anne sit beside her talking about the comfort of religion.

Her son's death was a disaster from which Sarah never really recovered. Up to this time her life had been fed by two arteries: her will to dominate, and her human, feminine impulse to love. With the death of her son, her maternal impulse dwindled; before the end of her own life she was to quarrel with every one of her four daughters. Her love now flowed intensely along one narrow channel toward her husband, while her will to dominate coursed through her even more strongly. At times she behaved like a woman possessed of a devil.

As if to strike a balance and to compensate for the military and domestic successes of 1702, everything went wrong in the following year. Even Nature seemed to think she had smiled for too long. There were terrible storms, in one of which the Eddystone lighthouse was completely destroyed. The loss of any lighthouse is serious enough, but the destruction of the Eddystone light was a disaster of depressing significance. It had been a fantastic structure, like a Chinese pagoda, fitted out by the inventor, Henry Winstanley, with winches and pulleys, balconies and porches. In the ebullient spirit of the new century, he had amazed all London with his curious contrivances as if to say, "This is the eighteenth century. With imagination and science we can do anything we will to do. Man is now master of his fate." Winstanley happened to be in his lighthouse and was killed when it was blown down in the great storm. Fate, it seemed, was still the master of man.

Military news was depressing too. Neither Marlborough in Flanders, nor his ally, Prince Eugene, the great Austrian general fighting in Italy, achieved any real success. Marlborough was hampered in every plan by the Dutch, who insisted on being consulted about every move and were unwilling to commit their forces to an offensive battle away from their own frontiers. Meanwhile, Louis's armies advanced all the way to the Rhine and were threatening Vienna, capital of Austria.

In England there was bitter complaint and criticism of Marlborough from optimistic souls who had expected the war to end with the successes of the previous year. But Anne wrote to Sarah, "I will never forsake your dear self, Mr. Freeman, nor Mr. Montgomery, but always be your constant faithful servant; and we four must never part till death mows us down with his impartial hand."

Marlborough was heartened by the Queen's backing, and he saw that he could not afford to be pinned down, fighting small actions in defense of Dutch fortresses. He must strike a decisive blow near Vienna to cripple Louis and save England's Austrian allies.

Concealing his exact plans from almost everyone, he persuaded the Dutch to let him lead the combined forces as far as the upper Rhine to attack the French armies there. He also succeeded in getting new troops from the King of Prussia, ruler of one of the many principalities with which Churchill had to work as an ally. Any other man would have been worn out with the bickering, the delays, the complaints, and the demands of the wrangling commanders of that campaign. Churchill never lost patience. He persuaded, he cajoled, placated, deceived, and before anyone knew what was happening, he had made a long, swift march with his allied forces from the North Sea to the Danube. About halfway between Nuremberg and Munich lay the little town of Blenheim. There, in the summer of 1704, Marlborough and Prince Eugene caught up with the combined French and Bavarian armies headed by Marshal Tallard, Marshal Marsin, and the Elector of Bavaria. The French had sixty thousand men, England and her allies about fifty-six thousand.

For months these vast armies had been inactive. Professional soldiers were expensive, and few leaders were anxious to commit them to battle. At times, the military scene in this war was so static that the great Louis himself could establish headquarters in the Spanish Netherlands with a retinue that included a Court painter and a theatrical troupe. Young English gentlemen who seemed unlikely to do well at college could be provided with a commission, a scarlet laced coat, a brace of silver-mounted pistols, and sent off to the Continent to follow the Duke's campaigns for a season or two. It was not necessarily a dangerous experience and was as good as an education. Great commanders lived in fine style. They did not merely eat well; they dined on many courses and from silver plates.

The English soldiers in camp together near Blenheim on the night of August 12, 1704, had reached this place at this time for a great variety of reasons. The colonel of each regiment was responsible for filling its ranks; some used press gangs, who picked up men on the streets, in taverns, or from their very homes. Carried away, bound or even drugged, they woke up to find themselves marching off to war.

Others were persuaded more easily. In George Farquhar's comedy, "The Recruiting Officer" (1705), Sergeant Kite knew all the usual motives for leaving domestic life in favor of the military: "If any gentlemen soldiers or others have a mind to serve her Majesty, and pull down the French king: if any prentices have severe masters, any children have undutiful parents: if any servants have too little wages; or any husband too much wife; let him repair to the noble Sergeant Kite . . . and they shall receive present relief and entertainment."

If gullible recruits expected "present relief and entertainment," they would be undeceived soon after enlisting. Life in the army was brutal, and navy life was even worse, if possible— "pox above, plague between the decks, hell in the forecastle, and the devil at the helm." Yet in battle, morale was high. At dawn on August 13, the men camped near Blenheim saw their great general, the Duke of Marlborough, riding along the lines. His calm face and bearing were outward signs of the indomitable will within, and gave his men a conviction that they too were invincible. They felt that he would lead them to a victory, and they waited with supreme confidence for the order to attack.

At about seven in the morning the French saw them coming. Between the wooded hills and the Danube, nine columns of Allied soldiers were advancing. When all were in place, the battle line was five miles long. At one o'clock in the afternoon the attack began, and raged with fearful loss of life at both ends of the line. Marlborough was everywhere, inspecting each position, ordering every maneuver. Late in the afternoon he led a cavalry charge in the center, over marshy ground and through a shallow stream. The French responded with a counterattack by foot soldiers and horse, but their cavalry paused to fire while Marlborough's gained the far side of the stream and galloped with drawn swords toward the wavering French lines. As the great English historian Trevelyan tells it, "The [French] center was swept away in one triumphant roar; the deserted infantry were ridden over and cut down; the cavalry were . . . herded towards the south, and driven over the steep river-bank, where hundreds found refuge or death in the wilderness of marshy shore and reedy island, divided by the broad, deep currents of the Danube." The enemy were in utter confusion. At one village after another, French soldiers surrendered, and handed over to English victors proud banners that had never known defeat until Blenheim.

By nightfall the battlefield was carpeted with the dead of both sides. Regiments of French dragoons, who had not even had a chance to fire, laid down their arms. Marshal Tallard and other generals were captured. English soldiers led Tallard ceremoniously to Marlborough's tent, where he surrendered his sword. The Duke returned it with a bow, saying in his "bad but agreeable" French, "I am very sorry that such a cruel misfortune should have fallen upon a soldier for whom I have had the highest regard."

Tallard responded, "And I congratulate you on defeating the best soldiers in the world."

"Your Lordship, I presume, excepts those who had the honor to beat them," Marlborough said with a smile.

He put the marshal courteously into his own coach with other captured French generals and started them, under parole, on the first stage of the trip to England. Writing a hasty note, he gave it to Colonel Daniel Parke,* of a regiment from the Virginia colony, to be delivered at top speed to the Queen. Then he rode off to inspect his own wounded and the French prisoners, asking questions as he went. He had been in the saddle for seventeen hours. To one French private he said, "If the King of France had many men like you, he would soon be victorious." The

* See page 267.

gallant young Frenchman replied, "It is not men like me he lacks, but a general like you."

At Versailles, Louis and his Court had received only one small piece of bad news since the first of August; *hélas,* the English had captured the fortress at Gibraltar! What had really occupied the attention of the Court for the past several days was a spectacular gala party, from which they were still recovering, and the question of who should precede whom at Court ceremonies. After the incredible news from Blenheim, they had something else to think about. The French and Bavarians had lost more than thirty thousand men, killed and wounded, besides fifteen thousand prisoners and three thousand deserters. All Bavaria was in Allied hands. Blenheim had dealt Louis a shattering blow. Trevelyan says, "His sun had set for ever on the banks of the Danube."

Colonel Parke reached Windsor ten days after the battle. The Queen was sitting in her boudoir overlooking the East Terrace from a tall bay window. Her mood was anxious and depressed; complaints and criticisms of her Commander-in-Chief were mounting on every hand in Parliament and among the public. The Tories, whom she herself had brought to power, were bitterly opposed to a war which demanded another year of high taxes. It was all very well for the Whigs, whose commercial interests would presumably profit in the long run by a victory over France, no matter how costly. But Tories represented landed interests, which could be wiped out by ruinously high taxation. They were furious with the Duke for taking the army to the Danube without orders. They would fall on him "like hounds upon a hare" if he failed. In the face of such opposition, Anne wondered how long her own loyal support could keep Churchill in control of military affairs.

Winston Churchill has described with his customary flair

the arrival of Colonel Parke in Anne's presence at Windsor: "A scarlet horseman has crossed the river. . . . They bring the weary messenger to her presence. He falls on his knee . . . hands her Marlborough's note to Sarah, and tells her that with his own eyes he has seen the first army of France broken in flight and ruin . . ."

Anne gave the note to Sarah. John had written, "I have not time to say more, but to beg you will give my duty to the Queen, and let her know her army has had a glorious victory. Monsieur Tallard and the two other generals are in my coach and I am following the rest."

When asked to name his reward, Colonel Parke requested a miniature of the Queen. It was granted, and with it went a gift of 1,000 guineas. All over England bells rang to express the relief and joy of the people. Trevelyan says, "Never were such demonstrations of joy since the laying of London stone."

Chapter XV

St. Paul's

Marlbrouk s'en va t'en guerre,
Mi ron ton, ton, ton, mi ron taine;
Marlbrouk s'en va t'en guerre,
Ne sais quand reviendra.
            French Folk Song sung to the tune
            "For he's a jolly good fellow"

WITH THE BATTLE OF BLENHEIM, Louis had lost the war, but since he did not recognize that fact, the fighting went on. The Duke of Marlborough came home, bringing with him French banners and generals captured at Blenheim. The banners were carried in triumph through the streets of London, but the generals were driven in the Queen's own carriages to commodious country houses where they would live as honored guests of England until the end of the war, which would surely not be long in coming. As Christmas approached, waits were caroling, "God rest ye merry, gentlemen." At St. Paul's Cathedral, choir boys practiced a new hymn, "While shepherds watched their flocks by night," with words by Nahum Tate, the Poet Laureate. There was a feeling of hope in the smoggy air of London.

During Advent, the Queen attended a service at St. Paul's and looked about her with awe and admiration. Rank above rank, stone columns and arches rose up to support the vast dome of the center cupola. This church was Sir Christopher Wren's masterpiece. Already, thirty years of work had gone into the building, and it was not yet completed, although services had been held here for the past seven years. The finishing touches were still to be added, and one could only hope that Sir Christopher would live to see them. Carvings of fruit and flowers by Grinling Gibbons would decorate the choir stalls, the Bishop's throne, the organ case. Golden Gates of magnificent gilded iron grillwork by the French master, Jean Tijou, were to guard the sanctuary. Yet in spite of its grandeur, St. Paul's was clearly English and Protestant in its inspiration. It seemed a place to collect one's thoughts and then, refreshed, return to the battleground of this world.

As Anne picked up her prayer book, the pages fell open at the healing service. Was she mistaken, or could she really read the words more easily than before? If so, she must thank God for her new doctor's good care and treatment of her eyes. Abigail Hill had read in the *Daily Courant* an advertisement by an oculist with the curious name of Dr. Read. He specifically claimed to cure "Defluxion of Humours," and he was now treating the Queen's eyes. Sarah said that he was nothing but a tailor and an itinerant fraud, but it seemed to Anne today that her vision was better, beyond a doubt. After all the years of constant trouble with her eyes, the improvement was like a miracle. It was a reminder, as if straight from God, that early in the new year she must again touch for the Evil. She had already done so on several occasions and found it a deeply moving though exhausting experience. She always abstained from meat for several days and fasted on the day before the service was to be performed. The great crowds of people, the fetid air, the emotion expended as each sufferer knelt to be touched, all of these taxed her strength to the limit. Yet touching for the Evil was one thing she had done about which she had no doubt or regret.*

During the sermon today, the Queen allowed her mind to follow other paths. The year's end was a suitable time for a personal accounting of those things left undone which she ought to have done, and those things done which she ought not to have done. There was the Toleration Act, for instance. Her father, James II, had sponsored it to allow Protestant Nonconformists to have their own places of worship and their own preachers. The Act had brought him more enemies than friends, but Anne had decided to continue it, and she could only pray that she had done right. The Quaker, William Penn, her father's old friend, had come to thank her for the renewal of the Act. He had recently returned home to England because of some legislation affecting his great tract of land in Western New Jersey, later to be called Pennsylvania. James had given it to him in payment of a debt to Penn's father. Now it was a refuge for Quakers, who, over the years, appeared to be a very good sort of people after all. Anne remembered the Quaker who had built the new Jewish synagogue in Plough Yard and had returned all of his profit to the Jewish congregation because, he said, it was a temple to the universal God whom all worshiped. Her own George had given a mast from a man-of-war of the English navy to be used as a beam in the roof of the synagogue. Times had indeed changed! England was becoming more tolerant.

To Anne, the Toleration Act had been a matter for much soul searching, and other decisions gave her growing concern. As Lord High Admiral, George was in command of the Admiralty Board, but much of the work fell to George Churchill, John's

* See page 269.

eldest brother. George Churchill was not liked. He was cold and autocratic, completely unlike John, and besides, there was some grumbling in Parliament about the inefficiency of the Board. If she could prevent it, her husband must not be the target for criticism. She had asked him to oversee changes and improvements in the gardens at Hampton Court, Windsor, and Kensington. Perhaps the gardens were more suited to his talents than was the Admiralty Board. Dear George! He had always thought that the air at Kensington agreed with him, and now for the sake of his health, he should be there as much as he liked. And perhaps he should resign from the Board before he was asked to do so.

After Divine Service, Anne paused at the door of the church to give her hand to Robert Harley, who bowed over it and followed the Queen into her coach. This astute and diplomatic man was now Secretary of State, replacing Lord Nottingham, an extreme Tory who had resigned in opposition to the war. As the coach rolled through the streets toward St. James's, Anne gave silent thanks that her new Secretary of State was a man of moderate views, who made a splendid triumvirate with Mr. Freeman and Mr. Montgomery. Strangely enough, Harley had first been called to her attention by Abigail Hill, who happened to be his cousin as well as a cousin of Sarah Churchill. Anne had taken Abigail as her bedchamber woman in order to please Sarah, who was always glad to find positions at Court for her poor relatives. The Queen was well repaid for her kindness. She had gained both Abigail and Harley.

And what a comfort Abigail had proved to be! She was a quiet, self-denying sort of person—"meaching," Sarah called it—but she played the harpsichord delightfully and was as fond of Mr. Purcell's music as Anne was. She was not brilliant and beautiful like Sarah, but at Mr. Harley's suggestion she brought most interesting newspapers and books to read aloud while Anne embroidered. Harley employed a certain Daniel Defoe, who rode about on horseback, a kind of traveling reporter, writing about what he saw, very cleverly, it seemed to Anne. She was sorry to learn that he had said rather too much in favor of Dissenters and had been put in the pillory for it. His style was easy, conversational, and so vivid that she thought she could never have learned so much about England in any other way. Abigail Hill said that Robert Harley knew more about England than any man alive, all because of Daniel Defoe. Sometimes she arranged for her cousin Harley to come privately up the backstairs to Anne's chambers. The Queen was always very glad to see him and to hear his comments on Mr. Defoe's most recent investigations. When she attended meetings of the House of Lords, some of the gentlemen appeared surprised that the Queen knew so much about distant parts of her realm, but she only smiled and never told how she knew.

It was nearly time for dinner when Anne returned with Harley from St. Paul's. She and George would dine with only a few friends today—Mr. Harley, Lord Godolphin, and an old friend, the Duchess of Somerset. Anne was quite aware that her formal Court gatherings were not well attended by the people who had swarmed around the Court of her uncle and her father, but with an intimate group like this one today she felt happy. The size and character of the Court had begun to change with William, who had not wanted to surround himself with Englishmen. This change was now confirmed by her own ill health, her shyness, and her refusal to let the palace be a market for the buying and selling of patronage. Sadly, she had to admit that patronage was still bought and sold, but it happened elsewhere, in the halls of Parliament, and in government offices. Not at Windsor, Hampton Court, St. James's, or Kensington were reputations made or wrecked these days, but in the great houses of the newly rich and the not-so-newly rich, where men of arts and letters now gathered.

Still, in her seclusion the Queen could accomplish a good deal in a quiet conversation with the men who counted most. Today she wished to have their opinion about a plan dear to her heart. Poor Mrs. Freeman had been so unhappy since the death of her son; she was so waspish that one could hardly talk to her in the old friendly way. Every conversation seemed to turn into a political argument. A gift, token of Anne's undying love and admiration, might help to heal many wounds.

When dessert had been removed, the Queen sat back in her chair, signaling to Abigail Hill, who handed her a scroll. Anne unrolled it on the table and broached the subject which was in her mind.

"I have here the drawings for a palace to be rebuilt at White-hall. You have all seen them." The gentlemen nodded.

"This palace," said the Queen, "will never be built. I do not want it. Parliament cannot afford it. But there is one man who should have a palace that will rival Versailles. It is the man who defeated the French King. I wish to ask Parliament for the gift of a piece of land to the Duke of Marlborough and to his heirs forever. I myself will pay for the building of a palace which will honor England's great victory by honoring the man who won the battle."

"Does your Majesty have in mind a particular piece of land?" asked Godolphin.

"Woodstock," answered the Queen. "It has a sweet prospect, the finest in Oxfordshire, as fine as any in England, I believe."

Since the Queen planned to pay for the building of the palace herself, there was no objection, nor was Parliament in a mood to make difficulties. Before the Duke returned to the Continent, he had accepted the gift and had chosen an architect, not Sir Christopher Wren, as might have been expected, but a much younger man, John Vanbrugh, a dramatist and a member of the Whiggish Kit-cat Club, whose members were delighted with his stage settings, especially those representing buildings. He knew how to "translate a Roman triumph into stone."

The foundation stone of Blenheim Palace was laid in June 1705. By the end of July the Duke was again in the thick of battle, and Harley was writing to him: "Your friends and servants cannot be without concern upon your Grace's account when we hear how much you expose that precious life of yours upon all occasions, and that you are not contented to do the part of a great general, but you condescend to take your share as a common soldier."

In her husband's absence, Sarah took on the supervision of Blenheim, and from the very first she was dissatisfied. Columns, pilasters, towers, porticoes, and colonnades began to rise around her, spreading over three acres. At the same time, planting and landscaping was going on for Blenheim's lawns, lakes, groves, and fountains. Not even Sarah could superintend the laying of every stone, the driving of every nail, the planting of every tree and shrub, but she tried. She must also manage her children and grandchildren, back the Whigs, oppose the Tories, control the Queen, and watch every penny spent in the process. The richer she became, the more she worried about money; the cost of Blenheim was a nightmare to her. Each year during the building of the palace, the Queen was to pay a sum to Parliament, Parliament would pay the Duke, and the Duke would pay the workmen. But what if the Queen should die? Then who would pay for Blenheim? Worst of all, no matter who paid, this hateful place *was* a monument, not a home. Generations of visitors, down to the present day, have agreed with her.

In 1706 the Duke won another victory for England. This time, the place was the Netherlands. In an action similar to that at Blenheim, Marlborough's troops made a march of twelve hours and defeated French and Bavarian armies in a bloody battle at Ramillies. Once again the Duke led the attack in person. His horse fell and he was thrown from the saddle, but he remounted under heavy fire. After Ramillies, both friend and foe believed him to be invincible, perhaps even immortal! The victory at Ramillies was followed by others in which a string of fortresses were captured. The Netherlands were freed from French domination. In Italy, Prince Eugene crushed Louis's hopes of establishing his empire there.

The only cloud on the horizon was over Spain. Ever since William's time, England had recognized the Archduke Charles, a descendant of Spain's Philip III, as heir to the Spanish throne. When Anne continued to support his claim, he thanked her with a gift of splendid jewels. Now in the midst of the war, he went through the motions of being crowned in Madrid, under the name of "King Charles." But "King Philip," grandson of Louis, still had strong support in France and in Spain. The outcome of events there remained uncertain.

At home in England, 1706 was called "The Year of Victory." Mr. and Mrs. Freeman had never stood higher in the Queen's favor. When the two remaining Churchill daughters were married, Anne gave dowries of £5,000, as she had done for the first two girls. She missed Sarah's company, but she realized that her friend must be very busy, and she only wrote uncomplaining affectionate letters to St. Albans or to the Royal Lodge at Windsor, begging the Duchess to come to her as soon as it was convenient. Meanwhile, she depended more and more on Abigail Hill for companionship and on Robert Harley for advice. Sometimes it was awkward to have to ask the absent Sarah for money

One of the entrances to Blenheim Palace

to pay a small bill or make a charitable gift. As Keeper of the Privy Purse, the Duchess kept its strings pulled tight and was in no hurry to loosen them. The wealth of the Marlboroughs was the talk of the town, but Sarah could work herself into a fine rage if one of Anne's old dresses got into the wrong hands. She knew exactly how much Queen Mary's robes had cost, and declared that Queen Anne was handsomely dressed at a fourth of the amount.

The Queen was thinking of more important matters. She had established what is still called Queen Anne's Bounty "for the relief of the clergy," using funds known as First Fruits, and Tenths, which came to her annually from the parishes of the Church of England. These funds had been used by the Crown for a variety of purposes, some of them scandalous, since the time of Henry VIII. Anne gave them to the small country churches, whose clergy often had no more than £20 a year. With such poverty, it was no wonder that the minor clergy resorted to all sorts of undesirable practices to add to their income. It was difficult for the Church to attract brains and ability to its pulpits. Already, Queen Anne's Bounty was strengthening the entire structure of her beloved Church, as she had so long wished to do.

She was pleased also with the activities of two organizations which she sponsored by her approval and with gifts of money. One of these was the Society for the Reformation of Manners, which had denounced the dramatist Vanbrugh as "a man who debauched the stage beyond the looseness of all former times." On the whole, the public agreed that the Restoration drama had gone too far. As the quality of the plays became more and more degraded, so did the behavior of the audiences, and decent people stayed home rather than risk a bloody nose. Fortunately, a new kind of drama, Italian opera, was becoming popular. The Queen was delighted.

Some liberal-minded people thought that the Society for the Reformation of Manners made itself ridiculous when it began to issue tracts against "drunkenness, swearing, indecency, and Sunday trading." Less laughable was the Society for the Propagation of the Gospel in Foreign Parts. One of its aims was to educate the American Indians and the poor at home, so that they could read the Bible. The army and the navy welcomed this Society's work among the many illiterate soldiers and sailors. The earnest young men who did the work exerted a quiet but pervasive influence both in England and abroad. They taught in the free schools which the Queen supported. They started parish libraries which would later become public libraries. They were among the first Englishmen to condemn the slave trade; their descendants would work to abolish it. These societies found their members in High Church and Low, and among all kinds of Dissenters. Even while they still argued questions of doctrine, they were united in working "to promote Christian life."

The Queen's interests did not flourish on all fronts. Politics was a source of constant trouble. Whichever side she favored on a particular issue, both parties found ways to distress her. In 1705 the question of the succession raised its head again due to Anne's ill health. When Sir John Clerk, one of the Scottish commissioners, came to London for meetings concerning the Act of Union, the Queen followed the negotiations with the greatest interest and care, but she was not always well enough to attend the conferences. Sir John went to Kensington with a progress report and found her Majesty "in extreme pain and agony. . . . Her face, which was red and spotty, was rendered something frightful by her negligent dress, and the foot affected [with gout] was tied up with a poultice and some nasty bandages." It was only one of the many occasions which led to rumors that the Queen might not live much longer. Her friends the Tories suddenly made the outrageous suggestion that her cousin, the Electress Sophia, be invited to live in England, presumably so that she would be ready to take the throne immediately on Anne's death. Anne was terribly hurt. She remembered all too well how the Hanoverians had felt about her own mother, "low-born" Anne Hyde. She still remembered the visit which Sophia's son George had made to England twenty-five years before, and how he had humiliated her. She refused to have either of them in England even for a week.

Meanwhile, the Whigs were determined to have their share of public office. One of the Churchill daughters had married the Earl of Sunderland, a Whig. He was very strong-willed, very able, but Anne disliked him heartily, both as a person and as a political extremist. The Whigs informed Godolphin that they would force him out of office unless the Queen took Sunderland as one of her two Secretaries of State. It was a high position, and she would much have preferred to find a moderate Tory for the post, but Sarah deluged her husband on the battlefield and Godolphin at home with letters demanding that they help persuade the Queen to make the appointment. At last she did so, reluctantly, writing to Godolphin, "All I desire is my liberty in encouraging and employing all those that concur faithfully in my service, whether they are called Whigs or Tories, not to be tied to one or the other; for if I should be so unfortunate as to fall into the hands of either, I shall look upon myself, though I have the name of Queen, to be in reality but their slave."

So the Queen made her way painfully along the path that was set before her, trying to take a middle course. It was often the most difficult one, but as she moved forward during the first years of her reign, all England moved with her in one of its most energetic and productive periods.

She and George needed to get away frequently from the stress and strain of town. They went to Windsor as often as possible. The woods were well stocked with pheasant and deer, the streams abounded in perch, eel, carp, trout, and pike. George could enjoy some shooting, beagling, or fishing. Anne would drive through the forest in a light open chaise, behind a spirited horse, handling the reins herself. She sometimes thought that being Queen of England was like a ride in a chaise behind a fast horse: it was hard to say which was in control, horse or driver. She knew now that she could not be another Elizabeth; in the last hundred years, much power had passed from the Crown to Parliament. She always held the reins, but she took care to drive with a light hand, and her steed responded well. Her people were enthusiastic about their Queen. Tokens of love and esteem came from many sources. One was a poem on Windsor Forest by Alexander Pope, who saw the Queen driving there one day and turned a graceful compliment by comparing her with Diana:

> Let old Arcadia boast her ample plain,
> Th' immortal huntress, and her virgin train;
> Nor envy, Windsor! since thy shades have seen
> As bright a Goddess, and as chaste a Queen.

In less lyric vein, Abel Boyer gave an almost clinical description of Anne at this period: "Her person was middle-sized and well-made, but after she bare children, corpulent; her hair dark brown, her complexion sanguine and ruddy; her features strong but regular; and the only blemish in her face was owing to the difluxion she had in her infancy on the eyes, which left a contraction in the upper lids, that gave a cloudy air to her countenance. . . . What was most remarkable in her personal accomplishments was a clear harmonious voice, particularly conspicuous in her graceful delivery of her speeches to Parliament."

She made one of these speeches early in March 1707, when the Union with Scotland was at last to become a reality. After a diplomatic opening in which she spoke of her great satisfaction in the Union and of the benefits to be enjoyed from it, the Queen gave a motherly admonition, saying, "I Desire and Expect from all my Subjects of both Nations that from henceforth they act with all possible Respect and Kindness to one another, that so it may appear to all the World, they have Hearts dispos'd to be One People." On May 1 she drove to St. Paul's, where a service of General Thanksgiving for the Union was celebrated with pomp and ceremony. The text of the sermon was, "Behold how good and pleasant a Thing it is, for Brothers to dwell together in Unity." But the Queen's Scottish people wanted to remind her Majesty that she had other horses in her stable besides the English thoroughbred racehorse; one of them was the balky old mare, Scotland:

> This auld mare's head was stiff,
> But nane sae well could pu';
> Yet she had a will o' her ain,
> Was unco ill to bow. . . .

In spite of many hesitations on both sides, the first Parliament of the newly united Great Britain met for the first time at Westminster on October 23, 1707, and the Scottish members lived to see the beginning of prosperity, at least in the Lowlands, where ship-building was to flourish on the Clyde, and a growing number of vessels would sail from Glasgow to bring back tobacco from the American colonies. With the nourishment of this new commercial growth, Scottish soil was ready to put forth fruit in scholarship and the arts. David Hume the philosopher, Adam Smith the economist, Burns and Scott, all would add luster to the eighteenth century in Scotland. Still, the "auld mare" did not enjoy admitting how much she owed to the Act of Union.

While driving her political horses, Anne never lost interest in real ones. She gave orders for the dirty, muddy streets of Newmarket to be repaved, and gave a gold cup for the racing at Ascot and Epsom Downs. She and the Prince were at Epsom one day when he had a frightening attack of asthma. A Dr. John Arbuthnot happened to be at the race track and came to George's help. His treatment was so successful that the grateful Queen made him one of her personal physicians. It was a wise appointment. No one could criticize it as they had done when Anne conferred a knighthood on "that quack," her oculist William Read. By contrast, Arbuthnot was a distinguished man, who had taken his doctor's degree at St. Andrew's University. The son of a Scottish Episcopal clergyman, he was a close friend of the leading statesmen now controlling affairs under the leadership of Robert Harley. One of his admirers was a clergyman of the Church of Ireland, named Jonathan Swift.

Swift was more than just a name to the Queen. Whenever he came to London, his friend Dr. Arbuthnot talked about him to her. She knew that he was trying to get some sort of preferment in the Church, for which her approval was needed. Dr. Arbuthnot admired him enormously, but admitted that Swift was a stormy petrel. Who else would ask for a bishopric on one hand, and on the other, attack the Church for its corruption and hypocrisy? His wit was sharp enough to dissever a head and leave the body standing.

He did not stop to consider that three ladies might be reading his satiric *A Tale of a Tub* as they sat in the sunny quiet of the

Orangery with Sir Christopher Wren had built on the grounds of Kensington Palace as a present to Prince George from his devoted wife. Abigail Hill read aloud while the Queen sat sewing with the Duchess of Somerset. There was no denying the wit of this book; every word rang sharp and clear. But Mr. Swift could hardly expect the Queen to take to her bosom a man armed with a rapier for piercing and a razor for slashing away at the Church.

Abigail closed *A Tale of a Tub* and glanced at the Queen, murmuring, "Irreverent!" She was even more High Church than Anne. The Duchess of Somerset agreed. They rose and followed her Majesty to a table set near a long window where the Prince joined them for dinner. Mr. Thomas D'Urfey, the writer, completed the table. He brought a new and funny song about the Electress Sophia. Anne did not mind irreverence on this sore subject, especially since some of her own Tory friends had hurt her feelings by suggesting that the old lady should come to England.

When Mr. D'Urfey had finished his song and bowed himself out of the orangery, Anne went to rest. Unable to sleep, she lay on a couch, thinking about a vexatious problem concerning the Tories and the Electress. Her old friend, John Sheffield, now Duke of Buckingham and Normanby, had betrayed her interests by favoring that unfortunate business of the invitation to Sophia. And Anne had made him a Duke as one of the first acts of her reign. She had given him land in St. James's Park for the new and splendid Buckingham House. How could he! Now he was out of office. Yet he had been one of the most useful members of her Privy Council, and already he had redeemed himself in her eyes by acting as one of the commissioners to arrange the Union. She would forgive that sad mistake about the Electress, and would reappoint Buckingham to office as soon as possible.

There were old, tender memories that would never leave her. It was he who had first made her feel the plight of disabled seamen. Now a handsome naval hospital was being built at Greenwich, an appropriate site for it near the sea, from which England's brave sailors so often came home sick or maimed in her service. Anne would rather see the hospital at Greenwich completed than own all the jewels in the world.

When Abigail Hill came into the Queen's chamber a little later, Anne wanted tea and asked her to read again. "Find something amusing, Hill. I am tired of Mr. Swift. He makes me uneasy."

Abigail had a book at hand, newly arrived from Dr. Bentley, who still held the office of Librarian to the Court of St. James's. "*Arabian Nights Entertainment,*" said Abigail, opening the volume. "Dr. Bentley encloses a note to say that it has just been done into English from the French, who took it from an Arabian manuscript. He thinks it diverting, and hopes that your Majesty will not find anything offensive in it."

As Abigail read, the Queen watched her with affection. Abigail was no beauty; unlike Sarah, she had a pale face and a red nose. But unlike Sarah, her presence was comfortable and homely. Sarah could not be asked to bring tea, to change a poultice, or to sleep at night on a trundle bed or a mattress, almost on the floor. Also unlike Sarah, Abigail was a good listener. She never tired of basset, and besides, she was *there.* Sarah had stayed away for too long, leaving a vacuum which Abigail filled more than adequately.

Anne thought with pleasure of a purse filled with golden guineas, now hidden in her jewel box. She had had no end of trouble in getting the money from the Duchess without saying why she wanted so much. It was a wedding present for Abigail, who was to marry Samuel Masham, George's Groom of the

Chamber. The match was perfectly suitable, and Anne had urged Abigail to tell the Duchess, but Abigail was afraid to stir up a hornet's nest. She knew what her cousin called Samuel, ". . . a soft, good-natured, insignificant man, always making low bows to everybody, and ready to skip to open a door."

In the end, Sarah was not told. Only the Queen was present when Abigail Hill married Samuel Masham in a private ceremony performed in Dr. Arbuthnot's rooms. Eventually news of the wedding reached Sarah. She was annoyed, but told Abigail that she would help her by informing the Queen of the secret marriage. When told that the Queen already knew, she was more than annoyed. Then the whole truth came out. The Queen not only knew about the wedding but had witnessed it and given a sizeable gift from the Privy Purse without Sarah's knowledge. This opened the hell gates. Swift once said of the Duchess, "Three Furies reigned in her breast, the most mortal enemies of all softer passions, which were sordid Avarice, disdainful Pride and ungovernable Rage." All three were let loose when she heard of Mrs. Masham's marriage and then learned that Robert Harley was winning Tory support from the Queen through "backstairs" visits arranged by Abigail. "A woman I took out of a garret!" stormed Sarah. "A woman I took from a broom!" Before long, everyone knew that there was a breach between the Queen and the Duchess.

Anne went with George to Hampton Court for part of the summer. It was pleasant to sit in the Water Gallery where Mary had once sat, watching the boats on the river. They were glad to get away from Sarah, from the heat of town and the heat of politics. Anne's great triumvirate had fallen apart. Robert Harley was trying to form a third party. Marlborough and Godolphin were threatening to resign. When she wrote, begging them not to desert their country, she was called weak. If she stood firm on an issue, she was called obstinate. The strain was very great. As a tonic, Dr. Arbuthnot prescribed a spoonful of brandy in a cup of tea, but someone said, in jest, that it was a spoonful of tea in a cup of brandy. The report spread. Now they were calling her "Brandy Nan." Somehow she would try to bear it. At the same time, she must take care of George. The Prince was in poor health, hardly able to attend to the affairs of the Admiralty. Everyone said that he drank too much. This was true, but his wife saw that he was also a very sick man. At St. James's he had spent most of the previous winter in a dark little room where he had some tools for woodworking. When spring came, the gardens at Kensington were a quiet joy and satisfaction, and he seemed better. Dr. Arbuthnot was doing everything in his power for his royal patient.

In March 1708 startling news arrived. James Francis Edward Stuart, "the warming-pan baby," the Pretender, now twenty years old, was at Dunkirk with a fleet of ships, ready to sail for Scotland. He had with him everything needed to set up a court and declare himself King of Scotland. He, or someone thinking for him, had planned it all down to the last detail, including a new flag and new coinage. In France he was called the Chevalier de St. George. There, his claim to the throne of England was considered stronger than ever, and it was now certain that he was a Stuart. Anne heard the reports about his appearance. "His gait has great resemblance to his uncle, King Charles II," read one letter, "and the lines of his face grow daily more and more like him." The description told her, beyond a shadow of a doubt, that this young man was indeed her father's son. If so, was she herself the usurper?

She had no sooner asked herself this question than it was answered by her people. At news of the Pretender's plans, all wrangling at home stopped. England was united solidly behind the Queen. For once, the Admiralty acted with speed; a fleet went out to intercept the Chevalier and his forces. Like his father, young James had a fatal knack of doing the wrong thing at the wrong time. The landing was prevented with the help of stormy weather and an attack of measles which laid the Pretender low at the crucial moment. He sailed back to France to wait for a better opportunity. From this time on, the Queen no longer felt guilty toward her half-brother; she understood that the throne was not his by Divine Right, but hers, by the will of the people.

In July, Marlborough won another major battle in the Netherlands at Oudenarde. Once again there would be a service of thanksgiving at St. Paul's, but Anne found it hard to rejoice. The Allies had suffered three thousand casualties, the enemy even more. One French company of horse and dragoons had volunteered to gallop into the town with bags of gunpowder strapped to their own bodies. They were literally blown to bits. "O Lord, when will this dreadful bloodshed cease!" cried Anne. She had learned that another victory was no guarantee of an end to the war.

Her premonition was right. After Oudenarde, Louis was willing to begin negotiations for peace, but the Allies' terms were too hard. He agreed to give up some important French forts, he would no longer recognize the Pretender or support his grandson's claim to the Spanish throne. But when he was told that he must actively fight with the Allies against his grandson, he refused. He would not fight against his own flesh and blood. Hostilities resumed.

Nevertheless, the service of thanksgiving took place at St. Paul's. On August 19, Sarah, as Mistress of the Robes, laid out the splendid garments that had been made for the occasion. She also chose the jewels that should be worn; pearls to be entwined in the Queen's hair, a diamond necklace and earrings, the diamond bracelets given by Louis himself, long ago. The Duchess then went to be dressed in her own robes and to wait for the Queen. Once again they would ride together in the royal coach, the Queen and her great friend the Duchess, wife of the victor of Oudenarde.

The Queen came slowly down the palace staircase, her robes covered by a flowing cloak. Behind her came Mrs. Masham, holding up the long velvet train. With some difficulty Anne was put into the coach and Sarah stepped in after her. The door was closed. The Duchess leaned forward and examined the Queen's hair. She looked more closely at other details and gave a little cry.

"Madam, you are not wearing your jewels! That woman . . . Masham forgot them!"

"She did not forget them," the Queen said in a low voice. "I did not wish to wear them."

"Not wear them! And why not, may I ask?"

"This is not a suitable time," replied Anne, almost with a sob. "Too many men have died in this last terrible battle."

Sarah stiffened. "I knew it! That woman . . . that *thing* is at the bottom of it. My husband and I no longer have any credit with you. He will be surprised to hear that when I had taken so much pains to put your jewels in a way I thought you would like, Mrs. Masham could make you refuse to wear them."

"That is not true," the Queen said indignantly. "Masham does not interfere with what I want to do."

"Your Majesty chose a very wrong day to mortify me, when you were just going to return thanks for a victory obtained by Lord Marlborough."

They had reached St. Paul's. The crowds, gathered around the flight of steps, saw the Queen and the Duchess ascending, still deep in conversation, and those nearest heard the Queen say, with an agitated look, "It is not true! It is not true!"

Her usually placid face was distorted with emotion. She seemed to be trying to explain something to the Duchess. As they stepped through the door, Sarah's voice was clearly heard in furious retort: "Do . . . not . . . answer . . . me!"

The two great ladies swept into the church and the choir began the Introit. "I was glad when they said unto me, let us go into the house of the Lord."

 *Kensington*

Oranges and lemons, Say the bells of St. Clement's; . . .
You owe me five farthings, Say the bells of St. Martin's;
When will you pay me? Say the bells of Old Bailey;
When I grow rich, Say the bells of Shoreditch;
When will that be? Say the bells of Stepney;
I'm sure I don't know, Says the great bell at Bow. . . .
                    Old English Nursery Rhyme

IN LONDON NEWSPAPERS there were constant references to the war as being "just and necessary," but after Oudenarde even the Duke of Marlborough was tired of it. He had fought through the battle with a high fever; his rugged health was beginning to break under the demands he put upon it. He wrote to Sarah that he longed to be at home with her, his "dearest soul," yet he would not come until the issues of the war were settled to his own satisfaction.

Prince George's health was less important to the country but supremely important to the Queen. In the autumn of 1708 the Prince was so ill that only a visit to Bath offered any hope. Jolting and swaying over the rough road, the long trip was very hard for both of them, but once again Bath seemed to work its magic. They found the city even more beautiful than before. New streets rose one above the other, with green stretches between. The old Abbey looked down on the pale gold of stone houses and public rooms which had been built since Anne and George, by their approval, had made Bath "the first pleasure-ground in the kingdom." Where rowdy young scamps had once prowled about at night, making mischief and damaging property, the streets were now lighted and clean. A night watch kept law and order. Sanitary arrangements in the baths themselves were about the same as before, but no one was worried about them.

Germs notwithstanding, George's health improved almost miraculously during this visit. He was able to walk about the handsome new Pump-Room and to attend a ball with the Queen. As social arbiter, Beau Nash had established new rules of conduct to combine elegance with common sense. A ball began at six and ended not later than eleven o'clock, so that invalids could enjoy it as dancers or spectators and still have a good night's rest.

Anne and George drove back to Kensington in high hope of a good winter, but almost at once the Prince's health took a turn for the worse. Anne nursed her husband day and night while he fought for breath. The battle was hopeless, and on October 28, the London papers sadly and respectfully reported the death of the Prince of Denmark. "His Royal Highness had been troubled for many years with a constant difficulty of Breathing, and sometimes with Spitting of Blood, which often endangered his life, . . . Her Majesty assisting in his last Moments, as well as during his whole Illness, in the most mournful and most Affecting manner 'till he expired. His royal Highness's Great Humanity and Justice, with his other Extraordinary Virtues, had so highly endeared him to the whole Nation, that all Orders of Men discover an unspeakable Grief for the Loss of so Excellent a Prince."

At the very moment of George's death, Sarah arrived at Kensington in a quarrelsome mood, demanding to see the Queen. She had come to argue politics, but with the Prince lying dead in the room even Sarah recognized that it was not an opportune time. It might, however, be an excellent chance to regain control over the Queen, who was in no condition to resist. Sarah's own coach was waiting. Totally ignoring Mrs. Masham, the Duchess put Anne into the coach and drove with her to St. James's, where she ordered a cup of broth as a restorative. Writing about the death of Prince George years later in her private correspondence, she unconsciously told more about herself than anyone else could have done: The Queen ". . . had bitts of great tenderness for the Prince, and I remember she wrote me a little note at which I could not help smiling, that I should send to My Lord Treasurer [Godolphin] to take care that some door might be taken down at the removing of the Prince to Westminster, for fear the dear Prince's body should be shook as he was carried out of some room, although she had gone long jumbling journeys with him to the Bath, when he must feel it, and when he was gasping for breath. I did see the tears in her eyes two or three times after his death upon this subject, and I believe she fancied she loved him, and she was certainly more concerned for him than she was for the fate of Gloucester, but her nature was very hard, and she was not apt to cry."

Anne spent the winter at St. James's, sitting by the fire in one of the small rooms where the Prince had kept his carpenter's tools. After his death, she always dined alone. She wrote to the King of Denmark, "I must confess to Your Majesty that the loss of such a husband, who loved me so dearly and so devotedly, is too crushing for me to be able to bear it as I ought." Church services, by the Queen's request, no longer included a prayer that she might be the happy mother of children.

Abigail attended the Queen faithfully. Anne could hardly have survived the first months of her widowhood without Mrs.

Masham. Jonathan Swift, who was so often at Court these days, admired her. "My Lady Masham," he said, "was a person of a plain sound understanding, of great truth and sincerity, without the least mixture of falsehood or disguise; of an honest boldness and courage, superior to her sex; firm and disinterested in her friendship, and full of love, duty, and veneration for the Queen her mistress."

Outside the dark little room, one of the coldest winters in history brought such misery both in England and in France that the people wondered how they could bear their lives, day by day, to say nothing of paying the crushing taxes for the war. The long, hard winter was followed by a cold, rainy summer with poor harvests.

In September 1709, Marlborough won another victory. This was the battle of Malplaquet, fought at a town on the border between France and the Netherlands. "In that tremendous combat," says Thackeray, "near upon two hundred and fifty thousand men were engaged, more than thirty thousand of whom were slain or wounded . . . and this dreadful slaughter took place because the great General's credit was shaken at home, and he thought to restore it by victory." Malplaquet was the bloodiest battle of the eighteenth century. Hardly any prisoners were taken. It was said that the ragged remnants of Allied troops stood silent when the Duke rode past to review them after the battle. "Cheer, damn you!" an officer shouted to his men. They could not cheer; too many of their comrades had fallen.

At Kensington, Anne was coming to a slow and painful decision about the Marlboroughs. With the news of Malplaquet, the Queen knew that she must remove the Duke from command. There was no other way to end the war, since he would evidently fight on as long as he lived. The French of course were praying for his death. French soldiers marched to a song:

Marlborough has gone to war,
Mi ron ton, ton, ton, mi ron taine;
Marlborough has gone to war,
Who knows when he'll return?

The song pictured the Duchess climbing to the top of a tower, looking down on the road where her page, clothed all in black, was arriving with the news, "Madame! Marlborough is dead, is dead and in his grave!" To the French, the death of the terrible Duke seemed their only possible salvation; his own countrymen were beginning to agree.

Sarah was blind to the situation. While Robert Harley was forming a Tory administration to end the war, and while the Queen's manner toward the Duchess of Marlborough gradually changed from warm, to cool, to cold, Sarah continued to attack Mrs. Masham as the sole cause of Anne's Tory sympathies. She wrote a long letter, listing all the services she had ever performed for Anne, and demanding a private interview. She only wanted a chance to explain herself, she said; Anne need not answer.

The Queen did not want to see her. She knew that she could not out-talk Sarah. She suggested, by letter, that Sarah should put in writing whatever she had to say. On April 6, 1710, Sarah finally forced her way into the Queen's presence at Kensington, and launched into a full-scale defense of herself, her actions, and her motives. Before such a blast, Anne retreated into silence. She had never been good at repartee. She could only repeat doggedly, whenever Sarah paused to draw breath, "You desired no answer, and shall have none." Or, "Whatever you have to say, you may put it in writing." At last Sarah gave up and went away. In time to come, she wrote down her recollection of this remarkable conversation. It was, she said, "the last I ever had with her Majesty." Still she could not believe that Anne would really dismiss her dear Mrs. Freeman.

"I will never forsake your dear self, Mr. Freeman, nor Mr. Montgomery, but always be your constant faithful servant; and we four must never part till death mows us down with his impartial hand." So Anne had written to Sarah only eight short years before, without knowing the hard necessities of the war that lay ahead. Now she must detach herself from those friends, one by one. The first to receive formal notice of his dismissal was Godolphin, "Mr. Montgomery," Marlborough's strongest friend and supporter. Anne dismissed Godolphin without even an audience, perhaps too ashamed to face the man who had carried the financial burdens of his country so long and so well. For more than a year he had been saying, "The life of a slave in the galleys is a paradise in comparison of mine." He may have found retirement more of a relief than a disappointment. He went to live at St. Albans in the Marlboroughs' house, and died in 1712, the first of the four to be "mowed down," in Anne's words, "with death's impartial hand."

While Anne, backed by the Tories, was making a desperate resolve to stop the war by dismissing her closest friends, a group of Whigs was making an even more drastic plan in support of the war effort. They asked Marlborough to seize the Queen, force her abdication, and put the House of Hanover on the throne. Marlborough refused. Nonetheless, he was ruined. Already, without his knowledge, secret negotiations were underway between England and France to make a separate peace. If all parties were brought into the conference, no agreements would ever be reached, but with England out of the war, the other Allies could not continue to fight.

The Duke returned to England in 1711, a tired, almost a

broken man. The frustration of diplomatic and political maneuvering with his difficult Allies was even more wearing than his military campaigns. Now he found that peace negotiations had been going on behind his back. Sarah was in a state bordering on frenzy. The Queen would not see her but was surrounding herself with Tories. Anne had actually created twelve new Tory peers, one of whom was none other than Samuel Masham. As Lord Masham, he no longer skipped to open a door, and the "meaching" Mrs. Masham was "meaching" no more, now that she was Lady Masham. She was boldly and openly scheming to make the Queen desert Marlborough. The Tory newspapers were full of scorching articles accusing the Duke of using the war for his own benefit. When Sarah complained of Britain's ingratitude toward her husband, "that man Swift" answered with a comparison between the rewards received by an emperor of ancient Rome and those received by the Duke:

A Bill of Roman Gratitude

	l.	s.	d.
Imprimis for frankincense and earthen pots to burn it in	4	10	0
A bull for sacrifice	8	0	0
An embroidered garment	50	0	0
A crown of laurel	0	0	2
A statue	100	0	0
A trophy	80	0	0
A thousand copper medals value half pence a piece	2	1	8
A triumphal arch	500	0	0
A triumphal car, valued as a modern coach	100	0	0
Casual charges at the triumph	150	0	0
Sum total	994	11	10

A Bill of British Ingratitude

	l.	s.	d.
Imprimis Woodstock	40,000	0	0
Blenheim	200,000	0	0
Post-office grant	100,000	0	0
Mildenheim	30,000	0	0
Pictures, jewels, etc.	60,000	0	0
Pall-Mall grant, etc.	10,000	0	0
Employments	100,000	0	0
Sum total	540,000	0	0

Swift did, in fact, recognize the importance of Marlborough's victories. He saw with his own eyes the terrible price the Duke had paid in body and mind through his long years of service, winning every battle he fought and taking every town he besieged. Still he called Marlborough "as covetous as hell and ambitious as the prince of it," and the Tories threatened the Duke with a scandal. They brought up the question of the commission paid to him by Solomon de Medina for the right to sell bread to the army. Medina testified, and Marlborough was able to clear himself in the eyes of all except those who wished to destroy him. He showed that he had used this money to establish his own Secret Service, but the Tories made the most of the furor against him. Anne too greeted him with bad news. She thanked him for his most recent military services, then reluctantly told him that Sarah must resign as Groom of the Stole and Keeper of the Privy Purse. She must return her Key of Office at the earliest possible moment. He had to carry this message to the woman whom he still ardently, passionately loved.

"Don't reproach the Queen," he advised Sarah. "In a dispute like this, after much kindness and friendship, reproaches only make the breach wider."

"Kindness, friendship!" stormed Sarah. "She doesn't know what kindness is. I have never known her to do anything handsome, either as a reward or as a piece of friendship. Even to those she says she loves, her presents are very few, and very insignificant."

On second thought, she decided she had a good deal to lose. She wrote to Anne, promising to make no more trouble, and signed herself not as "Mrs. Freeman," the equal of "Mrs. Morley," but as her Majesty's "most dutiful and most obedient subject and servant, S. Marlborough." John carried the letter to Anne. The victor of Blenheim, of Ramillies, Oudenarde, and Malplaquet knelt humbly at her feet and begged her to reconsider. It was too late. Anne had made up her mind. The Duchess of Somerset would replace Sarah as Groom of the Stole, and Lady Masham could be keeper of the Privy Purse. Sarah might be contrite at this moment, but she was still Sarah and a violent Whig; she must go. The great days were over, those days when, it has been said, "Sarah managed the Queen, Marlborough managed the war, and Godolphin managed the Parliament." The executive power in England would never again be in the hands of three such people, nor would it ever again be managed quite so efficiently.

When John brought back the Queen's final word, Sarah flung her Key on the floor and told him to do with it whatever he wanted. He took the Key to the Queen. Sarah prepared to move into a new house at the edge of St. James's Park, built for her by Sir Christopher Wren on land granted to the Marlboroughs by the Queen in happier times. It was the "Pall-Mall grant" noted by Swift in his "Bill of British Ingratitude." Before leaving her apartments at St. James's Palace, Sarah removed everything she herself had paid for, including the locks on the doors and some of the mantels. She still had not learned that the

Queen was "Queen indeed." When Anne saw what Sarah had done to her rooms, she said, "Why should I pay for her house when she tears down mine?" Then she stopped payment on the building of Blenheim Palace. Marlborough returned to the Continent, and the war went on.

In time, Anne relented and began again to pay the bills for Blenheim. The great house grew and grew. Sarah drove out to see how it was getting on, quarreled with all the workmen, down to the last and least, and wandered about the formal gardens, the very model of a disconsolate lady waiting for her lover to return from the war.

On Marlborough's next return to England at the end of 1711, Anne had steeled herself to cut the last tie. On the advice of her Privy Council, she wrote to her Commander-in-Chief, dismissing him from all of his offices, and refused to see him in person. Of all painful and futile interviews, this would have been the worst. She had given him free rein to make himself the most powerful man in the western world. No one had admired him more than Anne. Perhaps she still did.

On battlefields, in halls of state, and in her own boudoir the Queen's drama with the Marlboroughs worked itself out, but her life also had its more peaceful, normal aspects. To relieve her loneliness at Hampton Court, at Windsor, at Kensington, she sometimes drove out on a fine day.

Mr. William Penn, who lived near Kensington, often saw her passing in her coach, drawn by a spanking pair. The Queen and the Quaker were poles apart on religious matters, but they had one thing in common, their interest in fine horses. He sympathized with her pleasure when "Pepper" and "Mustard" from her own stables won races. He understood her regret that she could no longer ride her sorrel hunter "Vinegar." Jonathan Swift was another who shared the Queen's high regard for beautiful horses. He was already making notes for a satirical tale of adventure in which an English sailor named Gulliver would visit several marvelous countries, one of them inhabited by noble horses whose behavior put humans to shame.

Anne did not live to read "Gulliver's Travels," but her last years saw the start of another famous adventure story. One day Lady Masham read to the Queen a newspaper article by Mr. Richard Steele, who had been a gentleman usher to the dear Prince. The account told of several years spent on a desert island by one Alexander Selkirk. When Daniel Defoe read the article, he was even more interested than the Queen. He began to spin a tale in his own mind, to be written later, if he could find the leisure to do it. He would call his story "Robinson Crusoe." Already, around the "dull" Queen and her "dull" Court, the Augustan Age of literature was shining.

Many distinguished guests arrived from exotic lands to see her. An ambassador, dark-skinned and dignified, came from "Barbary" in North Africa to congratulate the British Queen on the capture of Gibraltar and to arrange for a pact with England against France and Spain. Long ago, Barbary had thought Dick Whittington's London cat an exotic animal. Now the ambassador brought exotic animals from Barbary to Queen Anne—two lions for the zoo in the Tower of London, besides some tiger skins and a gift of gold dust and jewels for herself.

On another occasion, Anne received at Court four Mohawk Indian chiefs from her American colonies. They came in their full ceremonial regalia to request help against the French, so that they might "enjoy peaceable hunting, and have much trade with the Great Queen's children." She could not reveal that she was trying to end, rather than begin, a long war with France, but she told them that she had passed an act to encourage trade with America. The chiefs were pleased, and remained in London to be entertained, as Pocahontas had once been, in all the great London drawing rooms.

Tributes came from lands as far away as India. Robert Harley, Earl of Oxford, brought her a splendid diamond, dug from the fabulous mines of Golconda. Through the interest of Jewish importers, the diamond market had moved from Goa to London, and diamonds were pouring into England. Anne thought that she had more than enough diamonds. Her jewel casket was filled with the diamonds which Sarah had pressed her to buy. When Harley told Anne that the House of Commons planned to purchase the fine Golconda stone for her, she said that "she would be sorry to see the people's money thrown away upon such a bauble for her . . . and thought it was a much greater pity that Greenwich hospital was not finished."

From Germany came a visitor who added special luster to the London of Queen Anne. This was George Frederick Handel, who had just been appointed Kapellmeister to George of Hanover, with a salary of 1,000 thaler. George had long wished for a court musician. In Handel, he now had a court musician beyond compare. But Handel had no sooner been appointed than he requested leave of absence and sailed for London, promising a speedy return. When he arrived in London, he was introduced at Court and soon realized that the Queen was eager to be a patron of music. There was a golden opportunity to write some good opera. England at this time had a newly acquired taste for opera in the Italian manner, but only the most foolish and absurd examples were being produced in London. Handel set to work on "Rinaldo," which was dedicated in flowery language to the Queen: "Madam, Among the numerous Arts and Sciences which now distinguish the Best of Nations and Best of Queens, Musick the most engaging of the Train, appears in Charms we never saw her wear till lately; when the Universal

Glory of your Majesty's Illustrious Name drew hither the most celebrated Masters from every part of Europe. . . . This Opera is a Native of your Majesty's Dominions, and was consequently born your Subject. . . ."

"Rinaldo" played to big audiences at the Queen's Theater in the Haymarket. Everyone was talking about the scene in which "Armida" appeared in mid-air, "in a Chariot drawn by two huge Dragons, out of whose Mouths issue Fire and Smoke." Or the following scene, "a delightful Grove in which [live] Birds are heard to sing, and seen flying up and down among the Trees." Or Act II, Scene 1, in which "Two Mermaids are seen Dancing up and down in the Water." But the *Spectator* sniffed: "The Boy who had the Direction of the Two painted Dragons and made them spit Fire and Smoke [had] but Two things wanting, . . . the keeping his Head a little lower, and hiding his Candle. . . . The Sparrows and Chaffinches either get into the Galleries or put out the Candles. . . . As to the Mechanism and Scenery, the Undertakers [stage hands] forgetting to change their Side-Scenes, we were presented with a Prospect of the Ocean in the midst of a delightful Grove." The bad review was probably due to professional jealousy. Joseph Addison and Richard Steele, who wrote for the *Spectator,* had productions of their own in other theaters at the same time.

After the success of "Rinaldo," Handel made England his second fatherland. In 1712 he began to compose an "Ode for the Birthday of Queen Anne." It was performed at Court on February 6, 1713, in an atmosphere of hope for the long-awaited treaties that would end the War of the Spanish Succession.

For months, a handsome and brilliant young man had been working secretly on the peace negotiations. He was Henry St. John, Viscount Bolingbroke. He was only twenty-five years old, a notorious rake, but a noted orator and an accomplished linguist in French. Working with him was the poet, Matthew Prior, another of the literary figures of the day who dealt in diplomacy and politics as easily as in polished verse. Early in April 1713, the signing of treaties between the various warring countries brought the long and bloody war to an end. The French Court agreed to recognize the Protestant succession in Britain and to expel the Pretender from France. Some French territories in North America were ceded to Britain, including those in the West Indies, Hudson Bay, Newfoundland, and Nova Scotia. England would continue to hold Gibraltar. France and Spain would remain separate. And England would have sole right for thirty years to import African Negroes as slaves into the New World. In later days, William Pitt, the Earl of Chatham, would call the Treaty of Utrecht "an indelible blot upon the age." The Duke of Marlborough, who had won the military victories, left England in disgrace, to live on the Continent, at Frankfort, with his Duchess. Harley and his administration, who had made the peace, got about as much thanks as Gulliver did when he put out the fire in the bedchamber of the Lilliputian Queen.

Handel, however, began work on a *Te Deum* and a *Jubilate* to be sung for the first time at St. Paul's Cathedral on July 7, a day of national thanksgiving. The Queen, who had longed for the peace, and had separated herself from her dearest friends to attain it, was not able to attend the service. She was too weak and ill. Over the past year, rumors had repeatedly swept London that Queen Anne was dead. Then she would be seen inaugurating the race meetings at Ascot. Again the word would fly from one coffeehouse to the next, "Queen Anne is dead!" and the next day she would appear in the Banqueting House, touching for the Evil. One little boy named Samuel Johnson was brought to be touched at this time. Not yet three years old, he had only "a confused but somehow a sort of solemn recollection of a lady in diamonds, and a long black hood." He kept his touch-piece, the gold "angel" strung on a ribbon around his arm by the Queen's chaplain during the ceremony. It can still be seen in the British Museum. Once more, "Queen Anne is dead!" was heard in all the streets of London. Then her people saw her driving in her coach to greet the eight hundred boys and girls at Christ's Hospital, well pleased to find them "so decently clad, cleanly lodged, so wholesomely fed, so admirably taught." There were five thousand children now in the free schools of London, another twenty thousand elsewhere throughout the country.

On July 7, 1713, the bells of thanksgiving rang out. From St. Bride's, St. Mary-le-Bow in Cheapside, from Christ Church in Newgate Street, from St. Clement Danes, St. Magnus, St. Martin Ludgate, St. James's Piccadilly, St. Stephen Walbrook, from St. Michael Paternoster Royal, up and down the scales, over and over, the chimes made a joyful noise unto the Lord. All of these churches, and forty more besides, were the work of Sir Christopher Wren.

He loved his church steeples, and his thoughts were in harmony with the bells as he made his way toward St. Paul's. In his pocket he carried a watch, a present from the Queen in recognition of his work. It was an appropriate gift. He himself was rather like a well-regulated watch with a good balance wheel, working smoothly and dependably through many years. He had been forty-three when the foundation stones of St. Paul's were laid; now he was eighty-one years old. The great cathedral was finished at last, and he was still alive to see it. He said with modest humor, "You might set it in St. Peter's, and look for a good while before you could find it." But Englishmen acknowledged it to be "the beauty of all the churches in the city, and of all the Protestant churches in the world." Wren too was proud of it. He said he "would answer for it with his head" that the columns would bear the weight of the dome. They would even stand a stone spire a hundred feet higher, and "nothing below should give way, no not one half quarter of an inch." St. Paul's dominated the view of London.

On this day, hymns of triumph and praise would echo in its dome. With the coming of peace, England's poets were joining her churchmen in a chorus of thanksgiving for the wonderful works of God. It was during this joyful time that Alexander Pope dropped his satirical mask and wrote, "Rise, crowned with light, imperial Salem, rise!" In the *Spectator*, Joseph Addison printed his own new poem, "The spacious firmament on high." It would be set to music by Joseph Haydn to become one of the most glorious hymns ever written in Anne's or any other age. Nahum Tate, the Poet Laureate, contributed "Jesus Christ is risen today." And Anne's friend, Thomas Ken, Bishop of Bath and Wells, had written a fine doxology, "All praise to thee, my God, this night." The last verse began, "Praise God from whom all blessings flow." In churches and chapels of all denominations, it would soon be almost as much a part of every Sunday service as the Lord's Prayer.

The Dissenters too had their new poets and new hymns which would be sung on this day of thanksgiving in chapels and meeting houses all over the land. Little Mr. Isaac Watts, barely five feet tall, carried under his huge wig a head full of poetic ideas to express his devotional fervor. Now that hymn singing was no longer forbidden in most dissenting chapels, he was pouring out his verses: "When I survey the wondrous cross"; "Come, Holy Spirit, Heavenly Dove"; "There is a land of pure delight." His greatest hymns were still to come.

In the Dissenters' Burying Ground, John Bunyan lay at rest. He too had contributed a hymn that would be loved in both

Church and Chapel. It was a verse from "Pilgrim's Progress":

He that is down needs fear no fall,
He that is low, no pride:
He that is humble ever shall
Have God to be his guide . . .

With the blessing of Queen Anne's Act of Toleration, all sorts and conditions of men set off that day to thank God according to the forms that suited them best. At the Synagogue in Plough Yard, the Jewish congregation, growing in numbers and in prosperity, would hear their cantor sing, "Hear, O Israel, the Lord our God, the Lord is One." They stood secure under their roof, one beam of which was the mast from a man-of-war in the Queen's navy. It was a covenant, symbolizing England's protection of their right to worship. Like the Catholics, they still suffered from various kinds of discrimination. As Jonathan Swift put it, "We have just enough religion to make us hate, but not enough to make us love one another." Nevertheless, open persecution had stopped.

On the day of thanksgiving, Mr. Ellis Gamble, a silverplate engraver, told his apprentice, young William Hogarth, that he might have a whole holiday, even though it was a Tuesday. William thanked Mr. Gamble and hurried off to a nearby church in Leicester Fields. After church he planned to spend the rest of the day in the taverns and coffeehouses around Covent Garden and Drury Lane. If he was lucky, he might reach Button's on Russell Street in time to catch a glimpse of Mr. Addison, Mr. Pope, or Dr. Arbuthnot. Button's was a Tory coffeehouse where the best writers congregated, and William was sketching them. The East India Company was bringing home tea and coffee for hundreds of coffeehouses in London, but Mr. Addison usually came to Button's. He used it as an editorial office and kept a box there into which the *Spectator*'s correspondents dropped their letters through a carved lion's mouth. William was a good young man and he admired the gentle, bashful Mr. Addison. But the artist's eye was also drawn to others—the waspish face of Mr. Pope or the round jolly Irish countenance of Richard Steele, who wrote like an angel and made a whole group of amiable characters come alive in the pages of the *Spectator*.

Walking through the streets of London after the solemn church service on that great day, the artist saw Londoners who, he thought, could have stepped out of the "Sir Roger de Coverley Papers." That country squire, strolling along with his hands clasped behind his back and with a benevolent look for all, might be Sir Roger himself. Hogarth spied another gentleman who could easily be the fashionable Will Honeycomb, on his way to a rendezvous at Vauxhall Gardens, his perfumed wig sweetening the air around him.

That stout merchant, stopping to take a pinch of snuff, might almost be Sir Andrew Freeport. He too was a *Spectator* character, typical of the gentry who owned stocks and bonds in a hundred enterprises. He probably had a house in the country, but he lived in London the greater part of the year in order to keep in touch with his business.

That soldier might be Captain Sentry, who had gone "over the hills and far away" to fight for the Duke in Flanders. Now he was home from the wars and hurrying off for an evening of pleasure in Drury Lane, where there were plenty of girls to vow that

> . . . of all the world's brave heroes,
>   There's none that can compare
> With a tow row row row row,
> To the British Grenadiers.

But not all of the soldiers would come home safe and sound, with money in their pockets. There went a poor fellow in a tattered uniform and hobbling along on a crutch. In behalf of men like him, the *Flying Post* made a plea: "Do not suffer those brave Spirits, who have born Hunger, Cold, Sickness, loss of Limbs, terrible Sieges, and bloody Battles; have seen their Companions, Friends, and Relations, drop down by 'em, the Sons who have lost their Fathers, and Fathers their Sons: Let not these Men, that have endured this for their Country, and to defend your Liberty and Property, be treated as common, idle, vagrant Beggars . . ."

William Hogarth thought how well the gentle *Spectator* would describe the sights and sounds of London as the good people poured out of their churches to end their great day of thanksgiving with a little fun or business. The cries of London filled the streets with their din once more. At an open window, a musician laid down his violin, looked out, and put his hands over his ears. Then he slammed the window shut. William Hogarth laughed to himself and walked on. He would sketch the scene one day.

That evening, with guns still booming, and bells ringing, fireworks flared in the sky of a long summer twilight. People sitting over their cups in taverns, in coffeehouses, in their own gardens, spoke of certain actors in the long tragedy of the war, who had failed to appear on stage for the applause at the final curtain. Godolphin was dead. The Duke and Duchess of Marlborough were abroad and in disgrace. It was a pity that the Queen had been too ill to drive to St. Paul's on this greatest day of triumph.

Soon afterward she left London for Hampton Court, glad to be out of the heat and noise of town. The night was warm at Hampton too, but there was always a fresh breeze from the river. The Queen lay alone in her bedchamber, staring up through the darkness at the canopy above her. Through the open window she could hear the sound of water falling in the basin of a fountain. If there were any ghosts abroad at Hampton Court tonight, she did not hear or see them. She was no longer afraid of ghosts. She had been through so much and she was so tired, that death, when it came, would be a friend. On the battlefields the war had ended, but at home, Whig still warred against Tory, and within the Tory ranks, Robert Harley was at odds with Henry St. John. Even in her own household there was friction; Lady Masham had fallen out with the Duchess of Somerset. Much of the wrangling was caused by personal jealousies and ambitions, but Anne's health was involved too. Once again there was a movement to bring the Pretender, James, to England, and to put him on the throne when she died. Some had thought he could be persuaded to renounce his faith but, like his father, he was too devout and too honest to do so. Harley said that the Pretender would always be a threat. He was urging Anne to put a price on the head of young James, but she could not bring herself to do it. If he would content himself with staying away from England, let him live and die in peace.

Here at Hampton Court, a century ago, her great-grandfather, James I, had brought together bishops and Puritans embroiled in their differences. The conference had failed, but out of it had come the King James Bible. Now Anne's support was being asked for a Schism Act which would close all Dissenter schools. For more than eleven years she had tried to walk a middle course between opposing factions. If she had failed, perhaps something would still be left when she was gone, something worthwhile. Surely the Union with Scotland would be counted as a jewel in her crown. There might be others. Time would tell.

In the morning when Dr. Arbuthnot came to inquire for her

William Hogarth's engraving, "The Enraged Musician"

health, he brought an anecdote to pass the time while the dresser was doing the Queen's hair.

"Your Majesty may remember young Lord Petre?"

Anne nodded without speaking.

The doctor continued. "They tell me he was here one day when Arabella Fermor was playing at cards. He stepped behind her and cut off one of her curls."

The Queen smiled faintly. "Was she very angry?"

"Very," said Dr. Arbuthnot. "And he refused to give back the curl. But the extraordinary thing is that my friend Pope has made a poem of it, with more to come. The first part has already appeared and I have a copy here, if your Majesty would care to listen. I think you might find it amusing."

With the Queen's permission he sat down beside her and began to read from "The Rape of the Lock":

> Close by those meads, for ever crowned with flowers,
> Where Thames with pride surveys his rising towers,
> There stands a structure of majestic frame,
> Which from the neighboring Hampton takes its name.
> Here Britain's statesmen oft the fall foredoom
> Of foreign tyrants, and of nymphs at home;
> Here thou, great Anna! whom three realms obey,
> Dost sometimes counsel take—and sometimes tea . . .

As soon as she was well enough to travel, she went on to Windsor. Little William had died here, yet in spite of its sad memories it was a place where she always loved to be. Here she had come with George after their marriage. Here she had received the news of the great victory at Blenheim. Towering on its steep cliff above the Thames, the castle grew more and more imposing with every passing year. She herself had done much to enhance the beauty of the castle grounds. Often during that summer she felt well enough to drive through the Great Park, but her attendants and advisers warned her against driving alone. Some men had been seen lurking about, both at Windsor and at Kensington. There were rumors of a plot against her life, perhaps by foreign agents, perhaps by the terrible London "Mohocks"; but Anne only said that God would take care of her. She was less likely to be assassinated, she thought, than to be driven to an early grave by the quarreling and conniving that went on around her. The one man who seemed acceptable to all political factions was the moderate Duke of Shrewsbury, often called "the King of Hearts." She begged him to intervene in the feud between Harley and St. John, but he was unable to bring them together again.

Lady Masham was constantly urging various causes, including that of Mr. Swift, who occasionally sat down to a game of cards at Windsor. He was still hoping to be made a dean, but it was hard to reward anyone who wrote so offensively. His sour, severe face, nervous manner, and high sharp voice made him an uncongenial guest, and he seemed utterly cynical. Who else would have hung about the Queen in hope of an appointment and at the same time openly called the Queen's close friend, the red-headed Duchess of Somerset, "Carrots"? Who else but Swift had such a low opinion of human nature? Even while he sat at cards, supposedly among friends, he could imagine what they would say when he died:

> My female Friends, whose tender Hearts
> Have better learn'd to Act their Parts,
> Receive the News in doleful Dumps,
> "The Dean is Dead, (and what is Trumps?)". . .

At last a vacancy was made for him in the bishopric of St.

Patrick's Cathedral, Dublin, but by this time he was so deeply involved in the politics of power at Anne's Court that becoming Dean of St. Patrick's was only of secondary importance. He was disillusioned with what he had seen of political maneuvering; both climbing and crawling were done on all fours, he observed. He went off to Dublin with a bitter farewell for Robert Harley, Earl of Oxford, his one-time friend: ". . . Like one at your levee, having made my bow, I shrink back into the crowd."

Dr. Arbuthnot was another who was disgusted with politics. During his years as the Queen's physician, he had written a scathing piece entitled, "The Art of Political Lying," and more recently, "Law is a Bottomless Pit; or the History of John Bull." He appears to have originated the name, known around the world by millions who never heard of John Arbuthnot.

When autumn came, the Queen was too ill to return to London. Once again, panicky speculation about the succession filled the coffeehouses as well as the Court. What would the Queen do? Would she declare her half-brother, James, heir to the throne? Jacobites were holding meetings to drink to "King James III," as they called the Pretender. They worked themselves up to a fine pitch of enthusiasm with a stirring song, "When the King enjoys his own again." But the Protestant succession was at stake, and Anne knew that she could not risk putting her scepter into the hands of a Catholic heir, no matter how strong his claim to the throne. The moment he set foot in England, there would be a Protestant insurrection which could not end without a blood-letting. In order to settle the issue in the minds of her uneasy people, she returned to London in February 1714, ill as she was, and in June put a price of £5,000 on the head of James Stuart. Now it should be clear to all that she had given her support to the House of Hanover. However, she disliked them as much as ever, and when, once again, it was suggested that the Electress Sophia should come to England, Anne wrote such a maddening letter to her that the elderly Sophia nearly had a stroke. She did, in fact, die a few days later, thus narrowly missing the chance to become "Queen Sophia I of England."

Robert Harley had been taking a high hand in managing his position as Lord Treasurer. It was almost as if he believed that he alone held the reins of government. What made his presumptuous and arrogant behavior most dangerous was the fact that he had been drinking heavily. On July 27 the Queen asked him to give up his Staff of Office, the white wand which was the insignia of his authority. Harley was furious. He swore to "be revenged and leave some as low as he found them."

That night a meeting of the Privy Council took place at Kensington Palace. It began with acrimony and insults, continuing in a crescendo of vituperation from all sides until two o'clock in the morning. The Queen sat through it to the very end. The effect of that meeting literally brought her to her deathbed. When she woke on the morning of the twenty-ninth, she knew that she had not long to live. "I am going," she said to the Duchess of Somerset, "but my hearty prayers are for the prosperity of this poor nation."

In her bedchamber stood a walnut highboy, its drawers filled with the relics of her lifetime. She would like to look at them again—a few sheets of music, a favorite lace scarf, a fan, toy soldiers, a Stuart tartan, letters from George, from Sarah. Someone must bring them to her. She signaled to a lady-in-waiting, who followed the direction of the Queen's eyes and went to the highboy. A Delft jar of potpourri stood upon it. Misunderstanding what was wanted, she brought it to the Queen and opened it. The fragrance filled the room—violets, rose leaves, lavender, myrtle, verbena, rosemary, gathered from the gardens which the Stuarts had made and loved.* Anne turned away her face and shook her head, too tired to say a word.

The Privy Council was meeting again at the Cockpit on July 29 when a messenger arrived with word from Dr. Arbuthnot that the Queen was dying. Confronted with this new crisis, the Council hurried to Kensington, asking the Duke of Shrewsbury to fill the place of Robert Harley as Lord Treasurer. Only Shrewsbury seemed to have a chance of bringing the boiling political pot down to a simmer. But "the King of Hearts" said that the Queen herself must confirm his appointment. Into her room they all came, ministers and members of the Privy Council, crowding around her bed to witness her last official act, which would put an end to Jacobite hopes, plans, and plots. When she opened her eyes, they gave her the Lord Treasurer's white wand. Shrewsbury stepped forward. She called him by name and put the wand into his hand. Those who stood nearest the bed heard her faint voice. "Use it for the good of my people."

On Sunday morning, August 4, Dr. Arbuthnot went to a window and waved a handkerchief to a silent, waiting crowd outside Kensington Palace. Soon afterward, the bells of London began to toll for the death of Queen Anne. Dr. Arbuthnot wrote to Swift, "Sleep was never more welcome to a weary traveler than death to her."

Jonathan Swift had said many sharp things about many people. Of Anne he said, "She was the only really good woman I ever knew."

With the news that George of Hanover was now King George I of England, a prayer of thankfulness went up from those who

---

* See page 272.

had feared the Pretender. That emotion found a voice in Isaac Watts, who wrote his finest hymn at this time:

> O God, our help in ages past, Our hope for years to come,
> Our shelter from the stormy blast And our eternal home . . .
> A thousand ages in thy sight Are like an evening gone;
> Short as the watch that ends the night Before the rising sun.
> Time, like an ever-rolling stream, Bears all its sons away;
> They fly, forgotten, as a dream Dies at the opening day.
> O God, our help in ages past, Our hope for years to come,
> Be thou our Guide while life shall last, And our eternal home.

QUEEN ANNE'S LACE

(Hampton Court)

Queen Anne's Lace grows high in Queen Anne's garden,
But Queen Anne's gone from there forever and a day;
Nobody to tease her now for places or for pardon,
Nobody to quarrel half the night and noon away;
Her sister Mary's tulips blow in waves along the mall,
Her uncle Charles' light ladies loll white-shouldered on the wall,
But the little crown is lifted from her high-tormented hair,
They've folded down her hoopskirts to her velvet and her vair,
They've patted flat the cover to her crowned and daised bed—
The news has gone along the land, that Queen Anne's dead.

It's never she, the foolish ghost runs weeping loud and praying
Along the haunted gallery, where empty rooms are dark;
Queen Anne is all too glad to sleep, to let her soul go straying
To scare a silly sentry in the palace or the Park;
Queen Anne's abed with all her little babies round her,
In the first unworried sleep the world has ever found her;
Purple George of Hanover may puff to be her heir,
But the last Stuart lady does not lift her lids to care;
She's pulled the marble round her tight, and covered up her head—
There's nobody so glad as she that Queen Anne's dead!

Margaret Widdemer

Afterword

Thaes ofereode: thisses swa maeg.
That trouble passed away: this also may.
> Refrain from "The Complaint of Deor," fragment
> of an early English poem, preserved in the Exeter
> Book.

ONCE MORE, George of Hanover arrived in London by way of a barge along the Thames. Once more, church bells rang for him, and from the Tower of London cannon boomed a welcome. The Pool was even more crowded with shipping than when he had seen it as a young man in 1680. Reflecting on that first visit, he doubted that the Princess Anne would have made him a better wife than the one he had married and kept imprisoned in the castle of Ahlden for the past twenty years. Now Anne was dead, and he got the English throne in spite of her. She had proved to be stiff-necked, like all the English. No matter; he did not expect to give love or to get it from these people. There was only one person he really wanted to see. That was George Frederick Handel. He had an account to settle with his runaway court composer.

Handel was in an embarrassing position. It was difficult to explain gracefully why he had stayed away from home for so long. The new King was not pleased. Month after month went by, and George commissioned no *Te Deums,* no Birthday Odes. Handel, whose income depended on royal sponsorship, finally thought of a way to heal the breach. George enjoyed boating parties on the Thames in pleasant summer weather. One evening, so the story goes, he heard enchanting music floating across the water from an unseen source. Carried away by its beauty, he inquired about the invisible orchestra. Handel and his musicians then appeared on another barge which had been hidden nearby, and finished playing for the King the "Water Music" composed for the occasion. George forgave Handel his past offense and never again withdrew his favor.

The Marlboroughs returned to England and were soon on good terms with George I. The building of Blenheim had ground to a halt; the workmen were unpaid. John begged the King to confer a knighthood on his architect, Vanbrugh, and promised that if Parliament would not pay the workmen's claims, he would do it himself. Work was resumed and the bills continued to mount in spite of Sarah's protests over every penny.

The cost of the palace itself was colossal, and to make matters worse, Vanbrugh built a bridge at the foot of the hill with three splendid arches to cross some small drainage canals. The bridge was 390 feet long; Sarah fumed that she had counted thirty-three rooms built into it, to sit in "while the coaches are driving over your head." Ruinously expensive and absurd. By 1718, John had had a stroke, the palace was still unfinished, and workmen were suing the Duke for £8,000 in unpaid wages. Sarah and Vanbrugh were at swords' points. He could no longer bear her "far-fetched, laboured accusations, mistaken facts, wrong inferences, groundless jealousies, and strained constructions." He resigned as architect, and the next day John had a second stroke. Blenheim did indeed seem to be, as Sarah called it, a "wild unmerciful house." In the end it cost £300,000, the nation paying four-fifths of the cost, the Marlboroughs paying a fifth. Sarah and Vanbrugh were involved in lawsuits until 1725 and, as if driven by a demon, she started other suits against all the workmen, down to the last and least. Vanbrugh said privately, "I wonder her family don't agree to lock her up."

John did not live to see Blenheim finished. He often drove over from St. Albans to Woodstock to picnic on the lawn under the trees with Sarah and to watch the palace growing. In 1720 they were able to move into the east wing while the building went on around them. The Great Court took shape like "a quarry of stone," as Horace Walpole called it, and at last, over the south portico, a huge bust of Louis XIV was hoisted into place, a trophy somewhat reminiscent of those severed heads which had once been mounted on London Bridge.

In spite of John's illness, Sarah's tempestuous nature, and differences of opinion about Blenheim, their love never lost its zest. Into old age she kept her fine high color and her beautiful fair hair. One day, on a senseless, uncontrollable impulse, she cut off her curls and, knowing how John loved them, left them on a table which he would pass on his way to her room. He never mentioned what she had done, but the curls disappeared. Telling the story years later, she would burst into tears, for after his death in 1722 she had found the curls in a cabinet where he kept his dearest possessions.

Sarah could have married again, more than once. The Duke of Somerset asked for her hand when his Duchess, Queen Anne's friend, died. Sarah answered, "If I were young and handsome as I was, instead of old and faded as I am, and you could lay the empire of the world at my feet, you should never have the heart and hand that once belonged to John, Duke of Marlborough."

Left alone, she went on to finish the great palace at Woodstock. She brought in William Kent and "Capability" Brown to carry on the landscaping begun by the Queen's great gardener, William Wise. Brown constructed a lake at the foot of the palace gardens. Today the arches of the famous bridge are reflected in the still, clear water of the lake, one of the glories of Blenheim. Sarah never replaced Vanbrugh with another architect, and Grinling Gibbons, who had been carving prodigiously in stone and in marble, from a workshop near the stables, was dismissed in favor of some cheaper workmen. Then, in 1735, Sarah unaccountably decided to order another work of art, if she could get a good price. "I am going to Rysbrack [the sculptor]," she wrote, "to make a bargain with him for a fine statue of Queen Anne, which I will put up in the bow window room with a proper inscription. . . . I have a satisfaction in showing this respect to her, because her kindness to me was real." It was a little late in the day for Sarah to recognize that kindness, but better late than never.

Sarah lived on into her eighties, keen as ever in mind. She dictated from memory an inventory of Blenheim's contents—"67 dozen napkins plus 5; 93 tablecloths 'of the best sort,' " and so on. She recorded how she had got the gold plate and the hangings from Sophia, Electress of Hanover, in exchange for a portrait of Queen Anne, another good bargain for Sarah. At last, her body began to fail. Rumors of her death flew about, as they had for her royal mistress thirty years earlier. When Sarah was eighty-two, Horace Walpole wrote: "Old Marlborough is dying —but who can tell! Last year she had lain a great while ill, without speaking; her physicians said, 'She must be blistered, or she will die.' She called out, 'I won't be blistered, and I won't die.' If she takes the same resolution now, I don't believe she will." She did survive for nearly three years longer, until 1744.

A hundred years after Sarah's death, Blenheim was showing

its age. But when an American beauty, Consuelo Vanderbilt, became Duchess of Marlborough, her money helped to bring the old palace back to a state of splendor. Another American beauty, née Jennie Jerome, brought new fame to Blenheim by giving birth to Winston Churchill in a bedroom of the palace. The streams of visitors who go there today learn that young Winston took Blenheim in stride. It had caused much anguish in its building, and brought little happiness to its first owners, but he thought it "great fun." Although he never owned Blenheim, he played there with a collection of a thousand toy soldiers, which are still on display in a glass cabinet. Having found the palace a satisfactory place in which to be born and to play, he chose it as the place for his wedding. And in the Long Library, the marble statue of Queen Anne looks toward a table where lies an illuminated manuscript, a tribute to Sir Winston from President John F. Kennedy. With it is a certificate of honorary American citizenship which was one of Churchill's treasured possessions. It was a token of gratitude from the free world to this descendant of the first Duke of Marlborough and his Duchess. No second Blenheim was needed.

Among the figures who surrounded Queen Anne, none is more melancholy than that of the Old Pretender. After her death, he reappeared on the scene, in 1715, in another unsuccessful effort to take the throne. The English people had never become fond of the House of Hanover; the Scots, still poor in spite of the Union of 1707, liked them even less. As late as 1745, a valiant band of Highlanders made a final desperate effort to overthrow the Hanoverians and to restore the Stuarts under the leadership of "Bonnie Prince Charlie," son of the Old Pretender. Young Charles Stuart hoped to regain the English throne for his father. He was only twenty-five years old, clever, gay, and handsome. He kept fit by constant exercise to train himself for physical endurance and had, in fact, all the qualities of a romantic hero. What he did not have was good judgment, or fidelity to his followers. Jacobite clubs, in England as well as in Scotland, had been drinking secret toasts to "the king over the water." Charles expected great numbers of them to come forward when he landed in the Western Isles of Scotland. Only five thousand of them did so, but he led them as far south as Derby, hoping to gather up recruits along the way. Few recruits volunteered, and Charles retreated to Scotland with his feudal army.

Their way of warfare was the old way of the Highlander—to fight with savage fury, win if possible, capture the booty, and go home. After each battle, Charles was left almost alone, and had to gather his army together again. George II sent his son, William, Duke of Cumberland, to put down the insurrection. William's army was conscripted and equipped by the new English bourgeois society. His men were well drilled and had strong artillery. By 1746, Charles's men were short of food, but still loyally following their Bonnie Prince. At Culloden, on a bleak moor in northeastern Scotland, they made a foolhardy attack on the Hanoverian army of nine thousand men. It was a short and bloody battle with no quarter given on either side. The Jacobites were quickly defeated, and the Duke of Cumberland gave orders calculated to stamp out the last vestige of Highland spirit. Men, women, and children were slaughtered; the wearing of the kilt and the playing of bagpipes were forbidden. Dressed as a woman, Charles went into hiding in a countryside that is as wild today as when he fled on foot and by small boat through the heather and across the misty lochs. The faithful Scots risked their lives to protect the Prince, but, like other Stuarts before him, he took what they gave without thought or thanks. Months later, he was finally able to get back to the Continent, and left Scotland forever. He ended his days as a hanger-on at Continental courts, growing fat and drinking himself to death. Anne was the only one of the Stuarts who had really valued friendship and loyalty.

The defeat of Bonnie Prince Charlie at Culloden sent a new wave of Jacobite refugees to the American colonies, where the events of Anne's lifetime had already had widespread repercussions. By the Treaty of Breda in 1667, Holland had ceded Delaware, New Jersey, and New York to England. The importance of this vast tract of wilderness was not recognized, but immigrants were constantly arriving. Some had come there directly from England, including Quakers driven from home by the so-called Clarendon Code in the early days when Anne's grandfather, the Earl of Clarendon, was Chancellor. Other settlers went first to New England and later moved south to the "Middle Colonies." Because of the wide mixture of religions and nationalities, the "Middle Colonies" made religious toleration the basis of political rights for their citizens. Some Jacobites found new homes in Maryland, where religious toleration was the rule under the leadership of the Catholic Calverts. Maryland's capital was later named Annapolis, for Queen Anne.

To the Southern colonies—Virginia, the Carolinas, and Georgia—came a steady trickle of refugees, even before the battle of Culloden. Some had arrived after Monmouth's Rebellion; others after the Glorious Revolution that toppled the throne of James II, bringing with them that Stuart trait, "a melancholy pride in never choosing the winning side." Stephen Vincent Benét so described them when he wrote about the Wingates in "John Brown's Body." There was a Scottish strain in their blood and it gave "a stiffening set" to the spines of these Cavalier descendants, who would later play their part in America's epic Civil War.

North and South, the settlers were all good fighters and, from the start, no generation in the New World had known much peace. The unbroken line of English settlements which now stretched all along the eastern seaboard had been wrested from the Indians and from the French, who also had vast holdings in America. "Queen Anne's War" was the name given to the early years of the French and Indian Wars fought during her reign.

As conditions in the colonies became more settled and stable, the "Queen Anne" style appeared on the American scene. White frame churches, designed like Sir Christopher Wren's London churches, raised slender spires above the trees of every New England village green. The transplanted Cavaliers of Virginia, worshipping according to the English Book of Common Prayer, took Holy Communion from silver Communion services which were gifts from the Queen and have survived to this day in Virginia churches.

Prosperous Americans ordered furniture from England, and skilled American craftsmen, emigrants from the Old Country, began to copy the style in walnut highboys, carved cherrywood tea tables, graceful chairs, cane-seated or upholstered in brocade. American silversmiths copied English silver pots for coffee, tea, or chocolate. They called their work "Colonial." English visitors recognized it as pure "Queen Anne." In the South the Cavaliers planted gardens like the English gardens the Stuarts had planted, the paths edged with fragrant box and surrounded by laurel, holly, and juniper clipped into formal shapes. There were no nightingales here, but mockingbirds sang in the moonlight.

The colonies also reflected English intellectual life in many ways. William and Mary College was established in 1693 as part of the English effort to train ministers for the Virginia colony and to spread the Christian faith among the Indians. In the main building, named for Sir Christopher Wren, hangs a fine portrait of Queen Anne. Robert Boyle, the great English physicist and chemist, gave funds for an Indian school to be conducted by the new college. Boyle was a member of the Royal Society which meant so much to the learned men of England under the Stuarts. In New England there were equally learned men—the younger John Winthrop, Increase Mather and his son, Cotton Mather—who corresponded with the Royal Society. "Curiosa Americana," a paper by Cotton Mather, was read before the Royal Society in 1713, and he became its first American member. Bishop Berkeley, like many other Englishmen, was enthralled by the possibilities of the burgeoning intellectual life in the raw new continent:

> There shall be sung another golden age,
> The rise of empire and of arts,
> The good and great inspiring epic rage,
> The wisest heads and noblest hearts. . . .
> Westward the course of empire takes her way;
> The first four acts already past,
> A fifth shall close the drama with the day;
> Time's noblest offspring is the last.

We shall never know, unless we meet him in heaven, whether the Bishop thinks that America has fulfilled the bright promise of its youth. But we can suppose that he is no longer

> . . . disgusted at an age and clime
> Barren of every glorious theme

as he looks back from the perspective of eternity on the England of his day.

True, there were no more Miltons, but Dryden knew how to manipulate words in a powerful and subtle way, and wrote not only poetry, but a new kind of prose which sounded like modern conversation. It was a startling innovation, soon picked up by the

Tatler and the *Spectator* as a fresh way to record the passing scene for readers of the new century.

Pope, the pupil of Dryden, never achieved the symphonic effect of Dryden's heroic couplets, but Samuel Johnson said of him, ". . . a thousand years may elapse before there shall appear another man with a power of versification equal to that of Pope. . . . The master passion in his breast was not his vanity, it was his veneration for what is great and noble in intellectual life. . . . He served literature neither for power, like Swift, nor for place and pay . . . nor for fame, but for her own sake."

If Swift used literature for the sake of political power, he nonetheless stands with the immortals of Anne's age and of all time. Like Bunyan and Defoe, he won that place through a single piece of writing. Carl Van Doren has observed that Swift's masterpiece "is one of the three most widely known English books, all of them written in the half-century when English literature began to use the prose still used in the present age. They are so familiar that none of them is commonly called by its correct title. . . . Each of the books is both a story and a commentary on human life: the story for everybody, the commentary for anybody who reflects on the plight and fate of men." Van Doren is speaking, of course, of *The Pilgrim's Progress from this World to that which is to come; The Life and Strange Surprizing Adventures of Robinson Crusoe, of York, Mariner;* and *Travels into Several Remote Nations of the World . . . by Captain Lemuel Gulliver.* All three books owe their being to the events of the lifetime of Queen Anne.

Insolent and overbearing he may have been, but Swift still emerges as the greatest writer of prose in the "Age of the Augustans," and certain glimpses of this controversial genius are not altogether unlovable. It is pleasant to think of him coming home early after dinner on a cold night in London during the years when he was in the thick of politics and was writing his *Journal to Stella*. He noted the fact that his landlady had given him a fur night cap to take the place of his old velvet one. Then: "I studied till ten, and had a fire; O ho! and now am in bed. I have no fire-place in my bedchamber; but 'tis very warm weather when one's in bed." So, lónely but cosy, Swift refreshed his body in the repose of his solitary bed, and his spirit in the intimacy of one or two cherished friendships. Next morning he would sally forth, like another Gulliver, to examine the queer societies where he found himself. He would never be the right size or shape to fit into any of them.

Like Defoe's *Review,* and the *Tatler* and *Spectator* of Addison and Steele, the *Examiner* was the newspaper in which Swift recorded his witty observations. It was only one of the many periodicals to which distinguished literary men were giving their genius during the reign of Anne. Never before had such talent gone into the writing of news, editorials, and essays for the general public.

Anne was not responsible for the brilliance of the Augustans. And she knew no science. She merely happened to be on the throne when Thomas Newcomen invented the first practical steam engine. She could not conceive of a typewriter, though she granted the patent for the first one. She was probably asleep while Edmund Halley was searching the skies for great comets. She conferred a knighthood on Isaac Newton, but if she read what he wrote about optics, about mathematics, and the law of gravitation, she almost certainly did not understand it. She accepted God on simple faith alone, though she must have applauded when Richard Bentley, her librarian, used Newton's law to prove the existence of an intelligent and omnipotent Creator. She has been called stubborn and obstinate, but she was capable of changing with the times; she loathed the principle of Hobbes's earthshaking *Leviathan,* which viewed the will of the people as the origin of all law, yet she herself unwittingly accepted this principle before her life ended.

During the early years of her reign, England was blessed with fair weather and bountiful harvests for which she could hardly take credit, but her quiet, steady-going ways did their part in nourishing a healthy national life and the economic growth of her country. She was more than a mere spectator passively viewing events from the isolation of a *camera obscura,* and beneath the chatter of the connivers and contrivers hurrying up the back stairs to "have the Queen's ear," she seemed always to hear the pulse of England, the real England of men working the fields, planting hedgerows and orchards, building cities, hoisting sails. Because she had "no interest, no end, no thought" but for England, she knew when and how to act in the things that mattered most to her country. Political intrigue darkened her last years, but if politicians used her for their selfish ends, she used them too, for higher ends. She backed Marlborough to the hilt when the English people were united in determination to break the power of French despotism. And she dismissed Marlborough when the war had gone on too long. She united England and Scotland, like a mother who sees that two children must stop quarreling if they are to enjoy a strong and harmonious family life.

Anne lost her own children, but she took under her special care the poor children of all England, who began to go to school, cleaner, better fed, and in greater numbers than ever before. No one saw anything wrong in country children earning their keep at four and five years, but when the chores were done, the young roamed, as if in Arcady, through nearby fields rich with king-cups and daisies. A favorite eighteenth-century dancing game still echoes in green English meadows:

Lady Queen Anne she sits in the sun,
As fair as a lily, as brown as a bun;
Come taste my lily, come smell my rose,
Which of my maidens do you choose? . . .

Anne was buried in Westminster Abbey, where so many of the great had been laid to rest before her: her grandfather, the Lord Chancellor, Earl of Clarendon; her mother, Anne Hyde; her uncle, Charles II; her sister Mary, united in death with William of Orange; Anne's husband, George of Denmark. Without expression her pale effigy gazes at the past and the future; the effigy of the great Elizabeth does the same. "Good Queen Bess" and "Good Queen Anne."

" 'Tis very remarkable," says Defoe, "that the royal vault in which the English royal family was laid, was filled up with Queen Anne." Disregarding the Pretenders, he continues, "Just as the family was extinct above, there was no room to have buried any more below. . . . The body of the church begins to be crowded with the bodies of citizens, poets, seamen, parsons . . . so that in time, the royal ashes will be thus mingled with common dust."

Queen Anne in History

1649   King Charles I is executed.

1653–1659 The Protectorate, under the Cromwells.

1660   King Charles II becomes King; the Restoration.

1665   Anne is born, St. James's Palace.

1671   Anne's mother, Anne Hyde, dies.

1673   Anne's father, James, Duke of York, marries Mary of Modena.

1680   George of Hanover visits England.

1683   Anne marries George of Denmark.

1685   King Charles II dies; Anne's father becomes King James II.

1688–1689 The Glorious Revolution. James goes to France with Mary of Modena and their infant son, later known as the "Old Pretender." James's older daughter, Mary, becomes Queen, and her husband, William of Orange, rules with her as King.

1694   Queen Mary dies.

1700   William, Duke of Gloucester, Anne's only surviving child, dies.

1702   King William dies; Anne becomes Queen. By the Act of Settlement, if Anne and George die without children, the throne will go to the House of Hanover.

1701–1714 War of the Spanish Succession. When Philip, a grandson of the French King, Louis XIV, inherits the Spanish throne, Allied powers oppose France, Spain, and Bavaria. Allies are England, Holland, Austria, Prussia, Portugal (and Savoy, after 1703). The chief Allied leaders are the English John Churchill,

Duke of Marlborough, and the Austrian Prince Eugene of Savoy. The scene of the war is in the Netherlands, the Danube valley, Italy, and Spain. In America it is called Queen Anne's War, and becomes part of the French and Indian Wars. In English politics, Whigs include moderates of the Church of England, middle-class tradesmen, London financiers, with some nobility and gentry. Dissenters (without vote) support Whigs. Most Tories are landed gentry and clergy of the Church of England. Interest in the Succession is mixed. Some in both parties favor the House of Hanover; some prefer James Stuart, the "Old Pretender."

1704   Marlborough and Prince Eugene win the Battle of Blenheim; as a result, Austria and Bavaria are brought under Allied control.

1706   By a victory at Ramillies, Allies win control of Spanish Netherlands.

1707   England and Scotland are united. Scotland is represented for the first time in British Parliament. Established Church in Scotland remains Presbyterian.

1709   Unsuccessful efforts at peace treaties.

1710–1714   Peace efforts continue.

1713   Treaty of Utrecht is signed. England withdraws from war.

1714   Queen Anne dies; George, Elector of Hanover, becomes George I of England.

Bibliography

A SELECTED BIBLIOGRAPHY ON THE LIFETIME OF QUEEN ANNE
FOR THE GENERAL READER

Bedford, John. *London's Burning*. Abelard-Schuman, 1966.
A vivid and detailed account of the disaster which destroyed London in 1666.

Burton, Elizabeth. *Pageant of Stuart England*. Scribner's, 1962.
Seventeenth-century houses, furniture, eating and drinking, recreations, medicine, cosmetics, inventions and gardens.

Churchill, Sir Winston. *History of the English-Speaking Peoples*. v. 3. Dodd, 1957.
"The Age of Revolution" from William of Orange through the years of Anne's reign, with a penetrating analysis of events and their significance.

Churchill, Sir Winston. *Marlborough, His Life and Times*. Scribner's, 1933–1938.
The definitive biography of the first Marlborough by his most famous descendant, who admired him enormously.

Clark, Sir George. *Later Stuarts, 1660–1714*. Oxford History of England. Oxford, 1955.
History, economics, exploration, arts, and sciences, from the restoration of Charles II to the death of Anne.

Ewald, W. B., Jr. *Rogues, Royalty, and Reporters*. Houghton, 1956.
The Age of Anne through its newspapers. A close look at the life of her people, the humble as well as the famous.

Green, David. *Sarah, Duchess of Marlborough.* Scribner's, 1967.
Witty and scholarly revelations concerning Sarah's last years are especially engrossing. Handsomely illustrated.

Kronenberger, Louis. *Marlborough's Duchess, a Study in Worldliness.* Weidenfeld and Nicolson, 1958.
The rise and fall of Sarah, her life-long passion for John, and the building of Blenheim.

Pearson, Hesketh. *Merry Monarch.* Harper, 1960.
A popular biography of Charles II, his friends, his enemies, and the women he loved.

Pepys, Samuel. *Everybody's Pepys,* ill. by E. H. Shepard. Bell, 1926.
An attractive edition with 60 spirited illustrations. Endpaper maps show London in the 1660's, the important buildings, and area of the Great Fire.

Rowse, A. L. *Early Churchills.* Harper, 1956.
The life and times of John and his tempestuous Sarah. Generously illustrated.

Thackeray, W. M. *History of Henry Esmond, Esq.* Great Illustrated Classics. Dodd, 1945.
A Virginia Cavalier remembers his own personal romance amid the intrigues, battles, and literary figures of Queen Anne's England.

Thomson, G. S. *Life in a Noble Household, 1641–1700.* University of Michigan, 1959.
The habits of a great country family are revealed through the letters they wrote and the expense accounts they kept.

Trevelyan, G. M. *England under the Stuarts.* History of England. v. V. Methuen, 1904.
Political and social aspects of the period analyzed by a master of English prose.

Trevelyan, G. M. *Illustrated English Social History.* v. 2, 3. Longmans, 1951.
Easy reading, copious information and pictures on England during Anne's lifetime.

Turner, E. S. *Court of St. James's.* St. Martin's, 1959.
The entertaining and sometimes scandalous doings of England's

royal families as they moved from palace to palace over the centuries.

Van Doren, Carl, ed. *Portable Swift*. Viking, 1948.
The best of Swift in one volume with a brilliant introductory essay on his life and his place in literature.

Ward, Sir A. W., and A. R. Waller. *Cambridge History of English Literature*. v. 9. Cambridge, 1964.
A goldmine of biographical information and literary criticism covering Defoe, Addison, Steele, Swift, Pope, Arbuthnot, and others.

White, T. H. *Mistress Masham's Repose*. Putnam, 1946.
Lilliputians are found alive in modern times on the property of a ruined palace given to Mrs. Masham by Queen Anne after the battle of Malplaquet.

Wibberley, Leonard. *Coronation Book: the Dramatic Story in History and Legend*. Farrar, 1953.
Brief but complete explanation of all that is involved in the crowning of England's monarchs. Generously illustrated.

Williams, Neville. *Royal Residences of Great Britain: a Social History*. Macmillan, 1960.
Includes Westminster, Tower of London, Windsor Castle, Richmond, Whitehall, Hampton Court, St. James's Palace, Holyrood, Kensington Palace.

Notes

MENU

Dover Castle, August 16, 1709

As evidence that English appetites had not fallen off since the days of Charles II, Lionel Sackville, 7th Earl and 1st Duke of Dorset, gave a dinner at Dover Castle on August 16, 1709, when Queen Anne appointed him Lieutenant of the castle with a yearly salary of £50.

The first course consisted of "5 Soups, 12 dishes of fish, 1 Westphalia Ham and five fowls, 8 dishes of pullets and oysters, with bacon, 10 Almond Puddings, 12 haunches of venison, roast, 6 dishes of roast pigs, 3 dishes of roast geese, 12 Venison Pasties, 12 white Fragacies with Peetets, 8 dishes of 'ragged' [ragouted] veal. 2nd course, 14 dishes of ducks, turkeys, and pigeons, 15 codlin [young cod] tarts, creamed, 12 dishes of roast lobster, 12 dishes of umble pies [made of heart, lights, and liver], 10 dishes of fried fish, 8 dishes of Chickens and rabbits; Ryders [in addition]—5 dishes of dried sweetmeats, 12 dishes of jelly, 6 dishes of selebub cream [a sweet thick cream, flavored with wine], 13 dishes of fruit, 8 dishes of Almond Pies gilt, 12 dishes of Custard Florentines, 8 dishes of lobster, 120 Intermediate plates of sorts: Side Table—a large chine of beef stuck with flags and banners, 1 loaf of double refined sugar, oil and vinegar."

A MOST EXCELLENT CAKE

A recipe from the household book of Patience Wise, whose husband was Queen Anne's gardener.

Take a pound & 2 ounces of fine Flower after it is well dryed, 2 pound & ½ of Currants after they are wash'd dryed & pricked, a good quantity of Nutmeg Mace & Cinnamon & 10 Cloves all dryed & beaten fine & a little Salt mingle all thereinto your Flower with 3 ounces of fine Sugar, then break into a Bason yr Yolks of 12 Eggs & 6 whites, beat into em a pint of good yeast, then Strain into yr Flower ye Eggs & ye Yeast & Set over ye Fire a Quart of good Cream & when it boyls take it from ye fire & put in a pound of good Butter cut in slices & as much Saffron as will Colour ye Cream. When ye butter is all melted & ye Cream no better than New Milk, then pour into ye Flower as much as will make it into a pudding or like a pudding but not thin, never offer to mould or kneed it but lift it up with Your hand till all ye Flower be wet all over, then flower a Cloath all over & lay Your Cake in it & lay it before ye fire for a quarter of an hour to rise, then put it into a frame well buttered and with a knife Dip'd in flower cut ye Cake cross down to ye bottom, prick it with a Bodkin & Set it into a quick Oven giving it an hours baking & draw it very gently for Shaking it when hot will make it heavy, then Ice it & Set it where it must Stand, not putting it any more into ye Oven for that Spoils ye Colour of ye Ice. When You would Add to the richness of this Cake put in 6 Spoonfulls of Sack, Some Ambergreece & Dryed Citron, Orange, Lemon & Date. If you like not Saffron leave it out.

The Iceing for the Cake

Take a pound of ye best Double Refined Sugar, beaten & Sifted, then take ye Whites of 2 Eggs well beaten with 4 or 5 Spoonfulls of ye best orange flower water, then put your Sugar to your Eggs, never leave beating till they look as white as Snow. Some Strong person must beat it & as Soon as ye Cake is drawn, while it is hot, lay it all over with a knife Sides & all.

COLONEL DANIEL PARKE

The letter is on display at Blenheim. Colonel Parke was known in both Virginia and England as a "sparkish gentleman" with a hot temper. His descendants were related through marriage to three famous Virginia families, the Custis family, the Washingtons, and the Lees. An article in the *Virginia Magazine of History and Biography,* October, 1912, pp. 372–381, says:

"It was at that time the custom in England to give the bearer of the first news of a victory a gratuity of £500, but Col. Parke begged that, instead, he might have the Queen's picture. His gallantry (in both senses of the word), fine appearance and handsome bearing pleased Queen Anne, and being patronized by the Churchills, he was, on April 25, 1704, appointed chief governor of the Leeward Islands. The government of these islands had been very lax, the settlers were inclined to be rebellious, and like those of the other West Indian Colonies had among them many desperate and lawless characters. The appointment of Parke was unpopular from the first, and the policy which he adopted in his administration, instead of wiping away the prejudice against him, wrought his complete undoing.

"Having repelled the French who had plundered the islands of St. Christopher and Nevis, Governor Parke endeavored to carry out some much needed reforms, and being sure of support at home, he aroused the displeasure of the colonists by disregarding the articles of a formal complaint against him drawn up by them, and made a somewhat ostentatious display of the small military force placed at his command. At least this is the account given by Parke's friends, . . . while on the other hand, the colonists claimed that their Governor's oppressions drove them to revolt. The savage cruelty, however, with which they treated him, would incline us to give judgment against them. Whatever the cause, a violent insurrection broke out in 1710, at Antigua, the seat of government. Col. Parke made a gallant resistance, and with his own hand killed Captain John Piggott, one of the leaders of the insurrection, but finally overpowered by numbers, and made helpless by a shot in the thigh, he fell into the hands of the rioters. They had now an opportunity of sending him away to what place and in what manner they think fit,' says [one] account, 'but instead thereof they use him with the utmost contempt and inhumanity. They strip him of his clothes, kick, spurn at, and beat him with the buts [sic] of their muskets, by which means at last they break his back. They drag him into the streets by a leg and arm, and his head trails and beats from step to step of the stone stairs at the entrance of the house, and he is dragged on the coarse gravelly street, which raked the skin from his bones. These cruelties and tortures force tears from his eyes, and in this condition he is left expiring, exposed to the scorching sun, out of the heat of which he begs to be removed. The good-natured woman, who, at his request, brought him water to quench his thirst is threatened by one Samuel Watkins to have a sword passed through her for her humanity, and the water is dashed out of her hands. He is insulted and reviled by every scoundrel, in the agonies of death, but makes no other return but these mild expressions, "Gentlemen, you have no sense of honor left, pray have some of humanity." He gratefully owns the kindness of friends, and prays God to reward those who stood by him that day. At last he was removed to the house of one Mr. John Wright, near the place where he lay, and there, recommending his soul to God, with some pious ejaculations, he pays the great debt of nature, and death, less cruel than his enemies, put an end to his sufferings.

"'After they had surfeited themselves with cruelties, they plundered the General's house and broke open his store-houses, so that his estate must have suffered by that day in money, plate, jewels, clothes, and household goods, by the most moderate computation, five thousand pounds sterling, for which his executors have obtained no satisfaction to this day. Thus died Colonel Parke, whose brave end shows him sufficiently deserving of the commission he bore, and his death acquired an honor to his memory, which the base aspersions of his enemies could not overthrow.'"

It would be interesting to know what happened to the medallion given to him by Queen Anne.

AT THE HEALING

Service used by Queen Anne from the Book of Common Prayer, 1708

Prevent us, O Lord, in all our doings, with thy most gracious favour, and further us with thy continual help, that in all our works begun, continued and ended in thee, we may glorify thy holy Name, and finally by thy mercy obtain everlasting life, through Jesus Christ our Lord. Amen.

The Holy Gospel is written in the 16th Chapter of Saint Mark, beginning at the 14th Verse.

Jesus appeared unto the eleven as they sat at meat, and upbraided them with their unbelief and hardness of heart, because they believed not them which had seen him after he was risen. And he said unto them, Go ye into all the world, and preach the Gospel to every creature. He that believed and baptised [sic], shall be saved; but he that believeth not, shall be damned. And these signs shall follow them that believe; In my name they shall cast out devils, they shall speak with new tongues, they shall take up serpents, and if they drink any deadly thing, it shall not hurt them; They shall lay hands on the sick, and they shall recover.

So then, after the Lord had spoken unto them, he was received up into heaven, and sat on the right hand of God.

And they went forth and preached every where, the Lord working with them, and confirming the word with signs following.

Let us pray.

Lord, have mercy upon us.
Christ, have mercy upon us.
Lord, have mercy upon us.

Our Father, which art in Heaven; Hallowed be thy Name. Thy Kingdom come. Thy will be done in Earth, As it is in Heaven. Give us this day our daily bread. And forgive us our trespasses, As we forgive them that trespass against us. And lead us not into temptation; But deliver us from evil: For thine is the Kingdom, The power, and the glory, For ever and ever. Amen.

Then shall the infirm Persons, one by one, be presented to the Queen upon their Knees, and as every one is presented, and while the Queen is laying Her Hands upon them, and putting the Gold about their Necks, the Chaplain that officiates, turning himself to Her Majesty, shall say these words following.

God give a Blessing to this Work; And grant that *these* sick *Persons,* on whom the Queen *lays* her Hands, may recover, thro(u) Jesus Christ our Lord.

After all have been presented, the Chaplain shall say,

Vers. O Lord, save thy servants.
Resp. *Who put their trust in thee.* *These Answers are*
Vers. Send them help from thy holy place. *to be made by*
Resp. *And evermore mightily defend them.* *them that come*
Vers. Help us, O God of our Salvation. *to be Healed.*
Resp. *And for the glory of thy Name, deliver us,*
and be merciful unto us sinners, for thy Names sake.
Vers. O Lord, hear our prayers.
Resp. *And let our cry come unto thee.*

Let us pray.

O Almighty God, who art the giver of all health, and the aid of them that seek to thee for succour, we call upon thee for thy help and goodness mercifully to be shewed upon these thy servants, that they being healed of their infirmities, may give thanks unto thee in thy holy Church, through Jesus Christ our Lord. *Amen.*

Then the Chaplain, standing with his face towards them that come to be healed, shall say,

The Almighty Lord, who is a most strong tower to all them that put their trust in him, to whom all things in heaven, in earth, and under the earth, do bow, and obey, be now, and evermore your defence, and make you know and feel, that there is none other Name under heaven given to man, in whom, and through whom you may receive health and salvation, but only the Name of our Lord Jesus Christ. *Amen.*

The grace of our Lord Jesus Christ, and the love of God and the fellowship of the Holy Ghost, be with us all evermore. *Amen.*

POTPOURRI

Recipe of Lady Betty Germain, lady-in-waiting to Queen Anne

Gather dry, Double Violets, Rose Leaves, Lavender, Myrtle flowers, Verbena, Bay leaves, Rosemary, Balm, Musk, Geranium. Pick these from the stalks and dry on paper in the sun for a day or two before putting them in a jar. This should be a large white one, well glazed, with a close fitting cover, also a piece of card the exact size of the jar, which you must keep pressed down on the flowers. Keep a new wooden spoon to stir the salt and flowers from the bottom, before you put in a fresh layer of bay salt above and below every layer of flowers. Have ready spices, plenty of Cinnamon, Mace, Nutmeg, and Pepper and Lemon-peel pounded. For a large jar ½ lb. Orris root, 1 oz. Storax, 1 oz. Gum Benjamin, 2 ozs. Calamino Rhodium. The spice and gums to be added when you have collected all the flowers you intend to put in. Mix all well together, press it down well, and spread bay salt on the top to exclude the air until the January or February following. Keep the jar in a cool, dry place.

Index